Erlang and Elixir for Imperative Programmers

Wolfgang Loder

Apress®

Erlang and Elixir for Imperative Programmers

Wolfgang Loder
Vienna
Austria

ISBN-13 (pbk): 978-1-4842-2393-2   ISBN-13 (electronic): 978-1-4842-2394-9
DOI 10.1007/978-1-4842-2394-9

Library of Congress Control Number: 2016960209

Managing Director: Welmoed Spahr
Lead Editor: Steve Anglin
Technical Reviewers: Massimo Nardone and Aleks Drozdov
Editorial Board: Steve Anglin, Pramila Balan, Laura Berendson, Aaron Black, Louise Corrigan,
    Jonathan Gennick, Robert Hutchinson, Celestin Suresh John, Nikhil Karkal, James Markham,
    Susan McDermott, Matthew Moodie, Natalie Pao, Gwenan Spearing
Coordinating Editor: Mark Powers
Copy Editor: Mary Behr
Compositor: SPi Global
Indexer: SPi Global
Artist: SPi Global

Distributed to the book trade worldwide by Springer Science+Business Media New York, 233 Spring Street, 6th Floor, New York, NY 10013. Phone 1-800-SPRINGER, fax (201) 348-4505, e-mail orders-ny@springer-sbm.com, or visit www.springeronline.com. Apress Media, LLC is a California LLC and the sole member (owner) is Springer Science + Business Media Finance Inc (SSBM Finance Inc). SSBM Finance Inc is a Delaware corporation.

For information on translations, please e-mail rights@apress.com, or visit www.apress.com.

Apress and friends of ED books may be purchased in bulk for academic, corporate, or promotional use. eBook versions and licenses are also available for most titles. For more information, reference our Special Bulk Sales–eBook Licensing web page at www.apress.com/bulk-sales.

Any source code or other supplementary materials referenced by the author in this text are available to readers at www.apress.com. For detailed information about how to locate your book's source code, go to www.apress.com/source-code/. Readers can also access source code at SpringerLink in the Supplementary Material section for each chapter.

Printed on acid-free paper

Contents at a Glance

Contents

About the Author

Wolfgang Loder has been programming software since the 1980s. He has successfully rejected all calls for management roles and has remained hands-on up to today.

His journey went from Assembler and C to C++ and Java to C# and F# and JavaScript, from Waterfall to Agile, from Imperative to Declarative, and other paradigm changes too many to list and remember.

Most of his career Wolfgang was a contract Enterprise Developer and the introduction of "new" languages, frameworks, and concepts is very slow in this field. Once he decided to develop his own products he was free of such constraints and ventured into all sorts of paradigms, be it NoSQL or Functional, and evaluated all the latest ideas, crazy or not. In other words, he has fun developing software.

Wolfgang was born in Vienna and lives in Austria, UK, and Kenya.

About the Technical Reviewers

Massimo Nardone has more than 22 years of experience in security, web/mobile development, and cloud and IT architecture. His true IT passions are security and Android.

He has been programming and teaching how to program with Android, Perl, PHP, Java, VB, Python, C/C++, and MySQL for more than 20 years.

He holds a Master of Science degree in Computing Science from the University of Salerno, Italy.

He has worked as a Project Manager, Software Engineer, Research Engineer, Chief Security Architect, Information Security Manager, PCI/SCADA Auditor, and Senior Lead IT Security/Cloud/SCADA Architect for many years.

Technical skills include: security, Android, cloud, Java, MySQL, Drupal, Cobol, Perl, web and mobile development, MongoDB, D3, Joomla, Couchbase, C/C++, WebGL, Python, Pro Rails, Django CMS, Jekyll, Scratch, etc.

He currently works as Chief Information Security Office (CISO) for Cargotec Oyj.

He worked as visiting lecturer and supervisor for exercises at the Networking Laboratory of the Helsinki University of Technology (Aalto University). He holds four international patents (PKI, SIP, SAML, and Proxy areas). Massimo has reviewed more than 40 IT books for different publishing company and he is the coauthor of *Pro Android Games* (Apress, 2015).

Aleks Drozdov is an architect, a team lead, and software engineer with more than 20 years of experience in analysis, design, and implementation of complex information systems using Lean Architecture and Agile methodologies.

He has extensive practical knowledge in service-oriented technologies; distributed and parallel systems; relational, non-relational, and graph databases; data search and analytics.

Aleks likes to learn new technologies and isn't afraid of starting a new project in a new field. Currently he is working on large scale, high performance system for machine learning and artificial intelligence.

In his free time, he likes to read, take a long walks, play guitar, and spend time with his grandson.

Foreword

Don't confuse essence with tools.
Declarative is a process ("magical spirit"), controlled by procedures.
Controlling complexity of large systems is Computer Science.

The quotes are from a lecture held by one of the authors of the book *Structure and Interpretation of Computer Programs*, Hal Abelson, at MIT in 1986[1]. At the time of the recording of the video I was sitting in Vienna in the Technical University to hear computer science courses as well. Unfortunately I did not hear similar interesting quotes, just barebones definitions. Let's interpret those quotes, keeping in mind which year they were made in.

Don't confuse essence with tools.

This remark was made while talking about the relationship of Computer Science to Computer. The computer is the tool, similar to a shovel used to dig a hole in the ground. Talking about digging is not talking about the shovel, but about the process of digging. The same with computers: they are just a tool. Of course, in 1986, a computer was a mainframe. The upcoming PCs were seen as a toy, and some people are still of this opinion. Nevertheless, mainframes then and mobile phones now are the same: a tool for our computing processes.

Similar is the relationship between programming languages and the program. The languages are the tools and the program is the essence.

Declarative is a process ("magical spirit"), controlled by procedures.

The magic in this quote refers to the inability to influence the process that is running on a computer. Today we may say that there are options to influence the process, but going down to the level of machine language there are not. More important is the idea that procedures or functions control the declarative process.

It mixes the concepts of declarative and imperative. Describe the process by combining procedures that themselves are a sequence of step-by-step instructions.

Controlling complexity of large systems is Computer Science.

---

[1]http://ocw.mit.edu/courses/electrical-engineering-and-computer-science/6-001-structure-and-interpretation-of-computer-programs-spring-2005/video-lectures/.

The definition of a large system is somehow arbitrary. What was large 30 years ago may be small today. What has not changed is the complexity of systems. Computer science tries to control this complexity with varying success. This starts with the development process itself and ends with handling huge amounts of data. Some may say that computer science did not make much progress; others will have enough examples to oppose this. I think that computer science is moving forward. Well enough, but the application and integration of the findings are not happening fast enough, either due to rapid progresses in hardware in the last decades or due to paradigm changes fueled by commercial pressures.

This book is about old and new, about concepts and implementation, and about paradigms.

Writing this book started with an idea to write about a journey and then the writing of the book itself became a journey. I hope you, the reader, will have as much pleasure as I had writing it.

Introduction

In December of 1988, Erlang was ready for use. Joe Armstrong, one of the creators, writes in *A History of Erlang*[2]: "By the end of 1988, most of the ideas in Erlang had stabilized." The language design and implementation started in 1986, and only two years later Erlang was stable enough to be used in production.

Let's put Erlang's first release in the historical context of the year 1988[3]:

Other languages at this time were Fortran 77, Cobol-85, Common Lisp was not yet a standard, and Haskell was not even defined. Stroustrup's *The C++ Programming Language*, released in 1985, was the reference for C++ with no official standard yet defined. The specification for C++ 2.0 was released in 1989. Microsoft published its C-Compiler in version 5, no C++ in sight. Zortech C++ 1.0, released in 1988, was the first native compiler on PCs, which means others were transpiling C++ to C and then compiling it, but the Zortech compiler was writing directly to machine code. The creator of that compiler, Walter Bright, later invented the language D. Java was not even a thought at this time.

Graphical interfaces as we know them today were not common; OS/2 1.1 got a GUI in October 1988 and Windows 2.1 was released in May of the same year.

So why, more than 26 years later, am I writing a book about Erlang? How is it that a new language, Elixir, was created just a few years ago to sit on top of the Erlang system? Why is Erlang relevant today?

Incidentally, the history of Erlang parallels my own software development career. In 1985, I started studying computer science after having worked with statistical packages to analyze social science problems. The languages we learned in the first two years were Pascal and Modula, 68000 assembler and Occam 2. This selection was not very helpful to get a job, but especially Occam 2 was interesting. It still exists, although without having a real impact, but the idea back then was to parallelize computing by using Transputers[4] and Occam was the language defined for that purpose. It put the finger on a problem we as an industry did not want to think about for 20 years: the physical limits of the CPU design.

We all disregarded the warning signs and hoped that the industry leaders would find a solution. In the meantime, the younger generation of developers did not have to deal with constraints that were prevalent in the 80s and beginning 90s: computation speed and memory management.

Now, in 2016, we are looking at the limits of physical CPU design and in fact the software has become the bottleneck. We have powerful CPUs with lots of memory and several cores that can compute in parallel, but the software development paradigms we use to create most enterprise applications are not taking advantage of this offer.

More than two years ago, I decided to create a product that needed to be fault tolerant and reliable, scalable, and fast. As a long-time user of the C-family languages (C/C++, C#, Java) the selection range was well defined for me. After using those languages and their corresponding standard libraries and frameworks for lots of projects, I knew about the problems, workarounds, and deficiencies. As a contract developer, one can't really decide which languages or frameworks are used, but for my own project I could.

My first thought was to use Node.js, but at the time of my final decision scalability and fault tolerance were issues and I really did not like the callback hell, although it is possible to ease that with Futures libraries and similar workarounds.

---

[2]http://dl.acm.org/citation.cfm?id=1238850&dl=ACM&coll=DL&CFID=495241682&CFTOKEN=12700222
[3]http://en.wikipedia.org/wiki/History_of_programming_languages
[4]http://en.wikipedia.org/wiki/Transputer

Then I remembered Erlang/OTP. I had played with it several times in the last two decades, but could not use it in any project. Now I saw that my upcoming product was a perfect use case. Also, Elixir as a language on top of the Erlang system was coming on nicely. So I decided to use Erlang/OTP and Elixir.

Coming from an imperative and object-oriented background I had to rethink my approach a little bit and this book is about this experience.

In **Part 1** I define the paradigms, talk about the history of Erlang and Elixir, and help you reset your mind away from imperative programming to functional and declarative programming.

Part 2 describes the original project and its features.

In **Part 3** you will set up your environment for development and production. While in development, you will focus on testing and continuous integration; in production, you must think about monitoring and scaling. For easier deployment you will have a look at Docker containers.

The implementation of the project will happen in **Part 4**. In it the languages and the framework will be introduced in the context of implemented features.

Part 5 describes the language and framework features you have used in the implementation in a more generic form. In this part, you work out the concept differences to and similarities with imperative and object-oriented languages.

All code for this book can be found on GitHub[5]. This repository also contains the basic Dockerfile to create Docker containers.

The GitHub repository contains directories named Erlang and Elixir with an example project in each. These examples are used in various chapters to explain different aspects of the development process and language features.

The service as described in Part 4 can be found on GitHub[6].

Appendix A gives some notes about modeling Erlang/Elixir applications.

Appendix B lists some resources for diving deeper into languages, libraries, and frameworks.

Appendix C shows a diagram with paths between service features, language and framework features, and corresponding patterns and concepts.

Appendix D gives a quick reference of the languages Erlang and Elixir. This appendix is not meant to learn the language; it's a help sheet for looking up the syntax of certain language constructs.

Please note: In Erlang and Elixir books you will often find a special syntax referring to functions. For example, the Elixir function

```
def example_function(arg1, arg2) do
{nothing}
end
```

would be referred to as example_function/2 to indicate the signature; the name is example_function and it has two arguments. I will not do this in this book and will refer to the above function simply as example_function.

---

[5]https://github.com/kujua/erlang-elixir-imperative-bookcompanion
[6]https://github.com/kujua/creative-common-dar

PART I

Before We Start

## CHAPTER 1

Imperative vs. Functional Programming

The title of this chapter could also read *Imperative* vs. *Declarative* vs. *Structured* vs. *Object Oriented* vs. *Functional* vs. (fill in the paradigm of your choice).

There are long and theoretical discussions about the definitions of each programming paradigm. The questions asked include the following:

- Is functional programming always declarative?

- Are functional languages pure or impure?

- Is SQL or HTML perfectly declarative?

It is important to keep those questions in the back of our minds, but it is also important to know that there are different answers depending on which paradigm is the basic point of view of the person who answers. This chapter gives simple definitions as a practical guide without going too deep into the finer details of the topic. The goal is to understand the differences and to put Erlang and Elixir into perspective.

Imperative and *functional* are the roots of two very distinct programming approaches. If we define it in an oversimplified way, the former tells the computer exactly what to do, step by step. The latter says: here are the high level functions, go calculate the result.

Imperative Programming

The essence of imperative programming is to provide statements to tell somebody how to do something. This is deliberately vague, because this paradigm is not restricted to computer programming.

Think of a cooking recipe: it specifies exactly what to do, given all that the ingredients are available. Figure 1-1 shows the equivalent programming constructs of the cooking recipe: statements, input arguments, and output data.

Electronic supplementary material   The online version of this chapter (doi: 10.1007/978-1-4842-2394-9_1) contains supplementary material, which is available to authorized users.

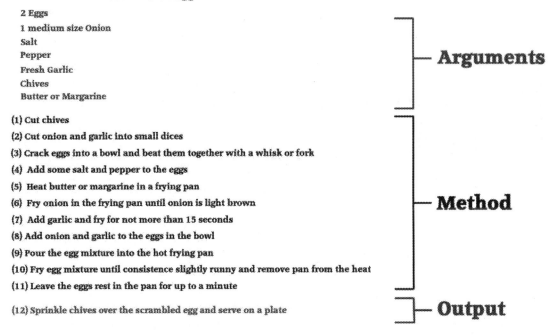

Scrambled Eggs

2 Eggs
1 medium size Onion
Salt
Pepper
Fresh Garlic
Chives
Butter or Margarine

(1) Cut chives

(2) Cut onion and garlic into small dices

(3) Crack eggs into a bowl and beat them together with a whisk or fork

(4) Add some salt and pepper to the eggs

(5) Heat butter or margarine in a frying pan

(6) Fry onion in the frying pan until onion is light brown

(7) Add garlic and fry for not more than 15 seconds

(8) Add onion and garlic to the eggs in the bowl

(9) Pour the egg mixture into the hot frying pan

(10) Fry egg mixture until consistence slightly runny and remove pan from the heat

(11) Leave the eggs rest in the pan for up to a minute

(12) Sprinkle chives over the scrambled egg and serve on a plate

Figure 1-1. *Imperative cooking recipe*

The ingredients, like eggs and salt, are the input arguments. Steps (1) to (11) describe how to cook the scrambled eggs. Since there is no "syntax" of a cooking recipe language, the description is more or less precise and the accuracy depends on the expertise of the writer. There's no process to check if the "statements" are correct or complete.

The output is the scrambled egg on a plate, ready for eating.

Initially, imperative programming was done in machine code, written in assembler or macro assembler languages, which were just thin wrappers around machine code. This way of programming was influenced by the physical design of von Neumann computers that expect to be told exactly what to do. I personally liked assembler programming and I still think that this is programming as it should be. Yes, it is tedious, with frequent restarts of the machine in case of an error, but on the other side one has to think exactly about memory, CPU registers, and code coordination. I would suggest that this is *pure* imperative programming. And it is the most error-prone programming as well! In the end, all compilers of any language, including functional languages, have to produce machine code or intermediary code that calls runtime libraries in machine code.

Problems with productivity, testing, and maintenance led to higher programming languages and to a more structured approach. Initially, simple structures and later procedures and modules were introduced. The *object-oriented programming (OOP)* approach lets programmers build smaller units that encapsulate properties and methods.

Objects

If machine code is influenced by physical machines, objects are influenced by a physical world that is seen as a concept. An *Animal* is a type that can be *hungry* or has a fur *color* and can *make noise* or *eat*. All this can be easily expressed with properties (also called attributes) and methods (which are procedures) of the type *Animal*. It is not a big step to create a type hierarchy from there. *Lion* and *Dog* are both of type *Animal*; we just need to override methods to implement derived types and perhaps add other properties. See Figure 1-2.

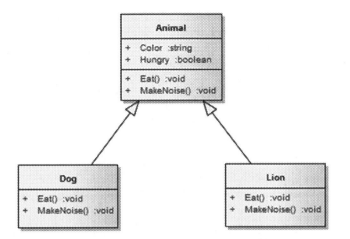

Figure 1-2. *OO diagram of Animal*

Eventually we will get a hierarchy model of the objects we see in the physical world and express them as types with inheritance, polymorphism, and encapsulation.

Memory

Throughout the development of imperative programming, memory access and memory management have been of great interest.

Having full access to memory is very powerful. In the C language, a programmer can get the address of memory as a pointer, which basically (internal implementation aside) has a value of type *integer* and indicates an *address* of a memory location. Being a number, the pointer can be manipulated as a number as well. Any programmer who has written programs in C knows about buffer manipulation. A sort algorithm is implemented by manipulating pointers instead of copying values. With this power, almost inevitably errors are made. Buffer overflows and exploits based on the same principles are probably the most common reasons for security problems, despite programming languages getting better at managing memory and checking boundaries. In most modern imperative programming languages, it is not possible to access memory with direct pointers without making it explicit with keywords like *unsafe* and compilers or standard library implementations checking for buffer overflows. Also, memory does not need to be allocated or freed in the program; a *garbage collection* program is part of runtime systems and does this automatically using sophisticated algorithms.

What has not changed in all the years is that values in memory can be changed from anywhere in a program and are mutable unless changes are prevented by the language. For example, in C#, the type *String* is immutable. More modern imperative languages make changes more difficult, but it is possible to change public properties of an object or change the whole object during a function call. This is especially difficult in multi-threaded situations, where memory locations that can be accessed from different threads need to be locked to prevent another thread from accessing the same memory location. It is very easy to produce deadlocks in such situations or introduce very subtle bugs with incorrect values because of race conditions.

Easy access to mutable values in memory also enables side effects by manipulating values that are accessible from various functions. Global variables are an obvious example, but it could also be a property in an object.

All this said, the imperative programming paradigm, especially in its object-oriented variation, has produced software that is reliable and does what requirements have specified. The industry has adjusted to the pitfalls by creating tools, runtimes, libraries, and better programming languages. For example, the new language *Rust* tries to tackle the memory problem by attaching an ownership model to each memory location that is referenced by a variable. It still allows a mutable variable, but since it needs to be explicitly set to *mutable*, the compiler can prevent unintended changes.

My personal experience in enterprise backend development shows that problems can be avoided with careful design. Critics coming from "pure" functional languages like Haskell often describe the imperative paradigm as if C was still used everywhere. In fact, even with C++ side effects, direct change of state can be prevented. It is the developer's responsibility and it is difficult, yes, but it is possible.

Functional Programming

How would a cooking recipe example look with the functional paradigm? The closest I can think of is the bread machine I use; see Figure 1-3.

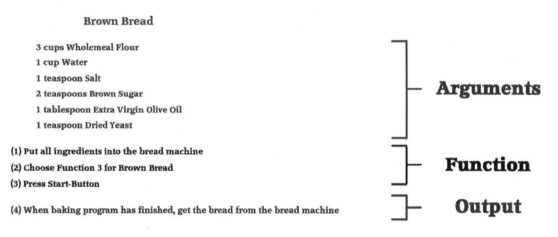

Figure 1-3. *Functional cooking recipe*

All the ingredients go into the machine and then I have to choose a function, press a button, and everything will be done for me. This is declarative and always produces the same bread as long as I get the measurements of the ingredients right.

Functional programming is based on the lambda calculus and can be explained from a mathematical point of view. It is the right approach for everybody who loves mathematics; for the rest of us, I would rather stick to simpler explanations.

Two features of the functional paradigm are the exact opposite of imperative programming: functional programming avoids side effects and mutable data.

The arguments of a function are all evaluated before the processing of the function starts and the only output is defined in the function. Immutability of data makes it impossible to change the value of data outside of the function.

Another interesting aspect of immutable data is that loop structures, like *for* or *while* as we see them in imperative languages, are not possible. A by-definition mutable index variable could not be changed and the loop would not work. Functional programming uses recursion for the same purpose. For programmers coming from imperative languages, this is quite unusual. Recursion is largely avoided in imperative programming because of possible stack overflows, and its use is rather discouraged. Functional languages get around this problem with tail recursion, which manipulates the stack so it does not grow. It is worth mentioning that tail recursion can be implemented in imperative languages as well. You will investigate this feature in more detail in Chapter 14.

In the example of the bread machine, I was talking about the declarative nature of the approach. It needs to be pointed out that a declarative style certainly goes hand in hand with the functional paradigm, but there is no permanent relation. There are plenty of discussions about it and, depending on the definition of *declarative*, the answers may be different.

Functional programming also does not deal with objects. As the name implies, the main focus is on functions, and these functions manipulate data. If a lion or a dog feeds on a piece of meat, it's not important. The end state is the same: the animal is still hungry or not. It is then a matter of another discussion how state is treated, either kept in a state structure or passed around from function to function.

Hybrid Programming Languages

In theory, both imperative and functional approaches should yield the same result, if they were applied to the same problem.

Example 1-1 shows a simple program in Erlang and C#. A range of numbers from 1 to 10 is the input, and then the function multiplies each number with 10. The output is a list from 10 to 100 in steps of 10.

Example 1-1.

```
1   [I*10 || I <- lists:seq(1,10)].
```

The Erlang code, shown in Example 1-2, uses a concept called *list comprehension*, which you will further explore in Chapter 14.

Example 1-2.

```
1   List<int> l = new List<int>();
2   foreach (var i in Enumerable.Range(1, 10)) {
3     l.Add(i*10);
4   }
```

The C# code clearly shows the imperative style. You tell the computer to go through the input list and add the result to the output list. The code is more verbose and very specific.

Both statement blocks have the same output, an array that is shown in pseudo-code in Example 1-3.

Example 1-3.

```
1   [10,20,30,40,50,60,70,80,90,100].
```

Many modern programming languages are hybrid languages and mix imperative and functional programming styles. F#, Scala, C#, and Ruby can be classified as both object oriented and functional; even Java 8 has added lambda expressions. The borders are not always clear, and developers who program in one of the more mainstream imperative languages have used the functional paradigm, often without knowing or noticing it.

How Do Erlang and Elixir Fit into the Schema?

Elixir and Erlang are certainly functional languages, although some functional programming communities will say they are "impure" functional languages. You will find features that constitute a functional programming style in Erlang and Elixir in every code listing of this book. The next chapter explains more of the ideas behind both languages.

CHAPTER 2

▓ ▓ ▓

From Erlang to Elixir

The language **Erlang** was inspired by Prolog's logical programming and concrete architectural requirements at Eriksson. Joe Armstrong has written a paper called *History of Erlang*, which describes in detail the evolution of the language from the perspectives of the creators and the company that sponsored the creation of the language.

This chapter describes the broad picture. If you want to get deeper into the history of Erlang, read Armstrong's fascinating paper, which also shows some of the syntax of the early language[1].

From the start, Erlang was built on three principles: fault tolerance, concurrency, and distribution. These principles were defined by the projected use case for this language in the telecommunication industry. A telephone switch can't simply die when bad data is processed, and it has to process data as fast as possible. When the switch needs to be updated, it can't restart and drop the existing data, which in this case are telephone calls. The *hot code swapping* feature in Erlang allows us to update code by keeping data and letting the data optionally be processed by other nodes in the distributed system.

Hot code swapping is also the cause for a language feature that haunts Erlang to this day: dynamic types. If types change, the code can't be easily swapped because the new code won't be able to handle the old types. But dynamic types have a habit of hiding type inconsistencies during compile time and springing up during runtime with the possibility of crashing the application or at least to pushing the application into a bad state.

Another critical assessment during the long life of Erlang is memory management. Erlang defines lightweight processes, which have nothing to do with operating system processes. Each process has its own heap, but large data will blow up the heaps and thus reduce the number of potential processes on one machine. The same problem applies to messages. Erlang implements a message system between processes to avoid shared memory, and large messages slow down the system because the data needs to be copied from one heap to another.

Knowing about possible problems is the first step to avoiding them. Erlang/OTP has reacted to them with new features. Throughout this book, you will see how developers who use Erlang/OTP can use architectural and design ways to avoid problems.

Elixir is an answer to Erlang's syntax and lack of modern tooling. The creator, Jose Valim, was involved with Ruby on Rails as core contributor and wanted to bring some of the Rails experience to the Erlang system. With the tooling, he and the community around Elixir certainly succeeded. The package manager **Hex** and the build tool **Mix** provide a unified experience for various developing tasks like scaffolding, running tests, compiling, and deploying.

Since Elixir uses the Erlang system, code and tools can be mixed. All code ends up in the byte code that is used by the Erlang virtual machine and runtime called BEAM (Bodgan's Erlang Abstract Machine). This means that the new language Elixir can use the experience of the last 25 years, especially when using OTP (Open Telecom Platform). This is the framework tightly coupled to the language itself and it implementing

---

[1] http://dl.acm.org/citation.cfm?id=1238850&dl=ACM&coll=DL&CFID=495241682&CFTOKEN=12700222

© Wolfgang Loder 2016

W. Loder, *Erlang and Elixir for Imperative Programmers*, DOI 10.1007/978-1-4842-2394-9_2

best practices that emerged in using the system in the last decades for system and enterprise-critical applications.

Elixir is still evolving: the 1.0 release was in September 2014 and it rapidly moved to 1.3 in 2016. Some Erlang developers are critical about features that mean to simplify usage, but are doing some magic in the background to satisfy the Erlang system. For example, syntactical sugar allows it to rebind variables, which means it looks as if a variable is not immutable, which is one of the fundamentals of Erlang. In reality, new variables are created for the rebound variables during compilation as the immutability rules demand, transparent to the developer.

Elixir brings new features to the system as well. Protocols are similar to interfaces or abstract classes, and pipe operators bind function calls together in one pipeline in a fluent way. One of the biggest changes to Erlang is that macros are at the core of the language. They manipulate the AST (Abstract Syntax Tree) at compile time and make it easy to integrate new language features. Some constructs in the core language are actually implemented as macros.

In this book, I mix Erlang and Elixir, but I use as much as possible the tooling of the Elixir system, which is, at the moment, simply more modern and flexible than the Erlang tools. These tools are currently worked on and many wish that the two communities would converge their tools eventually.

This is only a quick glimpse into Erlang/OTP and Elixir. In later chapters of this book, I will dive much deeper into the language features.

CHAPTER 3

■ ■ ■

Setting Your Mind

Coming from a background of imperative languages, it is important to meet Erlang/OTP and Elixir with a mind that is not preset.

The following rules are my recommendations for setting your mind before you get into the actual implementation of a project:

1. Don't try to translate from an OO (object-oriented) model to a functional model and don't try to express OO constructs in Erlang or Elixir.

2. Think in a declarative way; do not write how it should happen, but what should happen.

3. Assignments are not actual assignments, but comparisons between the left side and the right side of an expression. In Erlang, this process is called pattern matching. In addition, the first assignment in the code is an initialization of a variable similar to *final* in Java or *readonly* in C#.

4. From the last rule follows that variables, despite their name, are immutable once they are initialized.

5. All types are dynamic. This does not mean that there are no built-in types; there are, but you don't specify the type at compile time.

6. Leave the concepts of classes and interfaces behind. There are similarities and similar constructs, but it confuses more than it helps.

7. When you hear *processes*, forget what you fear about working with threads or operating processes. They are something completely different and there is no shared memory to hurt you.

8. There are no objects in an OO sense. There are processes and we send messages between them. And yes, this does not only sound like the Actor model, it is an implementation of it.

9. The language knows exceptions with the usual try-catch blocks. Now that you know this, you won't hear it again in this book. I adhere to Erlang's *Let it fail* premise. It sounds scary, but it works.

10. Libraries and frameworks are important, especially OTP. Erlang and Elixir as languages are only part of the whole.

You will see that all of the new concepts and patterns are not complicated. They are just different to the ones you, as a mostly imperative programmer, have encountered so far.

So keep these few rules in mind, and have more fun and less headaches.

© Wolfgang Loder 2016

W. Loder, *Erlang and Elixir for Imperative Programmers*, DOI 10.1007/978-1-4842-2394-9_3

PART II

The Service

CHAPTER 4

■ ■ ■

Service Overview and Design

The original commercial service that is based some of the examples is named *Digital Asset Repository (DAR)* and helps to manage digital assets like images, videos, scanned documents, online forms, spreadsheets, and similar. In fact, everything that is in digital form can be saved to the repository.

This service would not help much if these digital documents are only stored, so additional features are added: security, workflow, document transformations, and more. The requirements diagram looks like Figure 4-1.

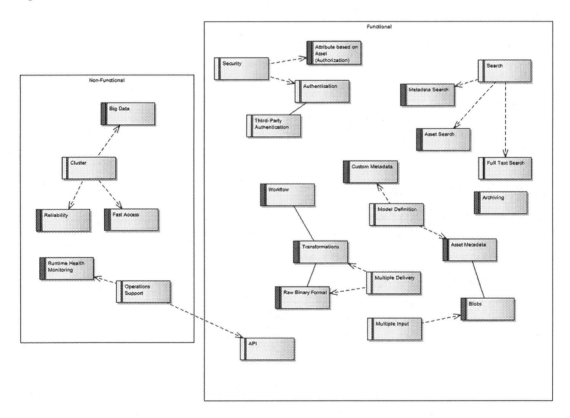

Figure 4-1. *Digital Asset Repository requirements*

W. Loder, *Erlang and Elixir for Imperative Programmers*, DOI 10.1007/978-1-4842-2394-9_4

These requirements describe the basis for real-world use cases described in the following sections.

Security

Images and videos from security cameras are sent to the repository. A workflow decides if and when these assets are archived. During the retrieval of images, a transformation provides smaller images and the full resolution image is only accessed on demand.

Live Media

Reporters take snapshots with their mobile cameras and send them to the headquarters. Workflow steps ensure that the images are appropriate for broadcast and sets the access rights appropriately. The images are then used in a live broadcast.

Insurance

Paper and online forms need to be processed. Paper forms are scanned and saved in the repository with custom metadata, which can optionally be filled by OCR processing (optical character recognition). Online forms are transferred directly into the repository. A workflow can be used to give access to assets to different workers.

Solicitor

Different paper documents, images, and digital documents are all saved in the repository. Metadata is used to connect them and a specialized full text search implementation provides information quickly.

Registries and Archives

Scanned documents need to be saved. The number is huge and data retrieval is unpredictable, so a cache cannot be used effectively. Data loss is not an option, so the solution must run in a fail-safe manner.

Online Shop

Images are used for shop item descriptions and need to be changed frequently. Access to the assets happens with high frequency and the access API needs to respond quickly to a high number of responses.

Mobile Apps

Images are delivered to a variety of devices. Transformations make sure that assets are sent in the right size and resolution.

The use case diagram for the commercial project looks Figure 4-2.

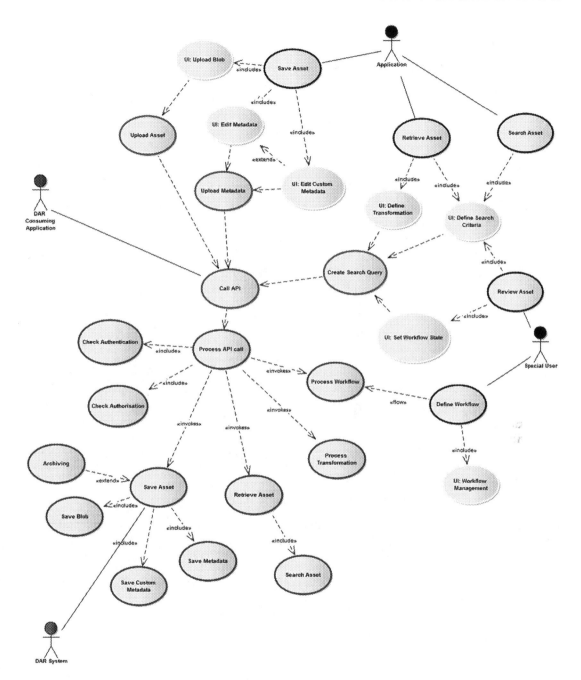

Figure 4-2. *Digital Asset Repository use cases*

All use cases in Figure 4-2 with green borders are the core system and their implementation will be at least partially described in this book.

The context is set with requirements and use cases, and the next step is to have a diagram to describe components involved, so see Figure 4-3.

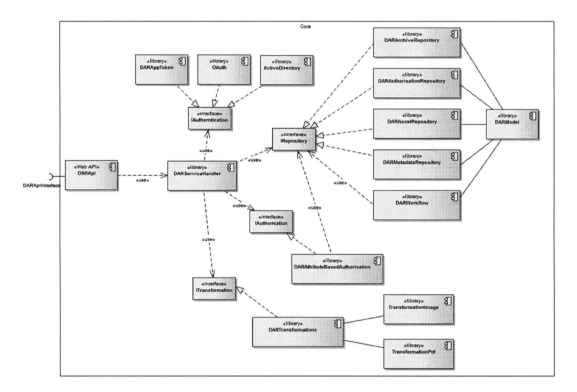

Figure 4-3. *Digital Asset Repository components*

Looking at this version of the component diagram reveals another difference between imperative programming and functional or declarative programming: the modeling needs a rethink. A description of interfaces and libraries, which are in fact sets of class types in object-oriented design, does not suffice for an Erlang/OTP/Elixir system.

A discussion about modeling of Erlang/OTP applications can be found in Appendix A.

The commercial project is partly closed source, so not everything can be shown. But I started an offspring from this project that is open source and specializes in storing and retrieving Common Creative licensed stories for children. This implementation is inspired by the African Storybook Project[1], which provides reading material for children in different languages.

This open source project uses some of the implementation of the commercial project, but does not show internal security protocols, deployment strategies, or enhanced features. It can be found on GitHub at `https://github.com/kujua/creative-common-dar`.

I will base the service implementation as described in Part 4 on this open source project.

---

[1]`africanstorybook.org`

CHAPTER 5

■ ■ ■

Service Features

The features of the commercial project *Digital Asset Repository* are

- Enterprise-Grade Security
- API Access
- Various Search Options
- Reliability
- Archive Option
- Transformations
- Multiple Input
- Multiple Delivery
- Workflow
- Custom Metadata
- Operating Support

The *workflow* component can define various tasks or steps that relate to the business process. For example, an image must get approved before it can be published or a scanned document must go through several processing steps.

Built-in *security* can be applied to any asset individually. For example, it is possible to have public access to some assets and private access to others or assign individuals to have write access to certain assets.

All features can be accessed with a standard web *API*. It is part of DAR and the project provides implementations for different platforms. This way it can guarantee that the repository is working as designed. The API runs on a web server in the cloud by default, but can also be installed on premises for custom solutions.

Search can query asset names and all related metadata. Additional options like full-text search can be implemented as custom solutions.

The retrieval of assets can use built-in *transformations* to serve, for example, different resolution of images or PDF-documents from other document formats like Office Word.

The repository is distributed to more than one server and data is replicated (backed up) to ensure *reliability*.

Access of popular assets and metadata is made faster by using a *cache* in server memory or on the file system; therefore it is not necessary to query the database every time, but to use a cached version of the asset.

© Wolfgang Loder 2016

W. Loder, *Erlang and Elixir for Imperative Programmers*, DOI 10.1007/978-1-4842-2394-9_5

Assets that are not used anymore or are expected to be infrequently retrieved can be stored in an *archive*. Internally, this is a different datastore, which is not accessed during normal operation like search queries. Of course, the archive can be accessed with the API.

DAR can be easily integrated via API calls. This is sufficient for most solutions, but other businesses may need further integration with already existing systems.

As for technical requirements, the repository and the API run on Microsoft Azure by default, either on Windows Server or Ubuntu server systems with a MongoDB datastore for assets, a PostgreSQL datastore for metadata, and an API implementation in Erlang.

The **open source version** provides the following features:

- API Access

- Some Transformations

- Workflow

These features are described in this book, but there are also examples of the commercial version slightly changed to obey license rules.

PART III

The Setup

■ ■ ■

## CHAPTER 6

Environment and Deployment

Installation

You need to set up Erlang/OTP and Elixir on your machine(s). The differences between development and production environments will be discussed in Chapter 7 and Chapter 8. For now, you will install the minimum applications and frameworks needed to run Erlang and Elixir code.

ℹ Docker If you don't want to install Erlang/OTP and Elixir on your physical machine, read later in this chapter about Docker containers.

From the web sites for Erlang Downloads[1] (the binaries are distributed by *Erlang Solutions*) and Elixir[2] either precompiled packages or sources can be downloaded. The process was straightforward for me on Windows (8.1, 10), Mac OS X (10.11.x), and Ubuntu 14.04/16.04 LTS 64-bit (in a VirtualBox VM on a Windows host and in a Parallels VM on Mac OS X).

⚲ If you use Ubuntu in a VirtualBox VM Don't forget to configure the Ubuntu machine to allow drag-and-drop and shared folders.

In the VirtualBox menu, set `Devices > Drag'n Drop` and `Devices > Shared Clipboard` to `Bidirectional`. For shared folders, run the statement `sudo adduser <username> vboxsf` in a shell and define a folder in the VM settings on your host to be shared.

Testing the Setup

Both Erlang and Elixir install a REPL (*read-eval-print loop*). As in similar language systems, expressions and other language constructs can be directly tested in the REPL. Elixir and Erlang are in fact starting a virtual machine when running the REPL, which can be done from the shell or by running a program in Windows.

---

[1] `www.erlang-solutions.com/downloads/download-erlang-otp`
[2] `http://elixir-lang.org/install.html`

© Wolfgang Loder 2016
W. Loder, *Erlang and Elixir for Imperative Programmers*, DOI 10.1007/978-1-4842-2394-9_6

A big difference in environments like Java or .Net is that no IDE is provided by default. The REPL is used to test out code snippets or run modules from a file. Ruby and F# developers will find this approach familiar, but others will miss the default integrated environment.

Let's see if your setup was correct and is working. You will define a function called double that multiplies its argument by 2. Then you will invoke double on a list of integers, which is done with a map function: each item in the list is an argument to double and the result is a new list.

Erlang

Run the Erlang REPL by opening a shell and typing erl in Linux or OS X; on Windows systems type werl or click the icon provided by the installation. You should see a line like that in Example 6-1.

Example 6-1.

```
Erlang/OTP 18 [erts-7.1] [source] [64-bit] [smp:8:8] [async-threads:10] [hipe] [\ kernel-
poll:false]    [dtrace]
```

The numbers *18* and *7.1* indicate the version of the Erlang system and the *Erlang RunTime System (erts)* and can be different in your case.

Type the statements in lines 5 and 7 from Example 6-2 (don't forget the dot (.) at the end of each statement line!). You will see the result shown in line 8.

Example 6-2.

```
1    Erlang/OTP 18 [erts-7.1] [source] [64-bit] [smp:8:8] [async-threads:10] [hipe]
2    [\kernel-poll:false] [dtrace]
3
4    Eshell V6.4 (abort with ^G)
5    1> Double = fun(X) -> 2 * X end.
6    #Fun<erl_eval.6.90072148>
7    2> lists:map(Double, [1,2,3,4,5]).
8    [2,4,6,8,10]
9    3>
```

Exit the Erlang REPL with Ctrl+Command+C and answer *a* when the information shown in Example 6-3 is displayed.

Example 6-3.

```
BREAK: (a)bort (c)ontinue (p)roc info (i)nfo (l)oaded
       (v)ersion   (k)ill (D)b-tables (d)istribution
```

Elixir

To see the Elixir REPL, you must type iex into the shell; you will see the lines shown in Example 6-4.

Example 6-4.

```
1    Erlang/OTP 19 [erts-8.0.2] [source] [64-bit] [smp:8:8] [async-threads:10] [hipe]\
2    [kernel-poll:false] [dtrace]
3
```

```
4    Interactive Elixir (1.3.2) - press Ctrl+C to exit (type h() ENTER  for help)
5    iex(1)>
```

The first line is the banner of the Erlang system. The fourth line shows the version of the Elixir system. As before, the numbers may be different from your output. Typing elixir instead of iex will bring up the help text for the non-interactive version of Elixir, which can be used to run scripts, start applications, or invoke other tasks; see Example 6-5.

Example 6-5.

```
$ elixir
Usage: elixir [options] [.exs file] [data]

  -v                 Prints  version  and  exits
  -e "command"       Evaluates the given command (*)
  -r "file"          Requires the given files/patterns (*)
  -S "script"        Finds and executes the given script
  -pr "file"         Requires the given files/patterns in parallel (*)
  -pa "path"         Prepends the given path to Erlang code path (*)
  -pz "path"         Appends the given path to Erlang code path (*)
  --app "app"        Starts the given app and its dependencies (*)
  --erl  "switches"  Switches to be passed down to Erlang (*)
  --name "name"      Makes and assigns a name to the distributed node
  --sname "name"     Makes and assigns a short name to the distributed node
  --cookie "cookie"  Sets a cookie for this distributed node
  --hidden           Makes a hidden node
  --detached         Starts the Erlang VM detached from console
  --werl             Uses Erlang's Windows shell GUI (Windows only)
  --no-halt          Does not halt the Erlang VM after execution

** Options marked with (*) can be given more than once
** Options given after the .exs file or -- are passed down to the executed code
** Options can be passed to the Erlang runtime using ELIXIR_ERL_OPTIONS or --erl
```

Type the statements in lines 5 and 7 (this time, with no dots at the end of statements) from Example 6-6.

Example 6-6.

```
1    Erlang/OTP 19 [erts-8.0.2] [source] [64-bit] [smp:8:8] [async-threads:10] [hipe]\
2    [kernel-poll:false] [dtrace]
3
4    Interactive Elixir (1.3.2) - press Ctrl+C to exit (type h() ENTER  for help)
5    iex(1)> double = fn x-> 2 * x  end
6    #Function<6.90072148/1 in :erl_eval.expr/5>
7    iex(2)> Enum.map(  [1,2,3,4,5],double)
8    [2, 4, 6, 8, 10]
9    iex(3)>
```

The result is the same in both cases, but even these short programs give you a first hint of the different syntax of Erlang and Elixir. In line 7, you could have also used Erlang's lists library with the same end result; see Example 6-7.

Example 6-7.

```
:lists.map(double,[1,2,3,4,5])
```

In Elixir, you can call any Erlang library by writing a colon (:) in front of the module name and then access functions with the dot operator, similar to object-oriented languages. The Elixir example shows another feature that will come handy when defining domain specific languages: most of the time the parentheses surrounding arguments can be omitted.

Please note: Erlang has strict naming conventions for variables (starting with an uppercase letter) and for atoms (which indicate *something* that is constant starting with a lowercase letter). X in the function declaration in the example above is a variable. The module name lists in the call to map is an atom. In Elixir, atoms start with a colon, hence the change from lists in Erlang to :lists in Elixir. All this will become much clearer in the following chapters.

REPLs are a nice way to try out some code, but for bigger projects an editor or better yet an IDE is needed. There are some editors with Erlang or Elixir syntax highlighting built in or available as an add-on. When you install Erlang on a machine with Emacs installed, it will add the Erlang mode for Emacs[3], which integrates the Erlang shell into Emacs and allows compiling from inside Emacs. There is also an Elixir mode for Emacs[4] available. Similar packages exist for Vim[5] and GitHub's Atom for both Erlang[6] and Elixir[7]. A mixed Vim-Emacs on the Mac is Spacemacs[8] which can run Alchemist[9], which is for many the best Elixir environment on the Mac.

A cross-platform development environment is IntelliJ IDEA[10]. It provides integration capabilities for Erlang and Elixir, and it can be used to edit and compile. The Community Edition is sufficient for developing non-commercial Erlang and Elixir programs.

For this book, I used a combination of Atom and shell on all platforms to ensure compatibility.

Docker Containers

It is very convenient to spawn a Docker container on a machine and work with REPLs without having to go through an installation process.

Of course, if you want to use the predefined Docker containers, you will need to install Docker. The Docker web site has detailed instructions for Windows[11], Mac OS X[12], and Ubuntu[13]. The Ubuntu installation has more steps than the one for Windows and OS X, which simply run installers. I also had to reboot Ubuntu a few times until the access rights for my user were picked up and I could successfully run Docker commands. Docker on Windows and OS X wraps Linux virtual machines because for obvious reasons it is not possible to run native Linux containers on these operating systems. The Ubuntu installation (and installations on different Linux systems, which I have not tested) is certainly the way Docker is supposed to be run. In March 2016, Docker started beta programs for more integrated applications on Mac and Windows[14]. They integrate

---

[3]www.erlang.org/doc/apps/tools/erlang_mode_chapter.html
[4]https://github.com/elixir-lang/emacs-elixir
[5]https://github.com/jimenezrick/vimerl
[6]https://atom.io/packages/language-erlang
[7]https://github.com/lucasmazza/language-elixir
[8]http://spacemacs.org
[9]https://github.com/tonini/alchemist.el
[10]www.jetbrains.com/idea/
[11]https://docs.docker.com/installation/windows/
[12]https://docs.docker.com/installation/mac/
[13]https://docs.docker.com/installation/ubuntulinux/
[14]https://blog.docker.com/2016/03/docker-for-mac-windows-beta/

tools and, judging from my first tests, make many tasks easier. The biggest advantage is that VirtualBox is not a requirement anymore and does not need to be installed on the machine that uses Docker, because these programs come with their own lightweight Linux embedded.

The Dockerfile shown in Example 6-8 creates a container based on Ubuntu (in this case a minimal Ubuntu image provided by Phusion) and installs Erlang and Elixir.

Example 6-8.

```
1   FROM phusion/baseimage:0.9.18
2   MAINTAINER Wolfgang Loder @wolfgang_loder
3
4   ENV REFRESHED_AT 2016-08-08
5
6   RUN echo /root /etc/container_environment/HOME
7
8   CMD ["sbin/my_init"]
9
10  # Set the locale
11  RUN locale-gen en_US.UTF-8
12  ENV LANG en_US.UTF-8
13  ENV LANGUAGE en_US:en
14  ENV LC_ALL en_US.UTF-8
15
16  # Set versions
17  ENV ERLANG_VERSION=1:19.0
18  ENV ELIXIR_VERSION=1.3.2
19
20  WORKDIR /tmp
21
22  # See : https://github.com/phusion/baseimage-docker/issues/58
23  RUN echo 'debconf debconf/frontend select Noninteractive' | debconf-set-selectio\
24  ns
25
26  # Get prerequisites
27  RUN apt-get update &&  apt-get install -y \
28      git \
29      make \
30      unzip \
31      wget
32
33  # Set up Erlang
34  RUN wget http://packages.erlang-solutions.com/erlang-solutions_1.0_all.deb && d\
35  pkg -i erlang-solutions_1.0_all.deb
36  RUN apt-get update
37  RUN apt-get install erlang -y \
38    && apt-get clean \
39    && rm -rf /var/lib/apt/lists/* /tmp/* /var/tmp/*
40
41  # Set up Elixir from precompiled zip on GitHub
42  WORKDIR /usr/local/elixir
43  RUN wget https://github.com/elixir-lang/elixir/releases/download/v$ELIXIR_VERSIO\
```

```
44   N/Precompiled.zip \
45     && unzip Precompiled.zip \
46     && ln -s /usr/local/elixir/bin/elixirc  /usr/local/bin/elixirc  \
47     && ln -s /usr/local/elixir/bin/elixir  /usr/local/bin/elixir  \
48     && ln -s /usr/local/elixir/bin/mix /usr/local/bin/mix \
49     && ln -s /usr/local/elixir/bin/iex /usr/local/bin/iex \
50     && rm -rf /var/lib/apt/lists/* /tmp/* /var/tmp/* \
51     && rm   /usr/local/elixir/Precompiled.zip
52
53   WORKDIR /
```

Notes:

- In lines 17 and 18, two environment variables are set to define the Erlang and Elixir versions you want to use. If you want to install different versions from the one shown in the Docker file, change them here. If you do this, be careful to choose an Erlang/Elixir pair that matches. For example, Elixir 1.0.3 did not work with Erlang 17.5. We are now (mid-2016) at Erlang version 19.2 and Elixir version 1.3.2, but at the publishing time of this book the version numbers will have changed.

- Elixir needs to run on a system with UTF 8 enabled; otherwise it won't work.

- The Elixir version is downloaded as a precompiled zip file from GitHub. It is also possible to download the source and compile Elixir during the creation of the Docker container.

- The script tries to clean up temporary files as much as possible, but the size of the created container is still about 700MB.

You can build the Docker image by executing the command shown in Example 6-9 on the command line in the folder that contains the Dockerfile.

Example 6-9.

```
1   docker build -t bookcompanionee:1.0 .
```

The container can then be run with the statement shown in Example 6-10.

Example 6-10.

```
docker run -t -i bookcompanionee:1.0 /bin/bash
```

Alternatively, a predefined container can be used. Docker Hub provides official images, amongst them Erlang[15] and Elixir[16]. The Elixir container builds on the Erlang container and has everything installed that is needed for development, including Rebar3. It can be pulled from the Docker Hub repository as shown in Example 6-11.

Example 6-11.

```
1   docker pull elixir
```

---

[15]https://hub.docker.com/_/erlang/
[16]https://hub.docker.com/_/elixir/

An additional option is to use Docker Compose[17] to spawn several containers with Erlang/Elixir in one and databases in the others.

It involves three steps:

- Create Dockerfiles for all your applications and services.

- Define all services that need to run for the application in a Docker Compose file.

- Execute composer commands to start or stop all services.

The file shown in Example 6-12 (`docker-compose.yml`) implements this scenario.

Example 6-12.

```
1   version: '2'
2   services:
3     elixir:
4       image: elixir
5       links:
6         - postgres
7         - mongo
8     postgres:
9       image: postgres
10      ports:
11      - "5432:5432"
12    environment:
13     POSTGRES_PASSWORD: postgres
14     POSTGRES_USER: postgres
15    mongo:
16      image: mongo
17      ports:
18        - "27017:27017"
```

You define three services: Elixir, PostgreSQL, and MongoDB. The Elixir service can communicate with the database servers via the defined ports.

Running all the containers is then invoked with the command shown in Example 6-13.

Example 6-13.

```
docker-compose run elixir
```

Listing all running containers will show (some columns were omitted) the output in Example 6-14.

Example 6-14.

```
1   $ docker ps
2   IMAGE        COMMAND              STATUS          PORTS
3   elixir       "iex"                Up 43 seconds
4   mongo        "/entrypoint.sh mongo"  Up 43 seconds  0.0.0.0:27017->27017/tcp
5   postgres     "/docker-entrypoint.s"  Up 43 seconds  0.0.0.0:5432->5432/tcp
```

---

[17]https://docs.docker.com/compose/overview/

The Elixir image runs iex and the official database images provide their services with predefined scripts. What you have not defined is that database files are on the host machines; if you stop the services, all data will be deleted as well.

When you don't need the containers anymore, you can issue the down command, as shown in Example 6-15.

Example 6-15.

```
1    $ docker-compose  down
2    Stopping docker_elixir_run_1 ... done
3    Stopping docker_mongo_1 ... done
4    Stopping docker_postgres_1 ... done
5    Removing docker_elixir_run_1 ... done
6    Removing docker_mongo_1 ... done
7    Removing docker_postgres_1 ... done
8    Removing network docker_default
```

? **Download or build containers?**   The answer to this question certainly depends on the trust you have towards the maintainer of the container. It is easier to download a container with the Docker tools and run it. Building the container from the Dockerfile is a process that takes its time; on the other hand, you know exactly what runs in the container.

Of course, it is not necessary to run Docker containers. The traditional way of having everything needed for development installed on one machine or in one virtual machine is still a good solution.

Deployment

Once a developer has written code in Erlang or Elixir, has tested it, and has confirmed that it runs locally, the next step is to deploy the application to a server on the network or in the cloud.

You may be surprised to learn that deployment of Erlang/Elixir applications is not straightforward. There is no obvious copy-and-paste solution or obvious one-click deployment. The reason is that the Erlang virtual machine or runtime must be available on a system that is running an Erlang or Elixir application.

? **What are *applications*?**   When we talk about *Applications* in the Erlang system, this does not mean an executable we can just run from the command line or by clicking an icon.

Applications are a set of modules that work together, but are not compiled into one binary file.

The Java world with JVM and the .Net world are similar, but those runtimes are either provided by the operating system (in .Net's case) or are most probably part of the operating system distribution, like the JVM.

In Erlang/OTP, the doctrine is to ship code with an embedded runtime and all dependencies. This makes sense from the point of view of guaranteeing that an application can start and run. Also, various applications on one machine can run different Erlang versions. Many developers know of the impact of incompatibilities between versions; Windows developers especially have experienced *DLL-hell*. The downside of embedded runtimes is that releases are quite large and the deployment on a distributed system or cluster needs to be planned carefully.

? **What is a *release*?**   A release copies the Erlang binaries and necessary libraries/beams/applications into a release directory and forms a self-contained Erlang system. It contains a boot script that defines how to start up the applications in the right order and keep them running.

You can mix Erlang and Elixir modules as you see fit to achieve your design goals. In a binary release, there is no difference between them because all code is compiled into the Beam-compliant code. Before getting to this stage, you must find out how to actually handle Erlang and Elixir source code to create a release.

In Chapter 7, you will look at the tools available to you for compiling, testing, and deploying code.

CHAPTER 7

▦ ▦ ▦

Development Setup

This development environment is a *continuous integration* environment (see Figure 7-1). The goal is to write code, and compile and run tests automatically in the background. The source code can be on the development machine or, if a container is used, on the host of the container, which may be the development machine as well. Optionally, you may have to install a database to run certain tests.

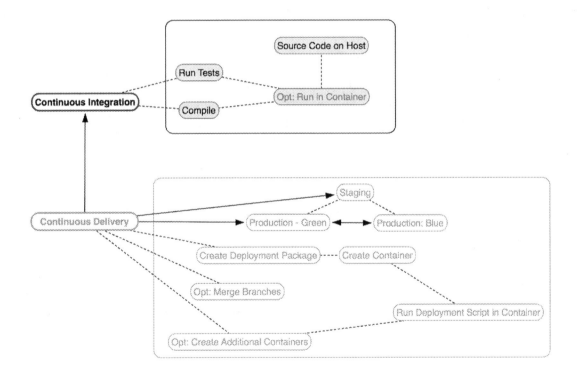

Figure 7-1. *Continuous integration*

If you do your coding in a folder on a host machine with containers, you must make sure to have different Erlang/Elixir versions and version combinations for compiling and testing available.

This chapter is an overview of various tools used during Erlang and Elixir development. After installing the tools, or using a container to have it prebuilt, your machine will be ready to do serious development work with Erlang and Elixir.

© Wolfgang Loder 2016
W. Loder, *Erlang and Elixir for Imperative Programmers*, DOI 10.1007/978-1-4842-2394-9_7

You'll use the example projects `erlangexamples` and `elixirexamples`, which are available on Github at `https://github.com/kujua/erlang-elixir-imperative-bookcompanion`.

Basic Tools for Continuous Integration

Continuous integration (CI) is a little bit more involved than running a REPL for Erlang or Elixir. In a nutshell, it means that you want to code, and a process watches the code folders and code files, and invokes tests whenever anything changes. These tests can be simple unit tests or more complicated integration tests. An example of a CI server for Erlang can be found at `https://github.com/greenelephantlabs/kha`. Unfortunately, the project has not been updated for a while, but perhaps somebody will pick it up and bring it up to the latest versions of Erlang, Rebar, and other requirements.

There are many discussions about the scopes of testing in CI, such as this google search on *scope of continuous integration*: `www.google.com/search?rls=en&q=ci+scope&ie=UTF-8&oe=UTF-8#q=scope+of+continuous+integration`. Topics include

- Do you want to run all tests all the time?

- Mocking or not mocking?

- Are databases included in the test setup?

- Where to keep the source code?

- How much to automate?

- Responsibilities of team members?

I touch on these topics without judging the need for the tools. For example, mocking libraries have their place in testing, but can be overused and may be just used for their own sake. Every developer team must make his/her own decision about mocking or other tools depending on managerial or technical requirements

---

⚷ Tools for Erlang and Elixir   The following two lists on GitHub give an overview of tools and libraries:

Awesome Elixir[1]

Awesome Erlang[2]

These lists are a good starting point to see what is going on in the Erlang/Elixir community. As expected, the list for Elixir is much larger and growing regularly. More resources can be found in Appendix B.

Rebar3

Rebar3 is Erlang's tool for building projects, but it is more than a build tool. It can create application templates, run tests, invoke scripts, and more. The previous version, *Rebar*, served Erlang developers for years, but some shied away from the configuration work and the fact that Rebar creates applications based on the OTP standard

---

[1]`https://github.com/h4cc/awesome-elixir`
[2]`https://github.com/drobakowski/awesome-erlang`

Rebar3 has changed a few things but stays as compatible as possible with older Rebar versions. One of the bigger changes is the integration of the package manager *Hex*, which is used in Elixir as well. This makes it possible to include (binary) packages that are created with Elixir. Another feature of Rebar3 is that it now *only* handles OTP applications and is more stringent with the folder structure of the projects, a fact that may put off some developers.

In this book, you will only use Rebar3 for Erlang projects because eventually this version will supersede the old version. The stable version 3.0 was released in February of 2016. The easiest way to install Rebar3 on your machine is to clone the GitHub repository[3] and run the bootstrap script for your operating system. Of course, Erlang must have been installed before that. Alternatively, get the compiled executable from the release page and copy it into a folder that is accessible on the path. You may have to set executable rights as well. The latter approach is preferable for updates, and the script approach is preferable for first-time installations.

The installation of Rebar3 links the executable to *rebar3* to avoid conflict with the previous version.

If you get a *command not found* or a similar message, you used the command rebar instead of rebar3.

The project erlangexamples in the directory Erlang/erlangexamples is an OTP application built with Rebar3. You can find the ready project in the GitHub repository, but let's walk through the creation and the configuration of this project to learn more about the tool.

Building a new application with Rebar3 is not difficult. The command will build a directory called erlangexamples and underneath it the directory structure and basic files for an OTP application. See Example 7-1.

Example 7-1.

```
rebar3 new app erlangexamples
```

Run the command, as shown in Example 7-2, from the newly created directory erlangexamples and the application will be compiled.

Example 7-2.

```
rebar3 compile
```

There is not much code in the project yet because the app-template of Rebar3 only creates the skeleton of an OTP application. Run the command and the compiled application will be brought into a form suitable for deploying, including a script to run the application from the command line. Doing this with a new application will just start a process with no functions to call, apart from the OTP skeleton callbacks, because you have not implemented anything yet. You will get deeper into the OTP code in Part 4. For now, see Example 7-3.

Example 7-3.

```
rebar3 release
```

In this example, you just created an OTP application, but there are more options that can be passed as arguments to create Erlang projects with Rebar3. The command shown in Example 7-4, without any arguments, reveals all templates that can be found on the machine.

---

[3]https://github.com/erlang/rebar3

Example 7-4.

```
rebar3 new
```

A vanilla installation of Rebar3 will print out the list shown in Example 7-5.

Example 7-5.

```
app (built-in): Complete OTP Application structure.
Cmake (built-in): Standalone Makefile for building C/C++ in c_src
escript (built-in): Complete escriptized application structure
lib (built-in):  Complete OTP Library application (no processes) structure
plugin (built-in):  Rebar3 plugin project structure
release (built-in):  OTP Release structure for executable programs
```

These are the default built-in template names with a brief explanation what they are creating.

Custom Templates

It is possible to implement custom templates[4]. These may be useful, for example, to provide more boilerplate code in the created files or to ensure project-specific headers. The following examples show the implementation of a custom template that creates an EUnit file in an existing project.

All custom templates reside in the folder ~/.config/rebar3/templates. On Windows, the ~ refers to the directory Rebar3 was installed into. This templates folder is read out automatically when you run the command new and all available custom templates are displayed together with the built-in templates. In the case of erlangexamples, the printout looks like Example 7-6.

Example 7-6.

```
app (built-in): Complete OTP Application structure.
cmake (built-in): Standalone Makefile for building C/C++ in c_src
cowboyapp (custom): Cowboy OTP-based application.
escript (built-in): Complete escriptized application structure
kujua_ctsuite (custom): Common Test Suite
kujua_eunit (custom): EUnit Test Suite
kujua_gsrv (custom): OTP gen_server
lib (built-in): Complete OTP Library application (no processes) structure
plugin (built-in): Rebar3 plugin project structure
release (built-in): OTP Release structure for executable programs
```

There are three custom templates with the prefix *kujua*, one of which will be described below, and one custom template for the web server Cowboy, which you will use in Part 4.

A template needs two files to function, one with the suffix .template and one Erlang code file with the default suffix .erl. Your example, kujua_eunit.template, is shown in Example 7-7.

Example 7-7.

```
1   {description, "EUnit Test Suite"}.
2   {variables, [
```

---

[4]www.rebar3.org/docs/using-templates

```
3     {name, "eunittestsuite"}
4   ]}.
5   {dir, "tests"}.
6   {template, "kujua_eunit.erl", "tests/{{name}}_tests.erl"}.
```

As often in Erlang, the configuration entries are just tuples:

- description will be shown when you run rebar3 new to get a list of all templates.

- variables defines variables in the form {key, "default value"} that will substitute placeholders in the Erlang file during file generation (shown later).

- dir creates a folder if it does not exist, but note that this is not automatically the place where the created files will be copied to.

- template is the heart of the configuration. It tells the generator which code file to use, where to put the new file, and which name to use. The {{name}} expression is Mustache[5], a template language widely used.

The Erlang file kujua_eunit.erl defines the output that should be created and defines the binding of Mustache placeholders to actual values; see Example 7-8.

Example 7-8.

```
1    %%%    @author      {{author_name}} <{{author_email}}>
2    %%%    @copyright   {{copyright_year}} {{author_name}}
3    %%%    @doc
4    %%%
5    %%%    @end
6
7    -module({{name}}_tests).
8    -author('{{author_name}} <{{author_email}}>').
9
10   -define(NOTEST, true).
11   -define(NOASSERT, true).
12   -include_lib("eunit/include/eunit.hrl").
13
14   -define(MODNAME, {{name}}).
15
16   %%% test generator
17   {{name}}_test_() ->
18       [].
```

In this example, you see placeholders like author_email that you did not define in the variables list in the template. These values are taken from a file global (without extension), which is the place to define key-value pairs for variables that are used in more than one template; see Example 7-9.

Example 7-9.

```
1    {variables, [
2       {copyright_year, "2016"},
```

---

[5]http://mustache.github.io

```
3       {author_name, "Wolfgang Loder"},
4       {author_email, "kujuasiokubahatisha@gmail.com"}
5    ]}.
```

The variables list in global will be merged with the variables for the particular template you want to create and then the bindings will be applied. The file global resides in the above mentioned templates folder.

Running the statement in Example 7-10 creates the file eunittemplate_tests.erl in the folder tests of the project you run the command in.

Example 7-10.

```
rebar3 new kujua_eunit eunittemplate
```

If test does not exist, it will be created during the processing of the template; see Example 7-11.

Example 7-11.

```
1    %%% @author      Wolfgang  Loder    <kujuasiokubahatisha@gmail.com>
2    %%% @copyright  2016  Wolfgang  Loder
3    %%% @doc
4    %%%
5    %%%    @end
6
7    -module(eunittemplate_tests).
8    -author('Wolfgang Loder <kujuasiokubahatisha@gmail.com>').
9
10   -define(NOTEST, true).
11   -define(NOASSERT, true).
12   -include_lib("eunit/include/eunit.hrl").
13
14   -define(MODNAME, eunittemplate).
15
16   %%%  test generator
17   eunittemplate_test_() ->
18       [].
```

Custom templates are useful, and you will see that the Elixir tool called *Mix* has a similar mechanism for creating custom templates.

Configuration and Shell

When Rebar3 processes a command, it relies on information in a configuration file to know what to do or if default values should be altered. The file rebar.config in erlangexamples looks like Example 7-12.

Example 7-12.

```
1    {erl_opts, [debug_info]}.
2    {deps, []}.
3
4    {relx, [{release, { erlangexamples, "0.1.0" },
5            [erlangexamples,
```

```
 6              sasl]},
 7           {sys_config, "./config/sys.config"},
 8           {vm_args, "./config/vm.args"},
 9           {dev_mode, true},
10           {include_erts, false},
11           {extended_start_script, true}]
12    }.
13
14    {profiles, [{prod,  [{relx, [{dev_mode, false},
15                                  {include_erts, true}]}]}]
16            }]
17    }.
```

Most of the commands in this file have to do with the release. The first two lines declare options (in this case, you want to have debug info in the binary) and dependencies. You will see in later chapters how to use dependencies and you will also use the files sys.config and vm.args that are linked to in the configuration in lines 7 and 8 and can be found in the directory config.

The syntax of the configuration file is Erlang code and consists of key-value pairs and lists. When you compile the example application with rebar3 compile, the output is as shown in Example 7-13.

Example 7-13.

```
===>  Verifying dependencies...
===>  Compiling    erlangexamples
```

Verifying dependencies refers to the *deps* declaration in rebar.config; in your example, this is an empty list.

The generated .beam file can be found in the folder _build. This folder has a structure that has to be described as "not obvious." Without going into the details, beam files in the erlangexamples project can be started in an Erlang shell from the directory Erlang/erlangexamples/_build/default/lib/erlangexamples/ebin, but there is a better way.

Rebar3 is a tool for OTP applications that are difficult to configure manually and difficult to run manually. Therefore, Rebar3 provides the option to build a release. The command rebar3 release uses another tool called *relx* and adds a folder named rel to the _build directory, which contains, among other files, scripts to run the application. Example 7-14 shows the output.

Example 7-14.

```
===> Verifying dependencies...
===>  Compiling    erlangexamples
===> Starting relx build process ...
===> Resolving OTP Applications from directories:
          /Users/Wolfgang/Projects/bookcompanion-ee/Erlang/erlangexamples/_build\
          /default/lib
          /Users/Wolfgang/Projects/bookcompanion-ee/Erlang/erlangexamples/apps
          /usr/local/Cellar/erlang/18.1/lib/erlang/lib
          /Users/Wolfgang/Projects/proper
          /Users/Wolfgang/Projects/bookcompanion-ee/Erlang/erlangexamples/_build\
          /default/rel
===>    Resolved erlangexamples-0.1.0
===>  Dev mode enabled, release will be symlinked
===>    release successfully created!
```

Again, it is possible to run the script manually, but it is likely that this will end in an error message. Rebar3 helps us with the command shown in Example 7-15 without relying on a release build.

Example 7-15.

```
rebar3 shell
```

This command opens a shell and boots your application with all needed dependencies and sets environment variables. One dependency you will see automatically loaded is *sasl*, the *System Application Support Library*. For production deployments, you will use the script as explained in the next chapter.

The shell also includes a Rebar3 agent, so it is possible to run commands in the shell like the one in Example 7-16.

Example 7-16.

r3:do(help).

This command displays the help page for Rebar3. More useful commands are compile, clean, or tree. You can also run tests this way, for example EUnit tests, such as the one in Example 7-17.

Example 7-17.

r3:do(eunit).

The list of commands in version 3.1.1 as printed by help is shown in Example 7-18.

Example 7-18.

```
1   Several tasks are available:
2
3   as                      Higher order provider for running multiple tasks in a sequence\
4    as a certain profiles.
5   clean                   Remove compiled beam files from apps.
6   compile                 Compile apps .app.src and .erl files.
7   cover                   Perform coverage analysis.
8   ct                      Run Common Tests.
9   deps                    List dependencies
10  dialyzer                Run the Dialyzer analyzer on the project.
11  do                      Higher order provider for running multiple tasks in a sequence.
12  edoc                    Generate documentation using edoc.
13  escriptize              Generate escript archive.
14  eunit                   Run EUnit Tests.
15  help                    Display a list of tasks or help for a given task or subtask.
16  new                     Create new project from templates.
17  path                    Print paths to build dirs in current profile.
18  pkgs                    List available packages.
19  release                 Build release of project.
20  relup                   Create relup of releases.
21  report                  Provide a crash report to be sent to the rebar3 issues page.
22  shell                   Run shell with project apps and deps in path.
23  tar                     Tar archive of release built of project.
24  tree                    Print dependency tree.
25  unlock                  Unlock dependencies.
```

```
26   update                Update package index.
27   upgrade               Upgrade dependencies.
28   version               Print version for rebar and current Erlang.
29   xref                  Run  cross reference analysis.
```

The most used commands in this list are certainly compile and shell. If you cloned the book companion GitHub repository to your local machine, just go to the directory Erlang/erlangexamples and run rebar3 shell. This command will compile the source and start the shell. Then run the statement shown in Example 7-19.

Example 7-19.

mapsexample:pizza_toppings_map().

You will get the return shown in Example 7-20.

Example 7-20.

```
1> mapsexample:pizza_toppings_map().
#{{ham,slices} => 6,
  {mozzarella,slices}  =>  8,
  {mushroom,spoon} => 2,
  {onion,spoon} => 2,
  {onionring,spoon} => 2,
  {sausage,piece} => 1,
  {spinach,spoon} => 2,
  {tomatosauce,spoon} =>  3}
```

Every function in the modules in the application erlangexamples can be run in the shell.

Rebar3 is more advanced than the few commands you have explored. Throughout this chapter and the rest of the book, you will use it and see many of the features. For now, I recommend a quick look at the Rebar3 documentation.[6]

Mix

Mix is the default tool to create and manage Elixir projects, similar to Rebar3 in Erlang or *npm* in Node.js.

Commands

The first command every Elixir developer will encounter is *mix new*. The line in Example 7-21 creates a simple project.

Example 7-21.

```
mix new  testproject
```

The output in Example 7-22 shows what was created and gives a few hints how to start.

---

[6]www.rebar3.org/docs

Example 7-22.

```
* creating README.md
* creating .gitignore
* creating mix.exs
* creating config
* creating config/config.exs
* creating lib
* creating lib/testproject.ex
* creating test
* creating  test/test_helper.exs
* creating test/testproject_test.exs

Your Mix project was created successfully.
You can use "mix" to compile it, test it, and more:

    cd testproject
    mix test

Run "mix help" for more commands.
```

Mix creates a subfolder with the name given for the project in the folder it runs in. Alternatively, a path can be supplied.

Running the command in Example 7-23 shows a help page for the command *new* with all the relevant options.

Example 7-23.

```
mix help new
```

Be careful not to write mix new help, as I did a few times; this will create a project called help in a subfolder of the current folder. The following help page output (Example 7-24) is formatted; the original has colors, and many more lines in between paragraphs.

Example 7-24.

```
Creates a new  Elixir project. It expects the path of the project as argument.

  mix new PATH [--sup] [--module MODULE] [--app APP] [--umbrella]

A project at the given PATH will be created. The application name and module
name will be retrieved from the path, unless --module or --app is given.
A --sup option can be given to generate an OTP application skeleton including a supervision
tree. Normally an app is generated without a supervisor and without the app callback.
An --umbrella option can be given to generate an umbrella project.
An --app option can be given in order to name the OTP application for the
project.
A --module option can be given in order to name the modules in the generated
code skeleton.

Examples
  mix new hello_world
```

```
Is equivalent to:
  mix new hello_world --module HelloWorld
To generate an app with supervisor and application callback:
  mix new hello_world --sup
Location: /usr/local/Cellar/elixir/1.2.5/lib/mix/ebinß
```

Important options are

- -sup for creating an OTP application with a supervisor

- -umbrella, which creates a project with an app folder to create applications in

You will see both options used in later chapters. Don't get too excited about these options; they produce skeletons, but not much more.

A useful application of mix new is that it can be invoked in an existing folder that has already files in it. Maybe you started writing some code and later decide to add tool support for packages or you want to use the code in a proper project. Run mix new . (note the dot) in the folder with your code and it will create a project structure with, among others, test files and a configuration file. If you had a mix.exs file in this folder, the new task will ask you if you want to overwrite it. After running the command, you will still have to copy your code into the lib folder manually, but it is better than doing everything else manually as well.

Mix uses the configuration file mix.exs to define everything about a project. The testproject you created before has the file in Example 7-25 (with all comments deleted).

Example 7-25.

```
1    defmodule Testproject.Mixfile do
2      use Mix.Project
3
4      def project do
5        [app: :testproject,
6         version: "0.0.1",
7         elixir: "~> 1.2",
8         build_embedded: Mix.env == :prod,
9         start_permanent: Mix.env == :prod,
10        deps: deps]
11     end
12
13     def application do
14       [applications: [:logger]]
15     end
16
17     defp deps do
18       []
19     end
20   end
```

This file is a normal Elixir script file that defines a module using Mix.Project, which has functions defined to support tasks in their work with projects. The function project is mandatory and needs to be defined in order for a project to work.

The file mix.exs is much more useful then the basic example shown. For example, it is possible to define functions that can be called from anywhere in the project. We can frown at global functions and global values, but sometimes they are necessary. The project dar_imagelib defines such a function; see Example 7-26.

Example 7-26.

```
1   defmodule DarImagelib.Mixfile do
2     use Mix.Project
3
4     def project do
5       [
6         app:  :dar_imagelib,
7         version: "0.0.1",
8         elixir: "~> 1.1",
9         build_embedded: Mix.env == :prod,
10        start_permanent: Mix.env == :prod,
11        deps: deps,
12        dialyzer:
13        [
14          plt_apps:  ["erts","kernel","stdlib","crypto","public_key","mnesia"],
15          flags:  ["-Wunmatched_returns","-Werror_handling",
16                    "-Wrace_conditions",  "-Wno_opaque"],
17          paths:  ["."]
18        ]
19      ]
20    end
21
22    def application do
23      [mod: {DarImagelib.App, []},
24       applications: [:logger,:mogrify]]
25    end
26
27    defp deps do
28      [
29        {:mogrify,path: "~/Projects/mogrify"},
30        {:dar_model,path: "~/Projects/creative-common-dar/Erlang/Libs/dar_model"},
31        {:ex_doc, "~> 0.11", only: :dev},
32        {:dialyxir, "~> 0.3", only: [:dev]}
33      ]
34    end
35
36    def getconstant(c) do
37      globdefs =  %{
38        respath:
39          "~/Projects/creative-common-dar/Elixir/Libs/dar_imagelib/test/res/"
40      }
41      case c do
42        :respath -> globdefs.respath
43        _    ->  ""
44      end
45    end
46
47  end
```

The function `getconstant` provides a way to get a global path for resources. It can be called in code as shown in Example 7-27.

Example 7-27.

DarImagelib.Mixfile.getconstant(:respath)

This example shows more features of mix configuration files. In the function deps, which returns a simple list of tuples, you can see path dependencies; see Example 7-28.

Example 7-28.

```
1   {:mogrify, path: "~/Projects/mogrify"},
2   {:dar_model, path: "~/Projects/creative-common-dar/Erlang/Libs/dar_model"}
```

Mogrify is an open source Elixir library (I will discuss it later in more depth) that I was forking to add new features for my project. The other dependency is dar_model, which is an Erlang project. When you compile the project with Mix, all dependent local Erlang projects will be compiled as well.

The function `project` also has configuration for Dialyzer on lines 12 to 18. You will learn more about Dialyzer later.

The command `mix help` displays the list in Example 7-29 (Elixir version 1.3.2 with the web framework *Phoenix* installed as archive).

Example 7-29.

```
Mix                        # Runs the default task (current: "mix run")
mix app.start              # Starts all registered apps
mix app.tree               # Prints the application tree
mix archive                # Lists  installed  archives
mix archive.build          # Archives this project into a .ez file
mix archive.install        # Installs an archive locally
mix  archive.uninstall     # Uninstalls archives
mix clean                  # Deletes generated application files
mix cmd                    # Executes the given command
mix compile                # Compiles source files
mix deps                   # Lists dependencies and their status
mix deps.clean             # Deletes the given dependencies' files
mix deps.compile           # Compiles dependencies
mix deps.get               # Gets all out of date dependencies
mix deps.tree              # Prints the dependency tree
mix deps.unlock            # Unlocks the given dependencies
mix deps.update            # Updates the given dependencies
mix do                     # Executes the tasks separated by comma
mix escript                # Lists installed escripts
mix escript.build          # Builds an escript for the project
mix  escript.install       # Installs an escript locally
mix  escript.uninstall     # Uninstalls escripts
mix help                   # Prints help information for tasks
mix hex                    # Prints Hex help information
mix hex.build              # Builds a new package version locally
```

```
mix hex.config              # Reads or updates Hex config
mix hex.docs                # Publishes docs for package
mix hex.info                # Prints Hex information
mix hex.key                 # Hex API key tasks
mix hex.outdated            # Shows outdated Hex deps for the current project
mix hex.owner               # Hex package ownership tasks
mix hex.public_keys        # Manages Hex public keys
mix hex.publish             # Publishes a new package version
mix hex.registry           # Hex  registry  tasks
mix hex.search              # Searches for package names
mix hex.user                # Hex user tasks
mix loadconfig              # Loads and persists the given configuration
mix local                   # Lists local tasks
mix local.hex               # Installs Hex locally
mix local.phoenix           # Updates Phoenix locally
mix local.public_keys       # Manages public keys
mix local.rebar             # Installs Rebar locally
mix new                     # Creates a new Elixir  project
mix phoenix.new             # Creates a new Phoenix v1.2.0 application
mix profile.fprof           # Profiles the given file or expression with fprof
mix run                     # Runs the given file or expression
mix test                    # Runs a project's tests
mix xref                    # Performs cross reference checks
iex -S mix                  # Starts IEx and runs the default task
```

The most important commands are

- mix deps.get: It scans the deps function output in mix.exs and downloads external dependencies to the machine. They are cached and reused, so they are not downloaded every time a project demands the dependency. The *Hex* package manager is used for this task and there are many options to tailor dependencies' management to the needs of the project. For example, it is possible to always override dependencies or to make them local to the project. You can specify dependencies from Hex (default), git including github, or local (path).

- mix compile: The project is compiled. If this task can't find dependencies, it will display a message to run the deps.get task first. It would be nice if running this command would be done automatically by default.

- mix test: All ExUnit tests of the project will be run. At the moment, there is no default task to run Common Test suites.

- iex -S mix: This is the equivalent of rebar3 shell. It starts the project in an Elixir REPL and loads all modules defined in the configuration. The option -S means to run a script, in this case mix.exs. You will hear more about iex when you look at debugging and monitoring.

- mix archive: Shows all registered archives, most notably that *Phoenix* is installed with an archive file (suffix .ez). Archive files are basically zip files with application and beam files.

- mix deps: Lists all dependencies for a project together with version information and if it is a mix (Elixir) or rebar3 (Erlang) package. It also indicates if a package was compiled with an old Elixir version, for example after an update (see Example 7-30).

Example 7-30.

```
* calendar (Hex package) (mix)
  locked at 0.16.0 (calendar) cf2dec9f
  the dependency was built with an out-of-date Elixir version, run "mix deps.com\ pile"
```

- mix deps.tree: Displays a graphical representation of the dependency tree with version information; see Example 7-31.

Example 7-31.

```
1   elixirexamples
2   ├── poison ~> 2.0 (Hex  package)
3   ├── dialyxir ~> 0.3 (Hex package)
4   ├── timex ~> 2.1.5 (Hex package)
5   │   ├── gettext ~> 0.10 (Hex package)
6   │   ├── combine ~> 0.7 (Hex package)
7   │   └── tzdata ~> 0.1.8 or ~> 0.5 (Hex package)
8   │       └── hackney  ~> 1.0 (Hex package)
9   │               ├── ssl_verify_fun 1.1.0 (Hex package)
10  │               ├── mimerl  1.0.2 (Hex package)
11  │               ├── metrics 1.0.1 (Hex package)
12  │               ├── idna  1.2.0 (Hex package)
13  │               └── certifi 0.4.0 (Hex package)
14  └── calendar ~> 0.16.0 (Hex package)
15          └── tzdata ~> 0.5.8 or ~> 0.1.201603 (Hex package)
```

- mix app.tree: Displays a graphical representation of the application tree, as shown in Example 7-32.

Example 7-32.

```
1   ==> dar_workflow
2   dar_workflow
3   ├── elixir
4   ├── logger
5   │   └── elixir
6   └── gen_state_machine
7       ├── elixir
8       └── logger
```

Both mix deps.tree and mix app.tree can create a *.dot*[7] file which can be transformed into other formats with the help of the command line tool *dot*[8], as shown in Example 7-33.

Example 7-33.

```
1   mix app.tree --format dot
2   dot -Tpng app_tree.dot -o app_tree.png
```

---

[7]https://en.wikipedia.org/wiki/DOT_(graph_description_language)
[8]www.graphviz.org

Figure 7-2 shows the application tree output for dar_workflow.

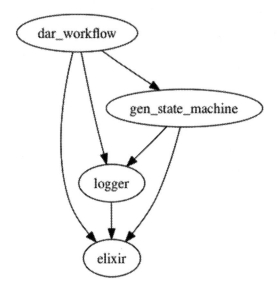

Figure 7-2. *Application tree output*

Custom Tasks

With Rebar3, you can define new templates; with Mix, you can do similar and more. I use the following custom task to insert headers into existing Elixir files (Example 7-34). It is a lengthy listing, but it can be easily used for your own custom tasks.

Example 7-34.

```
1   defmodule Mix.Tasks.Kujua.AddHeader do
2     use Mix.Task
3
4     @shortdoc "Generates a file header"
5     @moduledoc """
6     Generates a file header.
7
8       Usage: *mix kujua.add_header path/to/file.ex*
9
10    This command will write an empty header to *file.ex*.
11
12    If a header exists it will be overwritten.
13    Only headers generated with this task can be deleted!
14
15    ##  Options
16
17    The following options fill fields in @moduledoc:
18    * `--description Description` (default: "")
19    * `--author Author` (default: "")
```

```elixir
20      *  `--authoremail Email` (default: "")
21
22      The following options fill fields in @doc:
23      *  `--documentation` (default: "")
24
25      The following option does not ask for confirmation:
26      *  `-- silent true` (default: false)
27      """
28
29  def  run(args)  do
30      {options, filename, _} = OptionParser.parse  args
31      fname = List.first filename
32      if fname == nil, do: display_usage
33      if !File.exists?(fname), do: exit_gracefully
34      text = header_text options
35      silent = String.to_atom(Keyword.get options,:silent, "false")
36
37      Mix.shell.info """
38        The following header will be added to #{fname}:
39        "#{text}"
40        """
41      case overwrite? fname, silent do
42        true -> write_header fname,text
43        false -> Mix.shell.info "No changes were made"
44      end
45  end
46
47    defp header_text(options) do
48        """
49        @moduledoc \"\"\"
50        Author:  #{Keyword.get  options,:author,""}
51        Email:  #{Keyword.get  options,:authoremail,""}
52        Date: #{Keyword.get options,:date,""}
53        #{Keyword.get options,:description,""}
54        \"\"\"
55        @doc \"\"\"
56        #{Keyword.get options,:documentation,""}
57        \"\"\"
58        """
59    end
60
61    defp write_header(filename, text) do
62      {:ok, file} = File.read filename
63      # if String.contains?(file,"@moduledoc, @doc"), do: l = get_header_endline
64      file
65      # File.write filename, text <> file
66      # Mix.shell.info inspect delete_any_header(file)
67      File.write filename, text <> delete_existing_header(file, String.contains?
68      (file,"@moduledoc"))
69    end
70
71    defp exit_gracefully() do
```

```
72      Mix.shell.info "File does not exist. No changes were made."
73      exit(:shutdown)
74    end
75
76    defp display_usage() do
77      Mix.shell.info """
78      Usage: mix kujua.add_header path/to/file.ex
79      """
80      exit(:shutdown)
81    end
82
83    defp overwrite?(filename, false) do
84      Mix.Utils.can_write?(filename)
85    end
86    defp overwrite?(_filename, true) do
87      true
88    end
89
90    def delete_existing_header(file, true) do
91      split =   String.split(file,"\"\"\"")
92      Enum.at(split,4)
93    end
94    def delete_existing_header(file, false) do
95      file
96    end
97  end
```

The file defining the custom task can be included into a project by just copying it into the lib folder or any subfolder of lib. At the moment, I am not aware of a global folder that can make custom tasks available in any project managed with Mix, but it is possible to create all custom tasks in one application and include this application in the project or import it as a package.

The only requirement for a custom task is to include (use) Mix.Task and to provide a function run. This function gets arguments from the console and can then process its task accordingly. When you run mix help and have included the custom task in a project, it will be in the list. Your example task will appear like Example 7-35.

Example 7-35.

```
mix kujua.add_header  # Generates a file header
```

The description comes from the @shortdoc directive (line 4). The @moduledoc directive (lines 5ff) defines what is displayed when the command mix help kujua.add_header is run. All built-in tasks have a help page, similar to a man page in Unix/Linux/Mac OS, and it is good practice to write one for your own tasks as well.

Rebar 3 and Mix

Languages and their use are dependent on available tools. Erlang has Rebar3 and Elixir has Mix with the package manager Hex. At the moment, it is possible to use Hex from Rebar3 and compile Erlang projects from Mix. I hope that the tooling will eventually merge into one tool that can mix Erlang and Elixir projects seamlessly.

Common Test and EUnit for Erlang

Common Test and *EUnit* are installed with the Erlang-runtime by default. The difference between the two tools is the scope of the tests. While both can do all tests, EUnit is more suitable for testing units or modules. Common Test is more used for system tests like testing OTP applications.

ⓘ Test Types   There exist a huge taxonomy for testing and different definitions may intersect. Any project I was working on had its own definition of testing, if at all, but this is a different problem.

Without going into a deep discussion about different types, one way is to divide tests according to their knowledge about the code to be tested. *Unit testing* is understood to be on a very low level and *integration testing* is on a higher level. Another description is *white box testing* (with knowledge of the code) and *black box testing* (without knowledge of the code).

Working with these definitions, *EUnit* is on a lower level and *Common Test* on a higher level of testing. Testing the public interface of a module with EUnit is black box testing so, as often, the distinction falls apart after first scrutiny.

Rebar3 can run Common Test tests with the command shown in Example 7-36.

Example 7-36.

```
rebar3 ct
```

EUnit tests can be run with the command in Example 7-37.

Example 7-37.

```
rebar3 eunit
```

These commands will run even if there is no test present. So how do the tools know which tests to run? The easiest way is to create a folder named `test`. In erlangexamples it is the folder `Erlang/er-langexamples/apps/erlangexamples/test`. The test runners in Rebar3 work with conventions, but these conventions can be overwritten if necessary.

Both Rebar3 test runner commands have options to specify several aspects of running tests or test suites. For example, the option `-app appname` runs tests for a specified app only. More information can be found on the Rebar3 web site.[9]

EUnit

Developers with experience in Java, C#, and other languages will recognize the name derived from the family of xUnit frameworks, where "x" could be "J" or "N" or even "S" for the original Smalltalk unit testing framework [10] that started it in 1998. In the case of Eunit, the "E" clearly stands for "Erlang."

---

[9]`www.rebar3.org/docs/commands`
[10]`http://sunit.sourceforge.net`

I assume all readers know what a unit defines. Similar to folder structures of projects, the definition of a unit or more generally a *system under test* (*SUT*) is sometimes hotly debated. In this chapter, I define functions and modules as unit for EUnit. Libraries, applications, or distributed processes don't fall into this definition. Furthermore, one test should only check one function or module function.

The command rebar3 eunit will compile and run all tests within the test directory. You can take a very simple example of a test file from erlangexamples in the folder test, shown in Example 7-38.

Example 7-38.

```
1    -module(patternmatching_tests).
2    -include_lib("eunit/include/eunit.hrl").
3
4    always_return_42_test()    ->
5      ?assertEqual(42,    patternmatching:always_return_42()).
6
7    return_42_if_when_true_test() ->
8      ?assertEqual(42, patternmatching:return_42_if_when_true(true)).
9
10   return_42_if_when_true_fails_test()    ->
11     ?assertEqual(0, patternmatching:return_42_if_when_true(false)).
```

All functions ending with _test in its name will be run by EUnit if the line in Example 7-39 is included in the module.

Example 7-39.

```
-include_lib("eunit/include/eunit.hrl").
```

This declaration automatically creates an exported function named test() that is used to run all tests. Rebar3 calls this function when issuing the command eunit, but it is also possible to run tests directly from the command line once all dependencies are loaded, as shown in Example 7-40.

Example 7-40.

```
patternmatching_tests:test().
```

In the case of your erlangexamples project, this can be done with the commands in Example 7-41 in a Rebar3 shell.

Example 7-41.

```
1    1> c("apps/erlangexamples/test/patternmatching_tests.erl").
2    {ok,patternmatching_tests}
3    2> patternmatching_tests:tests().
4      All 3 tests passed.
5    ok
```

This method just shows that the test can be run directly from the shell. To do this, you must compile the test file first and then run the test() function. Normally you won't do this because it creates a *beam* file in the code folder, and you will want to run the tests by calling Rebar3.

When you look at the test code in the example, you can see that you could mix module functions and test functions by adding an include declaration to a module. As in other development environments, this is not a good idea. The downside of separation is that private functions cannot be tested; on the other hand, this means that only the public interface will be tested because a consumer will see the module.

❓Testing private functions?   Sometimes it may be necessary to test private functions. This is a problem that comes up in any development paradigm, either functional or imperative.

Let's put the question aside over whether the need for doing this is caused by a design fault, and have a look how it can be done.

Languages with reflection (like Java, ECMAScript, C#, PHP, Ruby, and others) can use reflection to invoke private methods or access private fields via helpers. Testing frameworks in the .Net or Java world can use byte code instrumentalization to inject helpers at runtime.

The Erlang VM does not have any way to call private functions from outside the module they are declared in. A workaround is to use `-ifdef(TEST).` with `-endif.` and put a test function into the block that will be called by EUnit during testing. Another more error-prone way is to export the function during development and set it private (i.e. not export it) for production.

Rebar3 defines several macros for expressing assertions. In the example, *?assertEqual* was used. Other assertion macros are *assertNotEqual, assertNot, assertMatch, assertNotMatch,* and a few others[11] to catch exceptions thrown by a function.

EUnit also defines macros to enable or disable testing or assertions and to put code into conditionals to avoid errors when test code should not be compiled. Again, the best way to avoid workarounds like this is to separate test modules from modules with production code.

Most of the time, you want to run several test cases and to define state and a running environment for those tests. EUnit helps you with this by allowing creations of *fixtures* and *test generators*; see Example 7-42.

Example 7-42.

```erlang
1    -module (fixture_tests).
2    -include_lib("eunit/include/eunit.hrl").
3
4    fixture1_test_()  ->
5        { setup,
6          fun setup/0,
7          fun cleanup/1,
8          ?_test(
9            begin
10               I =  42,
11               ?assertEqual(42,I)
12            end
13          )
14        }.
15
16   fixture2_test_()  ->
17       { setup,
18         fun setup/0,
19         fun cleanup/1,
20         [
```

---

[11]http://erlang.org/doc/apps/eunit/chapter.html#Assert_macros

```
21              {"assert true",
22              fun() ->
23                  ?assert(false)
24              end},
25              {"assert 42",
26              fun() ->
27                  I =  42,
28                  ?assertEqual(42,I)
29              end}
30          ]
31      }.
32
33  setup() ->
34      {ok}.
35
36  cleanup(_Pid)  ->
37      {ok}.
```

The functions fixture1_test_ and fixture2_test_ define fixtures with two tests each. The tests are not doing much and are just examples to show the structure. The functions end with test_ (note the underscore at the end), which indicates that it defines a test generator. This simply means that tests are defined, but not run immediately when encountered in the source code. In fact, functions are returned for later execution. The fixture functions do more than define tests; in your case, they define setup and teardown functions and a list of tests. The atom *setup* tells EUnit to run setup and cleanup once for the fixture. If you use the atom *foreach*, it would run it for each test.

The tests can be defined either with a macro *?_test* (fixture1) or inline (fixture2) with a tuple:

- The macro wraps the test in an anonymous function fun and adds more information like line numbers. The code block is between the begin and end keywords.

- The first element of the tuple in the inline version is a description that will be shown during test execution. The second element is an anonymous function.

If the test can be expressed in one line as an assert, the *?_test* macro syntax can be reduced to one line, as shown in Example 7-43.

Example 7-43.

```
?_assertEqual(42,patternmatching:always_return_42())
```

The underscore before assertEqual lets EUnit wrap the assertion with the _test macro. Running the test fixtures you get the output shown in Example 7-44.

Example 7-44.

```
$ rebar3 eunit
===> Verifying dependencies...
===> Performing EUnit tests...
.F.
```

```
Failures:
  1) fixture_tests:fixture2_test_/0: assert true
     Failure/Error: ?assert(false)
       expected: true
            got: false
     %% fixture_tests.erl:36:in 'fixture_tests:-fixture2_test_/0-fun-2-/0'
     Output:
     Output:
Top 3 slowest tests (0.000 seconds, 0.0% of total time):
   fixture_tests:fixture1_test_/0:21
     0.000 seconds
   fixture_tests:fixture2_test_/0: assert 42
     0.000 seconds
   fixture_tests:fixture2_test_/0: assert true
     0.000 seconds

Finished in 0.021 seconds
3 tests, 1 failures
===> Error running tests
```

One test is failing and two tests are succeeding as expected.

EUnit has more features like lazy generators or nested tests. Information about them can be found in the user guide.[12]

Common Test

The Common Test framework is mostly used for integration and system tests. It has greater expectations on the structure of projects and test files than EUnit and organizes tests in suites. The command rebar3 ct will look for files ending with _SUITE (yes, in uppercase).

Example 7-45 tests the DAR API implementation.

Example 7-45.

```
1   -module(api_SUITE).
2
3   -compile(export_all).
4   -include_lib("eunit/include/eunit.hrl").
5   -include_lib("common_test/include/ct.hrl").
6
7   -define (BODY_HOME, "<html>\n <body>\n \n DAR API\n \n </body>\n</h\
8   tml>\n").
9   -define (BODY_TEST_GETASSETS, "<html>\n <body>\n \n Test: get assets\n \
10        \n </body>\n</html>\n").
11
12  suite() ->
```

---

[12]http://erlang.org/doc/apps/eunit/chapter.html

```
13        [{timetrap,{seconds,10}}].
14
15   init_per_suite(Config) ->
16   Config.
17
18   end_per_suite(Config)  ->
19       Config.
20
21   all() ->
22     [
23       http_get_home_message,
24       http_test_getassets
25     ].
26
27   %%%  Tests
28
29   http_get_home_message(_Config) ->
30       {ok, {{_Version, 200, _ReasonPhrase}, _Headers, Body}} =
31           httpc:request(get, {"http://localhost:8402", []}, [], []),
32       ?assertEqual(Body, ?BODY_).
33
34   http_test_getassets(_Config)   ->
35       {ok, {{_Version, 200, _ReasonPhrase}, _Headers, Body}} =
36           httpc:request(get, {"http://localhost:8402/test?testmode=get_apiassets",
37           [\]}, [], []),
38       ?assertEqual(Body, ?BODY_TEST_GETASSETS).
```

Similar to EUnit, you need to include the definition file for Common Test in the module, like in Example 7-46.

Example 7-46.

```
-include_lib("common_test/include/ct.hrl").
```

Common Test defines several callbacks for setup and cleanup. Here you use the per_suite callbacks, although they are not doing any useful work in this example. The suite functions define a timetrap value of ten seconds (line 11). If the execution time of a test case including setup and teardown functions exceeds the time trap value a timeout error is thrown.

The function all defines the tests that should be run. If a test is not on the list, it won't be executed. The tests as such are sending requests to the API server and checking the responses. The example combines Common Test with asserts from EUint, but this is not necessary. You can let the test fail and perhaps write some messages to the console. In any case, Common Test will create detailed results in the folder _build/ test/logs if you run it with the command rebar3 ct. It creates HTML pages, like the one in Figure 7-3.

Test Results

Mon Jun 13 2016 09:34:14

COMMON TEST FRAMEWORK LOG

Test Name	Ok	Failed	Skipped (User/Auto)	Missing Suites
lib.darapi	3	0	0 (0/0)	0
Total	3	0	0 (0/0)	0

Test run history | Top level test index

Copyright © 2016 Open Telecom Platform
Updated: Mon Jun 13 2016 09:34:16

Figure 7-3. Common Test results

It is possible to drill down into details for each test and also open log files. Be aware that if you do not run it with Rebar3 but directly with `ct_run`[13] from the root of your project, Common Test will put HTML and JavaScript files into this folder and create its log folders as well in the root.

Common Test has many more features, such as defining test case orders with groups or running tests in parallel. It depends on your willingness to use a TDD (*test-driven development*) approach how much you will use EUnit (and ExUnit in Elixir) and Common Test in your projects. In the Elixir community, Common Test does not seem to have arrived as a viable testing tool. If you search Elixir Forum[14] for the search term *Common Test,* you get exactly zero results at the time of writing this.

ExUnit

ExUnit is the Elixir equivalent of Erlang's EUnit. When you create a project with Mix, you get a folder named `test` and a file with an example.

According to the paradigm *convention over configuration,* ExUnit will compile and run all tests in files with the name ending in `_test` and it will read the contents of the file `test_helper.exs` to start the tests and configure them.

---

[13]`http://erlang.org/doc/man/ct_run.html`
[14]`http://elixirforum.com`

ℹ️ **Files with suffix *exs*** The suffix exs shows that this file is an Elixir script file that is intended to run on a command line, but not to be compiled into a file. For example, with the command

```
elixir test_helper.exs
```

the script file test_helper.exs will be executed.

The code of the script file will still be compiled before execution, but in memory.

The test_helper.ex in Example 7-47 is from the project dar_db*lib*.

Example 7-47.

```
 1   options = [
 2       trace: true,
 3       capture_log: true,
 4       exclude: [wip: true]
 5   ]
 6
 7   ExUnit.configure(options)
 8   ExUnit.start()
 9
10   case :gen_tcp.connect('localhost', 27017, []) do
11     {:ok, socket} ->
12       :gen_tcp.close(socket)
13     {:error, reason} ->
14       Mix.raise "Cannot connect to MongoDB" <>
15                 "  #{:inet.format_error(reason)}"
16   end
```

In a newly created project, this file will only contain line 8: ExUnit.start(). This is the command that prepares the running environment to run tests.

There is some configuration in lines 1 to 5. This is a simple key-value list with configurations to define output options. You will come back later to the exclude key; the other options simply say you want to see log and trace information.

Before the statement ExUnit.start, you tell ExUnit in line 7 to apply your options. Lines 10ff will run before any test. In this case, you check if a TCP connection to a MongoDB server on its default port *27017* can be established. If so, you close the connection and move on to run the tests; otherwise, you raise an exception and halt the test run. The implementation uses one of the low-level servers defined in Erlang/OTP to access TCP. You will see similar servers for HTTP and UDP in Chapter 10.

Running code in the test starting script is very useful to check for data stores, files, or other crucial dependencies like web servers that must be available to run tests successfully.

ExUnit defines many asserts. Let's examine first the more common ones; see Example 7-48.

Example 7-48.

```
 1   defmodule ExUnitAssertions do
 2     use ExUnit.Case, async: true
 3
 4       @tag :wip
 5     test "assert" do
```

```
 6          assert 1 + 1 == 2
 7        end
 8
 9      test "refute" do
10        refute 1 + 1 == 3
11        end
12
13      test "assert_in_delta" do
14        assert_in_delta 1,4,5
15        end
16
17      test "refute_in_delta" do
18        refute_in_delta  1,4,3
19          end
20    end
```

This file defines a module and is importing the module ExUnit.Case, which amongst other things defines test to define test cases. Note that *test* is a macro, not a keyword.

ℹ️ **use vs. require vs. alias vs. import**   These directives (*alias, require, import*) and one macro (*use*) are a very confusing topic in Elixir. All of them have to do with referencing other modules from Elixir code.

- *alias* gives a module passed in as argument a name that can be used in the module instead of the fully qualified name.

- *require* gives a hint that the module passed as argument is compiled. According to the documentation, this is needed for using macros from that module.

- *import* references all functions or a subset of functions from a module passed in as argument so they can be called without the module name.

- *use* is a macro that compiles to a require statement and then calls a callback *using* in that module that can inject some necessary code.

My take is that *alias* and *import* are for convenience, *require* is for defining compile order in case macros are needed, and *use* is for special cases like ExUnit that injects code, such as the *test* macro. For normal cases, I guess *import* is the right approach, but it would be nice to have only one way to handle this task.

You run the tests with mix test in the console and get all output to the console as well.

The tests themselves are straightforward: *assert* checks if the assertion is true, *refute* checks if the assertion is false. Interesting are *assert_in_delta* and its negative pendant, *refute_in_delta*. It checks if two arithmetic expressions are inside or outside a given delta.

The async: true configuration in line 2 tells the ExUnit runtime that it may run tests concurrently. This option is not always feasible, for example if data stores or any other shared resources are used.

The @tag :wip on line 4 in the example defines that the following test is marked with the tag wip. If you look again at the example test_helper.exs above, you see in the options list the line exclude: [wip: true] that excludes all tests with the tag wip from the test run. The same effect can also be achieved by running the tests with mix test -exclude wip. There are also atoms and arguments defined for including only tests with certain tags.

ℹ️ Property-based testing   Tests written with EUnit and ExUnit are important, but they can't test all scenarios. For example, you won't be able to test all combinations of input parameters with different value ranges.

Tools can help with this task. They dynamically create input values and monitor the execution of a program or function. A commercial tool (with a free offering that does not provide all features of the commercial version) is *QuickCheck*[15] , which was originally implemented for Haskell. Open source tools are `PropEr`[16] for Erlang and `PropCheck`[17] which is an Elixir wrapper around PropEr.

You have looked at the most used assert statements so far, but Erlang and Elixir are about sending messages between actors. ExUnit has some asserts to make testing those scenarios easier; see Example 7-49.

Example 7-49.

```
1   defmodule ExUnitAssertionsReceive do
2       use ExUnit.Case, async: true
3
4       test "assert_receive" do
5           send self, {:hello, "world"}
6           assert_receive {:hello, "world"}
7       end
8
9       test "refute_receive" do
10          send self, {:hello, "world"}
11          refute_receive {:hello, ""}
12      end
13
14      test "assert_received" do
15          send self, {:hello, "world"}
16          assert_received {:hello, _}
17      end
18
19      test "refute_received" do
20          refute_received {:hello, _}
21      end
22  end
```

You see here again the pair *assert* and *refute*.

- The *receive* assertions indicate that a message will be received in future. The assertions have a parameter named `timeout` which can be set for this purpose. Its default is 100ms.

- The `_received_assertions` check if a message is in the mailbox. There is no waiting time set, so the test will return immediately after checking the mailbox.

---

[15]www.quviq.com/products/erlang-quickcheck/
[16]https://github.com/manopapad/proper
[17]https://github.com/alfert/propcheck

All receive tests will also fail if the received message does not pattern match with the expected message.

So far you have been shown simple tests and in practice this is what tests in a project will be. Sometimes there are more complex setups needed. ExUnit provides, as do other unit testing frameworks, callbacks to set up the test context; see Example 7-50.

Example 7-50.

```
1   defmodule ExUnitContext do
2     use ExUnit.Case, async: true
3
4     setup_all context do
5       IO.puts "Setup All:"
6         Enum.each context, &IO.puts(inspect &1)
7           {:ok, [arg1: "setupallarg0", arg2: fn x -> x*x end]}
8       end
9
10    setup context do
11      IO.puts ""
12      IO.puts "Setup:"
13      Enum.each context, &IO.puts(inspect &1)
14       on_exit fn ->
15          IO.puts ""
16          IO.puts "on exit"
17        end
18        {:ok, [setuparg: "setuparg1"]}
19    end
20
21    test "assert", context do
22        assert 2 + 2 == context.arg2.(2)
23    end
24
25    test "refute", context do
26        IO.puts "test:"
27        Enum.each context, &IO.puts(inspect &1)
28        refute 2 + 2 == context.arg2.(1)
29    end
30  end
```

The callbacks in the example work as follows:

- The function setup_all will be called before any test in the test case.

- The function setup will be called before each test.

- A callback on_exit can be defined that runs within the test process whenever a test has finished. A teardown callback on case process level existed in earlier versions, but was deprecated in favor of on_exit.

The setup callbacks have context as argument which is a key-value metadata map. Example 7-51 shows the output of the test.

Example 7-51.

ExUnitContext
Setup All:
{:case, **ExUnitContext**}
      * refute
Setup:
{:arg1, "setupallarg0"}
{:arg2, *#Function<4.83785844/1 in ExUnitContext. ex_unit_setup_all_0/1>*}
{:async, true}
{:case, **ExUnitContext**}
{:file, "/Users/Wolfgang/Projects/creative-common-dar/Elixir/Libs/dar_dblib/test\
/dar_dblib_test.exs"}
{:line, 25}

{:test, :"test refute"} test:
{:arg1, "setupallarg0"}
{:arg2, *#Function<4.83785844/1 in ExUnitContext. ex_unit_setup_all_0/1>*}
{:async, true}
{:case, **ExUnitContext**}
{:file, "/Users/Wolfgang/Projects/creative-common-dar/Elixir/Libs/dar_dblib/test\
/dar_dblib_test.exs"}
{:line, 25}
{:setuparg, "setuparg1"}
{:test, :"test refute"}

on exit
  * refute (3.2ms)
  * assert
Setup:
{:arg1, "setupallarg0"}

{:arg2, *#Function<4.83785844/1 in ExUnitContext. ex_unit_setup_all_0/1>*}
{:async, true}
{:case, **ExUnitContext**}
{:file, "/Users/Wolfgang/Projects/creative-common-dar/Elixir/Libs/dar_dblib/test\
/dar_dblib_test.exs"}
{:line, 21}
{:test, :"test assert"}

on exit
  *assert (0.2ms)

Finished in 0.04 seconds (0.04s on load, 0.00s on tests)
2 tests, 0 failures

Randomized with seed 442205

The initial context map in setup_all contains only the case name. You add two more keys (arg1 and arg2) to the map. This is done by returning a tuple from the function with the return atom *:ok* and a list of key-value pairs. The map will then be passed to the setup function, which by default automatically adds more keys, such as the file name or the test name. You can see the keys you added as well.

You can add more keys in setup, in your case setuparg. All this will now be passed to the test and can be used there if necessary. The context could be used to pass constants like text or field names for testing data stores. In your example, you pass a function as value of key arg2. If the function comes from another library, this could be used to dynamically change test assertions to cover different use cases.

The ExUnit documentation[18] describes more features with several examples.

Meck

Meck is a mocking library for Erlang that can be used in Elixir as well. Mocking is a controversial topic for many developers, and I won't go into this discussion here. Figure 7-4 just shows one way to mock.

The left side shows the implementation entities: *dblib client* is dependent on *dblib* and the library is dependent on *MongoDB* (driver and database). The right side shows test instances for the client and the library.

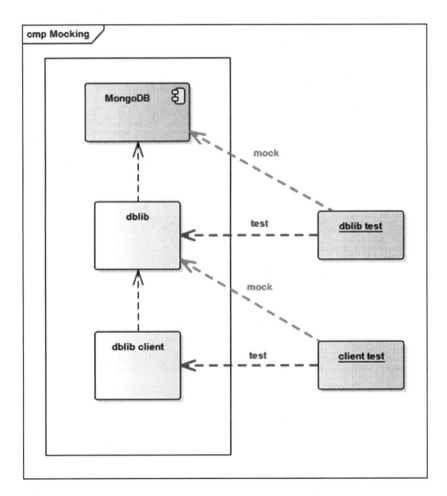

Figure 7-4. Mocking

---

[18]http://elixir-lang.org/docs/stable/ex_unit/ExUnit.html

When you test the client, you want to test how the client behaves in different situations. The library returns lists of *documents*, for example. This list could be empty, too big, or it could contain wrong types. In the *client test*, you can mock the library and tailor the response for your various test cases.

Similar thoughts apply to *dblib test*, which tests the library that in turn uses a third-party driver and database. Mocking *MongoDB* lets you test scenarios where connections are dropping, or where database or, in this case, collections are not available. You also can prepare data exactly as it is needed for the tests.

Mocking is not a replacement for integration tests in production environments, though. It can help in unit tests to separate module implementations from each other and thus have fewer variables that can influence test results.

❓How about dependency injection (DI) for testing?   Many developers have adopted the test approach of injecting dependencies via configuration or at runtime.

In OO languages, *interfaces* are used with sometimes elaborate DI libraries. It is no coincident that Elixir defines something similar to interfaces called *@behaviour*, which should not be confused with the *OTP term _behaviours*.

The problem with DI is that implementations are injected that are not tested themselves. Therefore, tests with DI are not a replacement for tests in production environments and have the same restrictions as mocking libraries. What DI can do is to reduce coupling. Testing against an interface will not be broken if implementation details change.

To access Meck you have to add the dependency in `rebar.config`, as shown in Example 7-52.

Example 7-52.

```
{deps, [
    {meck,{git, "https://github.com/eproxus/meck.git", {tag, "0.8.4"}}}
]}.
```

After this you can use the library in your tests. See Example 7-53 in Erlang.

Example 7-53.

```
1    -module(meck_mock_tests).
2
3    -ifdef(TEST).
4    -include_lib("eunit/include/eunit.hrl").
5
6    -define (FILETESTWRITE, "filetestwrite").
7    -define (FILETESTCONTENT, <<"test_from_gfslib">>).
8    -define (DARDB, "dar").
9
10   save_to_gfs_mocked_test() ->
11       M = #{name => ?FILETESTWRITE,origin=>"test",timestamp=>100, gfsid=>"66"},
12       ok = meck:new(dar_gfslib_process_files),
13       meck:expect(dar_gfslib_process_files, save_to_gfs, fun(?FILETESTCONTENT,M,?D\
14       ARDB) -> {nodb,?FILETESTWRITE} end),
15       R = dar_gfslib_process_files:save_to_gfs(?FILETESTCONTENT,M,?DARDB),
16       ?assert(meck:validate(dar_gfslib_process_files)),
```

```
17        ?assertEqual({nodb,?FILETESTWRITE},  R),
18        ok = meck:unload(dar_gfslib_process_files).
19
20    dar_model_assetmetadata_empty_mocked_test()  ->
21        ok = meck:new(dar_model),
22        meck:expect(dar_model, assetmetadata_empty, fun() -> changed end),
23        ?assertEqual(dar_model:assetmetadata_empty(),changed),
24         ok = meck:unload(dar_model).
25
26    -endif.
```

These tests show various Meck functions and are not real mocking tests. They mock the functions in modules you call, so they test more or less the mocking library.

In save_to_gfs_mocked_test on line 10 you create a new mock-entity and tell it to create one for the module *dar_gfslib_process_files*. At this moment there are no functions in this mocked entity, so you define one on line 13. The meck:expect line says that whenever in module *dar_gfslib_process_files* the function save_to_gfs is called, you run the defined function. In your example, it just returns {nodb,?FILETESTWRITE}. *?FILETESTWRITE* is a macro you define at the beginning of the module. You also make sure that you define the correct number of arguments for the mocked function to obey the original signature.

On line 15 you call the function save_to_gfs as you would in your code, but hit the mocked function instead. The statement on line 16 checks if the mocked function was actually called, which does not make so much sense here because you check the result in assertions, and the statement on line 18 reverts the changes Meck has made.

The function dar_model_assetmetadata_empty_mocked_test is a similar test for a different module. It can be written in Elixir as well, as shown in Example 7-54.

Example 7-54.

```
1    defmodule ExUnitMeck do
2        use ExUnit.Case
3
4        test "dar_model_assetmetadata_empty_mocked_test" do
5            :ok = :meck.new :dar_model
6            :meck.expect :dar_model, :assetmetadata_empty, fn -> :changed end
7            assert :meck.validate :dar_model
8            assert :dar_model.assetmetadata_empty == :changed
9            :ok = :meck.unload :dar_model
10       end
11   end
```

This is the equivalent of the previous Erlang example. The module mocked is actually an Erlang module (*dar_model*).

With the knowledge of the trivial examples you can write a test with proper mocks; see Example 7-55.

Example 7-55.

```
1    -module(dar_gfslib_process_files_mock_tests).
2
3    -ifdef(TEST).
4    -include_lib("eunit/include/eunit.hrl").
5
6    -define (FILETEST, "filetest").
```

```
7    -define (FILETESTWRITE, "filetestwrite").
8    -define (FILETESTCONTENT, <<"test_from_gfslib">>).
9    -define (DARDB, "dar").
10   -define (NOTDARDB, "notdar").
11
12   save_to_gfs_no_connection_mocked_test() ->
13       M = #{name => ?FILETESTWRITE,origin=>"test",timestamp=>100, gfsid=>"66"},
14       meck:new(mongodb,[passthrough]),
15       meck:expect(mongodb, is_connected, fun(def) -> false end),
16       ?assertError({badmatch,false}, dar_gfslib_process_files:save_to_gfs(?FILETES\
17       TCONTENT,M,?DARDB)),
18       ok = meck:unload(mongodb).
19
20   read_from_gfs_no_connection_mocked_test()    ->
21       meck:new(mongodb,[passthrough]),
22       meck:expect(mongodb, is_connected, fun(def) -> false end),
23       ?assertError({badmatch,false}, dar_gfslib_process_files:read_from_gfs(?FILET\
24       EST,?DARDB)),
25       ok = meck:unload(mongodb).
26
27   connect_to_server_mocked_test() ->
28       meck:new(mongodb,[passthrough]),
29       meck:expect(mongodb, is_connected, fun(def) -> false end),
30       R = dar_gfslib_process_files:connect(),
31       ?assert(meck:validate(mongodb)),
32       ?assertEqual(false,  R),
33       ok = meck:unload(mongodb).
34
35   -endif.
```

These tests check how functions in the module *dar_gfslib_process_files* behave when there is no database connection. In the previous trivial examples, you mocked a function from this module, but now you mock a module that is called by functions from this module.

The module *mongodb* is part of *erlmongo*, which is used to access GridFS in your project. On lines 14, 21, and 28, you create a mock entity for this module and in the lines after creating the mock entities you define that the function is_connected should return false to indicate that there is no connection.

The code in dar_gfslib_process_files to connect to MongoDB is shown in Example 7-56.

Example 7-56.

```
1    connect() ->
2        mongodb:singleServer(def),
3        mongodb:connect(def),
4        mongodb:is_connected(def).
```

You can see that two more *mongodb* functions are called before is_connected. You will see explanations of this module later, but for now it is necessary to know that this library returns the atom *ok* on lines 2 and 3 even if there is no server or no connection. To make sure you have a connection, you have to call is_connected. This is the reason why your creation of the mock entity is stated as shown in Example 7-57.

Example 7-57.

```
1    meck:new(mongodb,[passthrough])
```

The argument `passthrough` in the call to create mock entities indicates that you want all non-mocked calls to be passed to the original module. When you run the tests, the functions called will go through the normal connect process, but will always have to handle the case that there is no connection.

Meck is certainly useful in some unit test scenarios. It is a good idea to indicate always what is actually tested; otherwise there is the danger of ending up with tests like the trivial examples above that do not test what is probably intended.

Debugger

Developers of languages like C++, Java, or C# are used to having IDEs that expose the debug abilities of those languages and language environments. In Erlang and Elixir, you do not have this luxury.

Erlang has its own debugger[19] that works on beam files no matter which language was used before compiling to the binary, so you can use it in Elixir development as well.

The debugger is started in an Erlang shell or a shell opened with the command *rebar3 shell* with the code in Example 7-58.

Example 7-58.

```
1>   debugger:start().
{ok,<0.41.0>}
```

This command will automatically open a monitor window, as shown in Figure 7-5.

Figure 7-5. *Debugger window*

---

[19]http://erlang.org/doc/apps/debugger/debugger_chapter.html

After starting, the window is empty so you need to load a module for debugging. You can use the menu item *Module ➤ Interpret* to choose a beam file or you can use the interpreter interface *int* to specify a module for debugging and setting a break point, as shown in Example 7-59.

Example 7-59.

```
2>    int:ni(mapsexample).
{module,mapsexample}
3>    int:break(mapsexample,38).
ok
```

The function `int:ni` searches all known nodes, the function `int:i` only the current node. You set a break point on line 38 in the module *mapsexample*. This line is a statement in the function `mapsexample:pizza_toppings_match_valid` and you want to stop before the function returns. The monitor window shows what you have defined; see Figure 7-6.

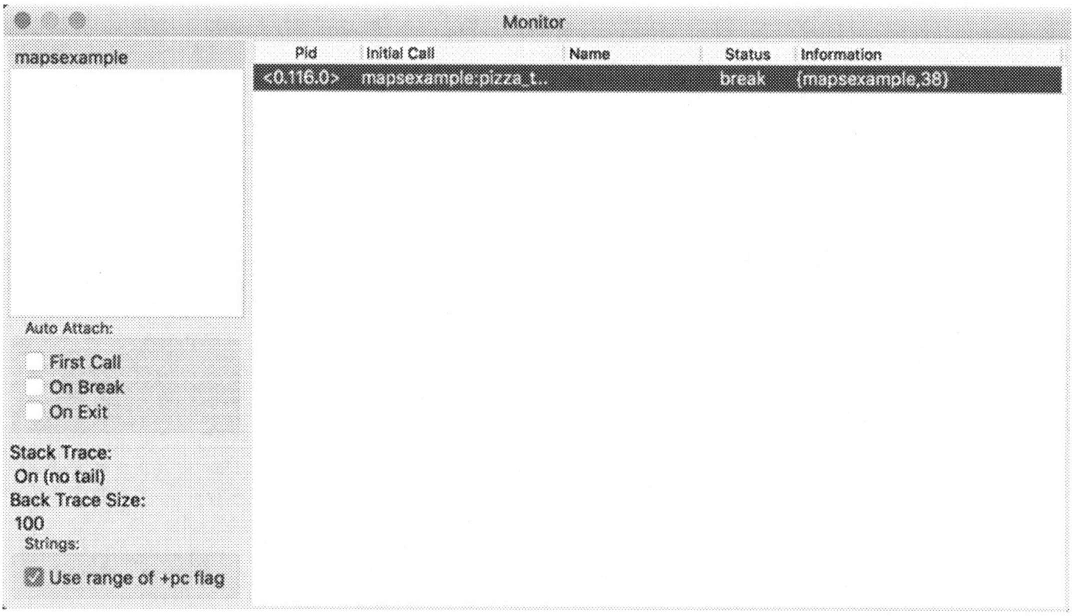

Figure 7-6. *Breakpoint set*

When you run now the function `mapsexample:pizza_topping_match_valid`, the execution will stop and you can double-click the break point. Another window opens with information about the state of the execution; see Figure 7-7.

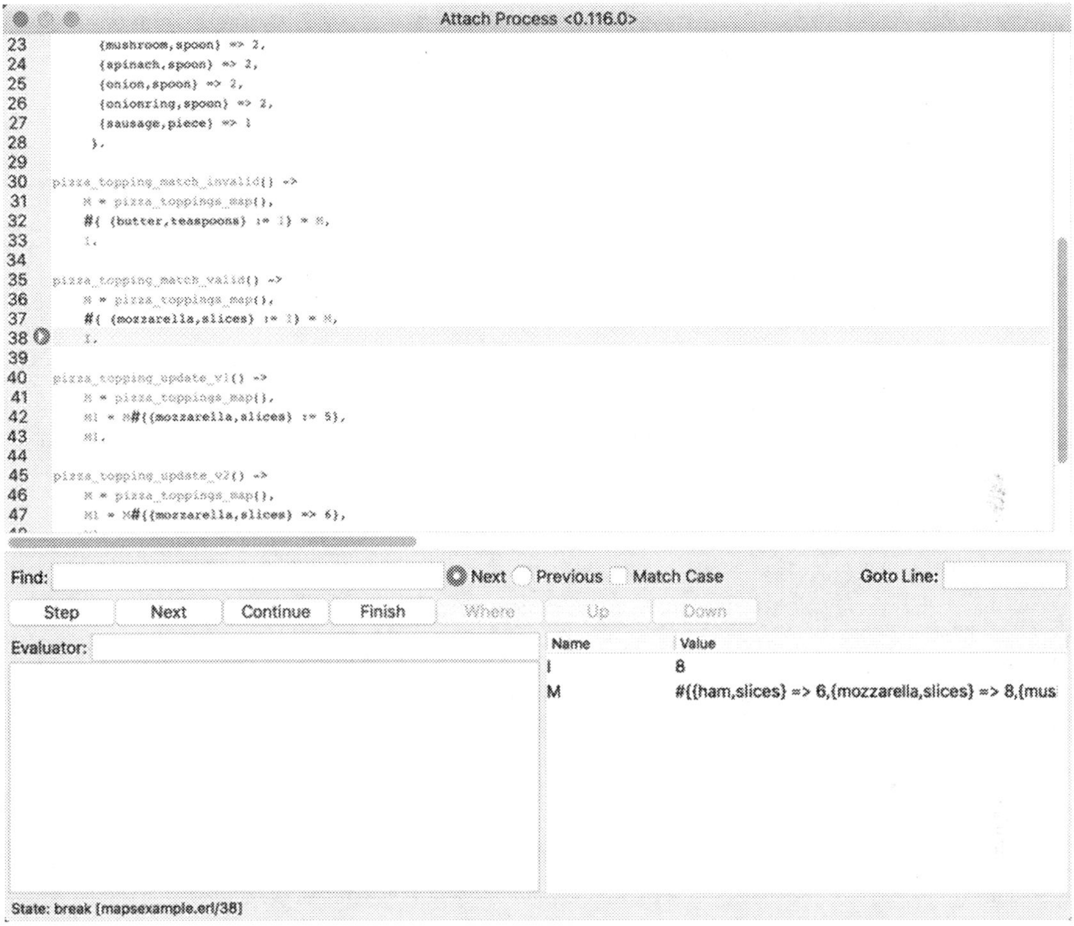

Figure 7-7. *Breakpoint reached*

Once a breakpoint has been reached, you can step into other functions, execute next statements line by line, or evaluate expressions. The UI of this debugger is certainly not as comfortable as in IDEs like Visual Studio, but it does its job.

Elixir has a tool for development environments called IEx.pry[20]. It requires a change of the source code to work, so it is not a solution for production.

You use the *append* function from *listsexample.ex* from the discussion about lists and tuples; see Example 7-60.

---

[20]http://elixir-lang.org/docs/stable/iex/IEx.html#pry/1

Example 7-60.

```
1   defmodule ListExample do
2     require IEx
3
4     def append([h|t], tail) do
5       IEx.pry
6       [h|append(t, tail)]
7     end
8     def append([], tail) do
9         tail
10    end
11  end
```

The module needs to require the *IEx* module where a macro called *pry* is defined. In line 5, you call this macro to get access to the state during execution at the time of the call to *pry*. An iex session with this code looks like Example 7-61.

Example 7-61.

```
1   iex(1)> c("listsexample.ex")
2   listsexample.ex:1: warning: redefining module ListExample
3   [ListExample]
4   iex(2)> ListExample.append [1,2],[3]
5   Request to pry #PID<0.194.0> at listsexample.ex:5
6
7           def append([h|t], tail) do
8               IEx.pry
9               [h|append(t, tail)]
10          end
11
12  Allow? [Yn]
13
14  Interactive Elixir (1.2.5) - press Ctrl+C to exit (type h() ENTER for help)
15  pry(1)> tail
16  [3]
17  pry(2)> h
18  1
19  pry(3)> t
20  [2]
21  pry(4)>   respawn
22  [1,2,3]
23
24  iex(1)>
```

After compiling the module, you call the function append. You are asked if you want to allow *pry*; if you do so, a pry-session will be started and the execution of the function will be blocked. You can now investigate variable values as in lines 15 to 20. Calling respawn will unblock the execution and start a new iex session.

This macro can help when a function does not yield results as expected. It certainly is not a replacement for a debugger, but it is easier than having print messages in the code.

Dialyzer

Erlang and Elixir are dynamically typed and there is a need to check types before deploying compiled code. Dialyzer[21] is a tool for this task by inferring types from usage and by getting hints with @spec attributes or directives. Dialyzer is not only used for finding type problems; the name stands for DIscrepancy AnalYZer for ERlang programs. It finds dead code, unreachable code, unnecessary tests, and other things.

Dialyzer is set up together with the Erlang system and should be available immediately. Once Dialyzer is on the development machine, it needs to have a first run to create a database of the core libraries and all other *beam* files specified; see Example 7-62.

Example 7-62.

```
dialyzer --build_plt --apps erts kernel stdlib crypto mnesia sasl
```

In earlier days, this may have taken some time, but in the days of 16GB of RAM and SSDs it does not need more than a minute or two.

The database is called *PLT (persistent lookup table)* and is used to store the analysis results of all specified *beam* files. This file database grows with time, so there is also an option to remove some results. If *beam* files change, the database values are updated for this file.

To see how Dialyzer works, use Example 7-63.

Example 7-63.

```
1   -module (specifications).
2   -compile(export_all).
3
4   -type returnvalue() :: {ok} | {error}.
5   -export_type([returnvalue/0]).
6
7   -spec numberfunction(number()) -> returnvalue().
8   numberfunction(T) ->
9     case T of
10      42 -> {ok};
11      _ -> {error}
b     end.
13
14  callnumberfunction_1() ->
15    numberfunction("test").
16
17  callnumberfunction_2() ->
18    numberfunction({}).
19
20  callnumberfunction_3() ->
21    numberfunction(0).
22
23  callnumberfunction_4() ->
24    numberfunction(42).
```

---

[21]http://erlang.org/doc/man/dialyzer.html

ℹ️ Option: *compile all* in Erlang   Sometimes you use the line

```
-compile(export_all).
```

in examples. This is an option that exports every function in the module. It is a convenience and should *never* be used in production code.

When you run Dialyzer with Rebar3 in the project *erlangexamples* you get the result shown in Example 7-64.

Example 7-64.

```
1   $ rebar3 dialyzer
2   ===> Verifying    dependencies...
3   ===> Compiling  erlangexamples
4   ===> Dialyzer starting, this may take a while...
5   ===> Updating plt...
6   ===> Resolving  files...
7   ===> Checking 156 files in "~/Projects/bookcompanion-ee/Erlang/erlangexamples/_b\
8   uild/default/rebar3_18.3_plt"...
9   ===> Doing success typing analysis...
10  ===> Resolving  files...
11  ===> Analyzing   35  files  with   "~/Projects/bookcompanion-ee/Erlang/
    erlangexamples/\
12  _build/default/rebar3_18.3_plt"...
13
14  _build/default/lib/erlangexamples/src/listsexample.erl
15    21: Cons will produce an improper list since its 2nd argument is 'someatom'
16
17
18  _build/default/lib/erlangexamples/src/patternmatching.erl
19    31: The test 'a' == 'b' can never evaluate to 'true'
20    32: The pattern 'true' can never match the type 'false'
21
22  _build/default/lib/erlangexamples/src/recursionexample.erl
23    24: Function nontailrecursiveloop/1 has no local return
24
25  _build/default/lib/erlangexamples/src/specifications.erl
26    14: Function callnumberfunction_1/0 has no local return
27    15: The call specifications:numberfunction([101 | 115 | 116,...]) breaks the c\
28  ontract (number()) -> returnvalue()
29    17: Function callnumberfunction_2/0 has no local return
30    18: The call specifications:numberfunction({}) breaks the contract (number()) \
31  -> returnvalue()
32  ===> Warnings written to ~/Projects/bookcompanion-ee/Erlang/erlangexamples/_buil\
33  d/default/18.3.dialyzer_warnings
34  ===> Warnings occured running dialyzer: 8
```

On line 7, it shows that is already has 156 files in the database. This is from previous runs with other projects on my machine. Line 11 shows that it is analyzing 35 files in the project. It has 8 warnings (line 34) and has written a text file to the build folder, which contains a list of all warnings.

You are interested in the warnings for your example; see Example 7-65.

Example 7-65.

```
_build/default/lib/erlangexamples/src/specifications.erl
  14: Function callnumberfunction_1/0 has no local return
  15: The call specifications:numberfunction([101 | 115 | 116,...]) breaks the
      contract (number()) -> returnvalue()
  17: Function callnumberfunction_2/0 has no local return
  18: The call specifications:numberfunction({}) breaks the contract (number())
      -> returnvalue()
```

The warnings tell you that some function calls are breaking a contract. Let's run Dialyzer with the line shown in Example 7-66 commented out.

Example 7-66.

```
-spec numberfunction(number()) -> returnvalue().
```

You can run Dialyzer just on one file in the folder where the code file is ; with the commented line you get the following, shown in Example 7-67.

Example 7-67.

```
$ dialyzer specifications.erl
  Checking whether the PLT ~/.dialyzer_plt is up-to-date... yes
  Proceeding with analysis... done in 0m0.52s
done (passed successfully)
```

Surprisingly, it was successful, Without the specification, Dialyzer can't infer the correct types. The specification says you expect a number and then a return value which is a type you have defined yourself with the code in Example 7-68.

Example 7-68.

```
1   -type returnvalue() :: {ok} | {error}.
2   -export_type([returnvalue/0]).
```

It defines that the value can have one of two tuples as values and you export this type to be available for other modules.

When you uncomment the @spec line, you get the warnings again. If you play with the example, you will see that most of the time dialyzer returns a success. The problem is that the example function does not actually do anything with the arguments. If you put in a line like that in Example 7-69 into numberfunction, you will get warnings even without specification.

Example 7-69.

```
T = T + 1
```

The warnings will be like those in Example 7-70.

Example 7-70.

```
The call specifications:numberfunction({}) will never return since it differs in the 1st
argument from the success typing arguments: (number())
```

The analysis infers that T must be a number because it is used in an arithmetic expression.

You can use Dialyzer in Elixir as well, since it analyzes *beam* files and can use a custom task in Mix, Dialyxir[22], to run the analysis.

Example 7-71 shows the Elixir version of your example.

Example 7-71.

```elixir
1   defmodule Specifications do
2     @type returnvalue :: {:ok} | {:error}
3     @spec numberfunction(number) :: returnvalue
4
5     def numberfunction(t) do
6       case t do
7         42 -> {:ok}
8         _  ->   {:error}
9       end
10    end
11
12    def callnumberfunction_1() do
13      numberfunction("1")
14    end
15
16    def callnumberfunction_2() do
17      numberfunction({})
18    end
19
20    def callnumberfunction_3() do
21      numberfunction(0)
22    end
23
24    def callnumberfunction_4() do
25      numberfunction(42)
26    end
27  end
```

First, you need to build the database. Dialyxir most probably uses a different folder than the Erlang analysis; see Example 7-72.

Example 7-72.

```
mix  dialyzer.plt
```

---

[22]https://github.com/jeremyjh/dialyxir

Then you can run the analysis, as shown in Example 7-73.

Example 7-73.

```
$ mix dialyzer
Starting  Dialyzer
dialyzer --no_check_plt --plt /Users/Wolfgang/.dialyxir_core_18_1.2.5.plt -Wunma\ tched_
returns -Werror_handling -Wrace_conditions -
Wno_opaque .
  Proceeding with analysis...
specifications.ex:12: Function callnumberfunction_1/0 has no local return
specifications.ex:13: The call 'Elixir.Specifications':numberfunction(<<_:8>>) b\
reaks the contract (number()) -> returnvalue()
specifications.ex:16: Function callnumberfunction_2/0 has no local return
specifications.ex:17: The call 'Elixir.Specifications':numberfunction({}) breaks\
  the contract (number()) -> returnvalue()
  done in 0m0.82s
done (warnings were emitted)
```

You get the same warnings as before, as expected. The example differs just in syntax and will most probably generate the same, or due to different internal calls a very similar, byte code as the Erlang version.

Working with Dialyzer does not always yield results that you as a human being might find logical. Looking through code you mostly find obvious defects. The harder ones should be found by automated tests and analysis. With a dynamically typed language, it is very hard to infer types at runtime and sometimes impossible. Tools like Dialyzer help with this task but can't be relied on. The most frustrating Dialyzer outputs are when it decides that the specification you gave is actually wrong. You know the specification is what you want, but the implementation is so far from the desired input that the tool simply thinks the hint you gave is wrong.

CHAPTER 8

■ ■ ■

Production Setup

The production environment is also the staging environment. See Figure 8-1.

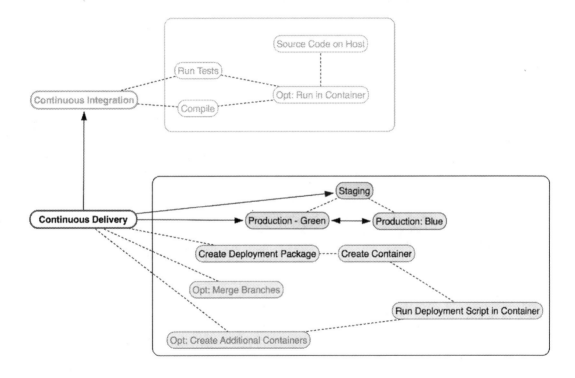

Figure 8-1. *Continuous delivery*

You're going to use a Blue/Green concept, where one server will run production code and the other will run staging code, which will be by definition a version different from the other server. Blue and green servers can be clustered. When a new version is deployed, the blue role and the green role switch between the servers.

Server in this case actually means a set of servers, because there may be various machines forming the deployment target, such as one web server and one or more application servers or nodes. Also, databases may be included or (most probably) excluded from the deployment.

© Wolfgang Loder 2016
W. Loder, *Erlang and Elixir for Imperative Programmers*, DOI 10.1007/978-1-4842-2394-9_8

You are now switching to continuous delivery, which not only means deployment, but also doing tasks like updating source control, preparing a database, and similar.

In Erlang and Elixir, *deployment* means to create deployment packages and in your case optionally Docker containers.

Release Management

Most of the time the easiest way is to develop applications on one machine even if production code will never run on a machine like the developer machine. Not only are hardware specifications different, but also the operating systems may be different. Many developers, including me, develop much of their software on a Mac with OS X, a system that does not even have a server version.

In Erlang and Elixir, you create release packages that contain everything the project needs to run, including scripts to start up the application(s) belonging to the project. In addition to deployment, the Erlang VM and all languages built on top of it have the option to upgrade or downgrade the system with special packages and scripts. Often it may be possible to change code on a running system, which is called hot code swapping.

In Erlang, you can use Rebar3 to create a release package for the project erlangexamples, as shown in Example 8-1.

Example 8-1.

```
1  $ rebar3 release
2  ===> Verifying dependencies...
3  ===> Compiling  erlangexamples
4  ===> Starting relx build process ...
5  ===> Resolving OTP Applications from directories:
6           ~/Projects/bookcompanion-ee/Erlang/erlangexamples/_build/default/lib
7           ~/Projects/bookcompanion-ee/Erlang/erlangexamples/apps
8           /usr/local/Cellar/erlang/19.0.2/lib/erlang/lib
9           ~/Projects/proper
10          ~/Projects/bookcompanion-ee/Erlang/erlangexamples/_build/default/rel
11 ===> Resolved erlangexamples-1.0.0
12 ===> release successfully created!
```

It compiles the projects as usual and then runs a build process with relx[1]. Relx can be used as a standalone tool with its own configuration file, but called from Rebar3 it can be configured in *rebar.config*. See Example 8-2.

Example 8-2.

```
1  {relx, [{release, { erlangexamples, "1.0.0" },
2            [erlangexamples,sasl]},
3          {sys_config, "./config/sys.config"},
4          {vm_args, "./config/vm.args"},
5          {dev_mode, false},
6          {include_erts, false},
7          {extended_start_script, true}]
8  }.
```

---

[1]https://github.com/erlware/relx

These keys define the values needed to create a release. Interesting is the key dev_mode that defines if the applications and configurations should be symlinked from source (true) or copied to the release folder (false).

The build process creates a release in the following folder: erlangexamples/_build/default/rel/erlangexamples/.

The script to start the release can be found in the following folder: erlangexamples/_build/default/rel/erlangexamples/bin/erlangexamples.

When you start the script elixirexamples you get the output shown in Example 8-3 to display the options.

Example 8-3.

```
1    $ ./erlangexamples
2    Usage: erlangexamples {start|start_boot <file>|foreground|stop|restart
3              |reboot|pid|ping|console|console_clean|console_boot <file>
4              |attach|remote_console|upgrade|escript|rpc|rpcterms|eval}
```

Let's run the script. See Example 8-4.

Example 8-4.

```
1    $ epmd -names
2        epmd: up and running on port 4369 with data:
3    $ ./erlangexamples start
4    $ epmd -names
5        epmd: up and running on port 4369 with data:
6        name erlangexamples at port 60477
7    $  ./erlangexamples   remote_console
8        Erlang/OTP 19 [erts-8.0.2] [source] [64-bit] [smp:8:8] [async-threads:10] [hi\
9        pe] [kernel-poll:false] [dtrace]
10
11       Eshell V8.0.2  (abort with ^G)
12       (erlangexamples@WL)1>
13
14   $ epmd -names
15       epmd: up and running on port 4369 with data:
16       name remshc958bdf4-erlangexamples at port 60495
17       name erlangexamples at port 60477
```

You first make sure by running epmd that no node is running on the machine. On line 3 you start the node with the option start. It does not give any positive feedback, but you can check with epmd again that the node erlangexamples was started. Now you can start a console with remote_host; in this case, you are on the same physical machine, but you can run a remote shell from another machine in the network. Opening another shell epmd reveals that there are now two nodes running (lines 14 to 17).

You just examined a barebone release, but most of the time more is needed. Relax provides ways to define variables specific to the operating system or to define that additional scripts or files need to be copied, such as for deployment on cloud services.

One problem is compiling for other operating systems. The compilation, scripts, and included ERTS (Erlang Runtime System) are specific to the operating system the build runs on. The key include_erts (see Example 8-tk) can be either a Boolean or a path to an Erlang system and an additional key system_libs can take a path to Erlang system libraries. So a release can be compiled for Linux on a Mac by providing the right files in the configuration. With the key include_src you can decide if you copy the source or the release (true) or not (false).

Once you have tested the release, you can create a tarball for deployment to other machines; see Example 8-5.

Example 8-5.

```
1   rebar3 tar
```

This creates a compressed archive in _build/default/rel/erlangexamples/erlangexamples-1.0.0.tar.gz. Without including ERTS, the size for erlangexamples is 4.8MB; with ERTS, it is 7.5MB.

In Elixir, you can create releases with Mix, but first you need to add a dependency to mix.exs, as shown in Example 8-6.

Example 8-6.

```
1   {:exrm, "~> 1.0.8"}
```

The release tool Exrm is the preferred tool for many Elixir developers, although there is a new project called Distillery[2] which should replace Exrm in the future. Since Distillery is still in beta, we will stick to Exrm in this chapter.

Once you have the dependency (mix deps.get) and have compiled it (mix deps.compile), you have new tasks in Mix; see Example 8-7.

Example 8-7.

```
1   $ mix release
2      Building release with MIX_ENV=dev.
3      ==> The release for elixirexamples-1.0.0 is ready!
4      ==> You can boot a console running your release with
5          `$ rel/elixirexamples/bin/elixirexamples console`
```

The task mix release creates a release in the folder rel, ready with scripts and without providing any additional configuration. In Elixir/elixirexamples/rel/elixirexamples/releases/1.0.0, you can find a tarball with a size of 16.9MB created. There are four different ways to configure Exrm, and Distillery adds another one, so I will not go into details of how to configure the release with different options.

Exam creates the same script as Rebar3 for starting the release node; see Example 8-8.

Example 8-8.

```
1   $ ./elixirexamples start
2   $ epmd -names
3      epmd: up and running on port 4369 with data:
4      name elixirexamples at port 62762
5   $ ./elixirexamples remote_console
6      Erlang/OTP 19 [erts-8.0.2] [source] [64-bit] [smp:8:8] [async-threads:10] [hi\
7      pe] [kernel-poll:false] [dtrace]
8      Interactive Elixir (1.3.2) - press Ctrl+C to exit (type h() ENTER for help)
9      iex(elixirexamples@127.0.0.1)1>
10
```

---

[2]https://github.com/bitwalker/distillery

```
11    $ empd -names
12        epmd: up and running on port 4369 with data:
13        name remsh-elixirexamples at port 62777
14        name elixirexamples at port 62762
```

The node can then be stopped with ./elixirexamples stop or, in the case of erlangexamples, with ./erlangexamples stop.

Monitoring

During development, you have access to the source code and can use tools like debugger. In production, you have to monitor a running application, often distributed on several nodes.

Erlang has tracing to see what is going on in an application. A tool called *dbg*[3] (not to be confused with *debugger*) is a wrapper around the tracing module and can be started with the command shown in Example 8-9.

Example 8-9.

```
1> dbg:tracer().
{ok,<0.501.0>}
```

This starts the application and a server to receive trace information. The application starts on the local node by default, but using arguments any node can be specified for tracing.

You also have to tell *dbg* what to trace; see Example 8-10.

Example 8-10.

```
1    2> dbg:tp(darapi_handler_assets,get_handler,2,[]).
2    {ok,[{matched,nonode@nohost,1}]}
3    3> dbg:p(all,c).
4    {ok,[{matched,nonode@nohost,198}]}
```

In line 1 you define the function get_handler with arity 2 in the module darapi_handler_assets to be traced. Line 3 says that all processes, current and created in the future, will be traced for calls. The processes can be restricted to one process PID and the trace pattern can be set to *messages sent*, *messages received*, and others.

Running the application, in your case of dar_api hitting the web server with localhost:8402/api/assets/1, prints the trace shown in Example 8-11.

Example 8-11.

```
4> <0.505.0>) call darapi_handler_assets:get_handler({http_req,#Port<0.89363>,
                        ranch_tcp,keepalive,<0.505.0>,<<"GET">>,'HTTP/1.1',
        {{127,0,0,1},61219},
        <<"localhost">>,undefined,8402,<<"/api/assets/1">>,undefined,<<>>,
```

---

[3]http://erlang.org/doc/man/dbg.html

81

```
        undefined,
        [{id,<<"1">>}],
        [{<<" host">>,<<"localhost:8402">>},
         {<<"user-agent">>,<<"curl/7.43.0">>},
         {<<"accept">>,<<"*/*">>}],
        [{<<"if-modified-since">>,undefined},
         {<<"if-none-match">>,undefined},
         {<<"if-unmodified-since">>,undefined},
         {<<"if-match">>,undefined},
         {<<"accept">>,[{{<<"*">>,<<"*">>,[]},1000,[]}]}],
        undefined,
        [{media_type,{<<"application">>,<<"json">>,[]}},{charset,undefined}],
        waiting,<<>>,undefined,false,waiting,
        [{<<"content-type">>,[<<"application">>,<<"/">>,<<"json">>,<<>>]}],
        <<>>,undefined},undefined)
```

Using tracing alone is not enough to monitor a system, especially when the trace are printed in a console together with log entries. Observer[4] combines traces with other information to provide an overview of a running system in a graphical interface. It is started in an Erlang environment with the command shown in Example 8-12.

Example 8-12.

```
1>  observer:start().
```

In an Elixir environment, you start it with the command shown in Example 8-13.

Example 8-13.

```
iex(1)> :observer.start
```

Once started, the GUI looks like Figure 8-2.

---

[4]http://erlang.org/doc/apps/observer/observer_ug.html

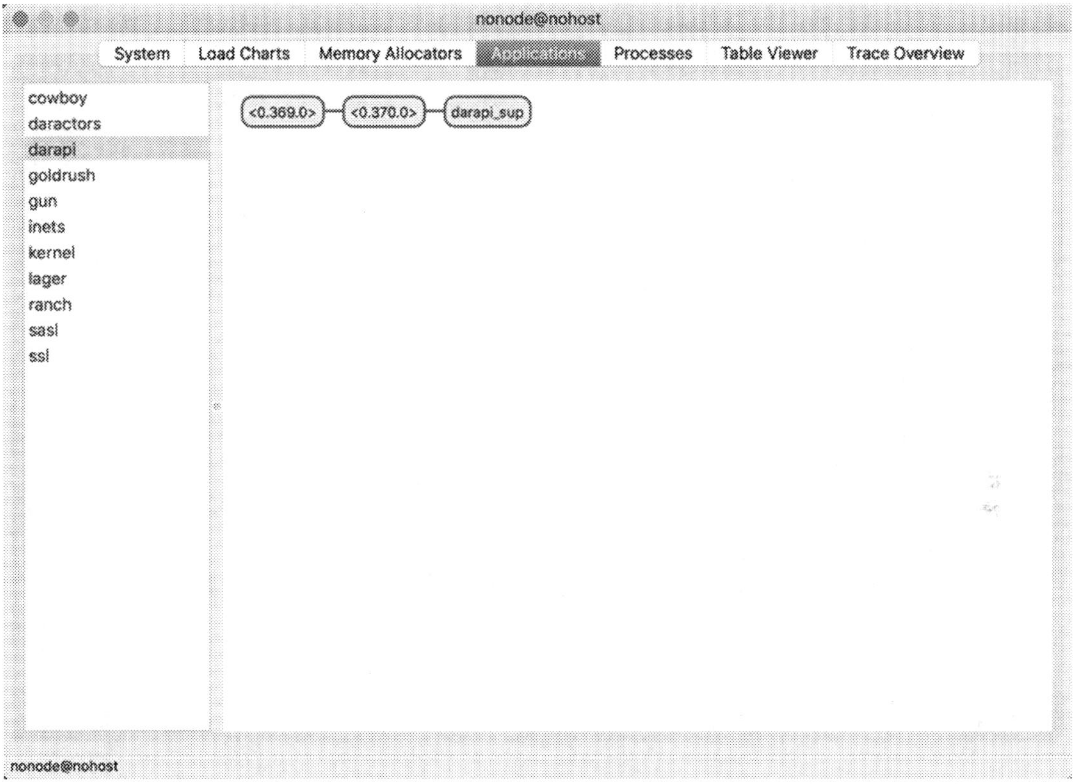

Figure 8-2. *Observer*

All running applications for the observed node are displayed. In the menu of the application, a node for observing can be chosen if others (besides the local node) are known.

Other tabs display information about memory usage, the system, the in-memory data store *ets*, and provide charts and list processes, as you can see in Figure 8-3.

Pid	Name or Initial Func	Reds	Memory	MsgQ	Current Function
<0.6.0>	application_controller	0	426952	0	gen_server:loop/6
<0.22933.1>	appmon_info	5235	42336	0	gen_server:loop/6
<0.11.0>	code_server	0	1202768	0	code_server:loop/1
<0.363.0>	cowboy_clock	140	5832	0	gen_server:loop/6
<0.362.0>	cowboy_sup	0	2864	0	gen_server:loop/6
<0.489.0>	daractors_sup	0	2824	0	gen_server:loop/6
<0.476.0>	darapi_sup	0	3968	0	gen_server:loop/6
<0.63.0>	disk_log_server	0	5840	0	gen_server:loop/6
<0.62.0>	disk_log_sup	0	6976	0	gen_server:loop/6
<0.3.0>	erl_prim_loader	0	689608	0	erl_prim_loader:loop/3
<0.5.0>	error_logger	0	109392	0	gen_event:fetch_msg/5
<0.19.0>	file_server_2	0	42376	0	gen_server:loop/6
<0.44.0>	ftp_sup	0	2824	0	gen_server:loop/6
<0.18.0>	global_group	0	2824	0	gen_server:loop/6
<0.14.0>	global_name_server	0	2904	0	gen_server:loop/6
<0.328.0>	gr_counter_sup	0	5872	0	gen_server:loop/6
<0.349.0>	gr_lager_default_tracer_counters	0	2864	0	gen_server:loop/6
<0.351.0>	gr_lager_default_tracer_counters_...	0	2864	0	gen_server:loop/6
<0.348.0>	gr_lager_default_tracer_params	0	2864	0	gen_server:loop/6
<0.350.0>	gr_lager_default_tracer_params_mgr	0	2864	0	gen_server:loop/6
<0.330.0>	gr_manager_sup	0	7056	0	gen_server:loop/6
<0.329.0>	gr_param_sup	0	5872	0	gen_server:loop/6
<0.327.0>	gr_sup	0	7096	0	gen_server:loop/6
<0.493.0>	gun_sup	0	2824	0	gen_server:loop/6
<0.48.0>	httpc_handler_sup	0	21648	0	gen_server:loop/6
<0.47.0>	httpc_manager	0	2824	0	gen_server:loop/6

Figure 8-3. *Observer*

Here I highlight the *darapi* supervisor.
Double-clicking this entry reveals more details about the process, as shown in Figure 8-4.

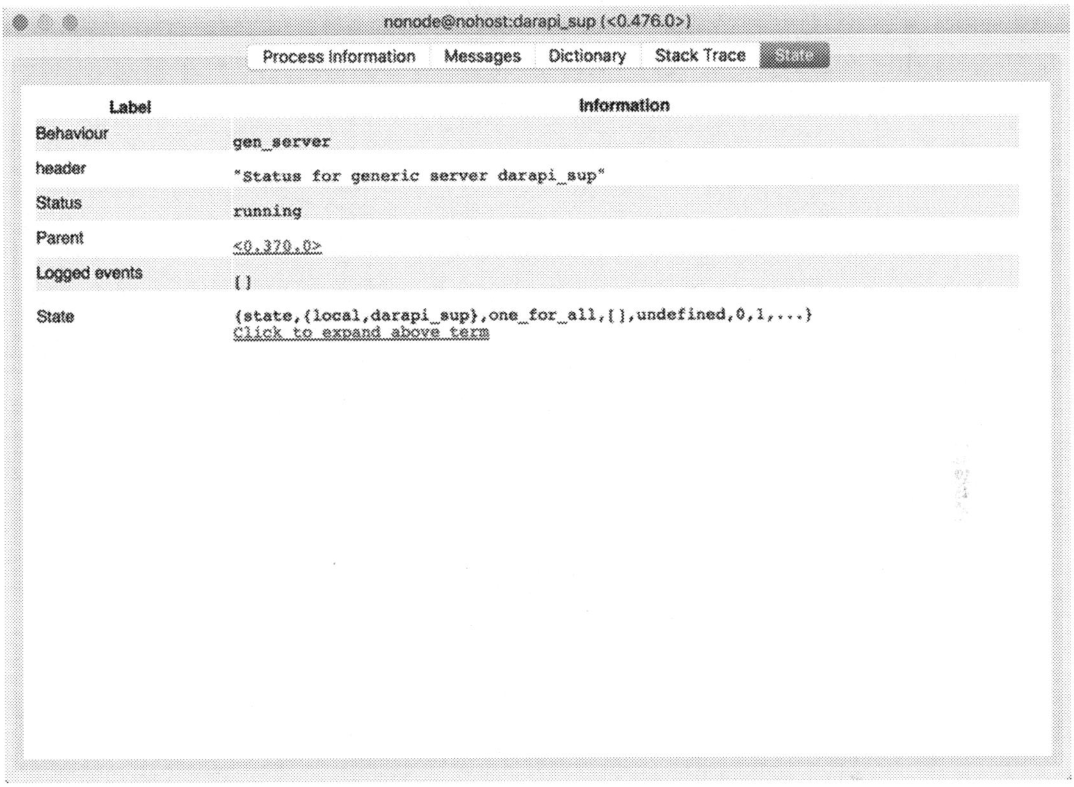

Figure 8-4. *Observer*

Observer can also monitor remote nodes. The menu item *Nodes* lists known nodes; choosing one of them will switch the observer to this node. Then all the information about the node can be read as if it was local. Before this can happen, a SSH tunnel may need to be set up to link ports from the local machine to the remote machine.

## PART IV

Implementing the Service

CHAPTER 9

Overview

Up to now you have not produced much code. Finally, this is the part of the book where you go deeper into code. I won't explain the syntax of Erlang or Elixir in this chapter; Appendix D lists the language features and compares the syntax of both languages.

You will examine a special *Hello World* application almost line by line to see how an application with distributed processes can be implemented in a few lines. At the end of the chapter, you will have a look at the standard libraries and also libraries the community provides.

This part and Part 5: Patterns and Concepts are intertwined and there are many links to the concepts that are explained in Part 5. I encourage you to jump between the chapters as your interest leads you.

A Deeper Look at Erlang and Elixir

Before you start, let's have a first look at Erlang and Elixir, a *Hello World* of a different kind. See Figure 9-1.

The following *Hello World* programs in Erlang and Elixir have the same functionality and only differ in syntax. The modules are basic examples of

- sending messages between processes and

- distributing processes on different machines.

I use two machines:

- On *machine 1* the recipient or listener is started.

- On *machine 2* a process is started that sends a message to the other machine.

The following code examples are the implementations of the above design. Erlang is in Example 9-1 and Elixir is in Example 9-2.

© Wolfgang Loder 2016
W. Loder, *Erlang and Elixir for Imperative Programmers*, DOI 10.1007/978-1-4842-2394-9_9

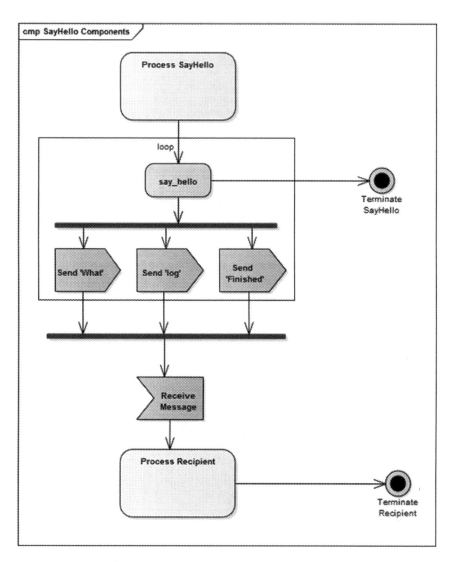

Figure 9-1. *Say Hello Design*

Example 9-1.

```
1  %%%--------------------------------------------------------------------
2  %%%  @doc
3  %%%  This module is a basic example of
4  %%%      (1) sending messages between processes and
5  %%%      (2) distribute processes on different nodes / machines.
6  %%%  Usage:
7  %%%  Machine 1: erl -sname precipient -setcookie scookie
8  %%%                 sayhello:start_recipient().
```

```
 9    %%%   Machine 2: erl -sname psayhello -setcookie scookie
10    %%%               sayhello:start_sayhello('precipient@machinename').
11    %%%   @end
12    %%%-----------------------------------------------------------------
13    -module(sayhello).
14
15    %%   API
16    -export([start/0, recipient/0, say_hello/2, say_hello/3, start_recipient/0, star\
17    t_sayhello/1]).
18
19    %% methods for distributed processes on more than one machine
20    say_hello(_, 0, Node) ->
21      io:format("Process arity 3 'say_hello' finished~n", []),
22      {precipient, Node} ! finished;
23
24    say_hello(What, Times, Node) ->
25      io:format("3: ~p~n", [What]),
26      {precipient, Node} ! What,
27      say_hello(What, Times - 1, Node).
28
29    start_recipient()  ->
30      register(precipient, spawn(sayhello, recipient, [])).
31
32    start_sayhello(InitNode)   ->
33      spawn(sayhello, say_hello, ["Hello", 2, InitNode]),
34      {precipient, InitNode} ! log.
35
36    %%  methods for processes on one machine
37    say_hello(_, 0) ->
38      io:format("Process arity 2 'say_hello' finished~n", []),
39      precipient ! finished;
40    say_hello(What, Times) ->
41      io:format("2: ~p~n", [What]),
42      precipient ! What,
43      say_hello(What, Times - 1).
44
45    %%   recipient  of  say_hello-messages
46    recipient() ->
47      receive
48        finished ->
49          io:format("Recipient process finished~n", []);
50        log ->
51          io:format("Recipient received log message~n", []),
52          recipient();
53        What ->
54          io:format("Recipient received ~s~n", [What]),
55          recipient()
56    end.
57
```

```
58   start()  ->
59   register(precipient, spawn(sayhello, recipient, [])),
60   precipient ! nomessagedefined,
61   spawn(sayhello, say_hello, ["Hello", 4]).
```

Example 9-2.

```
1    defmodule SayHello do
2    @doc """
3    This module is a basic example of
4       (1) sending messages between processes and
5       (2) distribute processes on different machines.
6    Usage:
7    Machine 1: iex --sname precipient --cookie scookie
8                 SayHello.start_recipient
9    Machine 2: iex --sname pinit --cookie scookie
10                Node.connect :"precipient@machinename"
11                SayHello.start_sayhello
12   """
13   def start_recipient do
14     precipient = spawn(SayHello, :recipient, [])
15     :global.register_name(:precipient, precipient)
16   end
17
18   def start_sayhello() do
19     spawn(SayHello, :say_hello, ["Hello", 2])
20     send :global.whereis_name(:precipient), :log
21   end
22
23   def say_hello(_, 0) do
24     IO.puts "Process 'say_hello' finished"
25     send :global.whereis_name(:precipient), :finished
26   end
27
28   def say_hello(what,  times) do
29     IO.puts what
30     send :global.whereis_name(:precipient), what
31     say_hello(what, times - 1)
32   end
33
34   # recipient of say_hello-messages
35   def recipient do
36     receive do
37       :finished  ->
38         IO.puts "Recipient process finished"
39       :log ->
40         IO.puts "Recipient received log message"
41         recipient
```

```
42      what  ->
43          IO.puts "Recipient received #{what}"
44          recipient
45     end
46   end
47
48   def start do
49     precipient = spawn(SayHello, :recipient, [])
50     :global.register_name(:precipient, precipient)
51     send precipient, :nomessagedefined
52     spawn(SayHello, :say_hello, ["Hello", 4])
53   end
54
55   end
```

The Elixir syntax looks a lot like Ruby, which is not a surprise considering that the creator was part of the Ruby core team. Otherwise, both modules show how concise implementations in Erlang and Elixir are. The *magic* lies in the underlying Erlang VM (BEAM). It handles the communication between processes; you just have to tell it what you need.

Let's dive deeper into the code without getting too much into syntax differences.

Module Definition

After the comment section on top, both implementations define the module. In Erlang, the module name needs to be an atom and also correspond exactly to the file name. See Example 9-3.

Example 9-3.

```
%   filename: sayhello.erl
-module(sayhello).
```

Elixir is here more forgiving; a file is just a container for definitions. See Example 9-4.

Example 9-4.

```
# filename: sayhello.ex
defmodule SayHello do
```

The module name can be anything, but Elixir translates the module name into an atom, as shown in Example 9-5.

Example 9-5.

```
1   iex(1)> is_atom SayHello
2   true
3   iex(2)> to_string SayHello
4   "Elixir.SayHello"
```

Internally the module name *SayHello* was transformed to the atom *Elixir.SayHello*.

> ℹ️ **BIFs (built-in functions)**   The function `is_atom` used in the example above is one of the built-in functions in Erlang that is also exposed in Elixir. Some of these functions are written in C for performance reasons. Another example of a BIF is *spawn*. In general, the definition of BIFs is not quite clear[1].
>
> Some of those functions can be found in the Erlang module *erlang*[2] and in the Elixir module *Kernel*[3] manuals.

Function Exports

In Erlang, you need to export functions explicitly, as shown in Example 9-6.

Example 9-6.

```
-export([start/0,
         recipient/0,
         say_hello/2,
         say_hello/3,
         start_recipient/0,
         start_sayhello/1]).
```

The line `-export` lists all the functions you want to access from outside the module.

Elixir implicitly exports all functions defined with `def`; functions defined with `defp` won't be exported and are marked as private functions.

Running on One Machine

If you look at the Erlang source code, you will see in the comments that you have two sets of functions for one and for multiple machines. This has to do with the way you register machine (*node*) names to show differences in possible implementations.

> ℹ️ **Nodes**   When the Erlang and Elixir applications are installed, they also have the VM runtime installed. The VM together with all the BEAM files that make up the application are called *nodes*. There can be more than one node on one machine, but normally they are distributed across several physical machines.

The function `start` is the entry point to the module on one machine; see Example 9-7.

---

[1] http://rvirding.blogspot.co.ke/2009/10/what-are-bifs.html
[2] http://erlang.org/doc/man/erlang.html
[3] http://elixir-lang.org/docs/stable/elixir/Kernel.html

Example 9-7.

```
1   start()  ->
2     register(precipient, spawn(sayhello, recipient, [])),
3     precipient ! nomessagedefined,
4     spawn(sayhello, say_hello, ["Hello", 4]).
```

The library function spawn takes the module name (*sayhello*) and the function to call as arguments. The additional list could send arguments to the function to call, but in your example you don't have any arguments and the list *[]* is empty. The output of this call is a process id (*PID*) and this is the second argument for the library function register; you pass it in without assigning it to a variable first. The first argument of register is the name you want to register (precipient) in the form of an atom. This name can be anything and does not need to correlate with module or function names.

ⓘ **PID**   A PID is a data type in Erlang and defines a process in the Erlang VM. Erlang's processes have nothing to do with threads or processes in an operating system. They are lightweight and can be called *green threads* (without going into the discussion of whether Erlang's green threads are comparable to those of other languages).

The structure of a PID can be seen in el_term.h[4] and the external representation in the Erlang documentation[5].

So you want the system to spawn an instance of the module *sayhello*, which is in fact the same module the function start is defined in. Then the system should name the instance precipient and call the function recipient without any arguments. The output of the spawn statement is an Erlang process, described by a PID, as mentioned above.

On line 3, you send an atom (*nomessagedefined*) to the process precipient, which is just a test message to see later in the log if the message was received.

On line 4, you spawn the second process. This time you run the function say_hello in the module *sayhello* and define two arguments in the list. The first one is a string and the second a number. The intention in this example is to send "Hello" four times to the recipient and then terminate.

What happens in say_hello? Conceptually the implementation of this function is a structural form of polymorphism; see Example 9-8.

Example 9-8.

```
1   %% methods for processes on one machine
2   say_hello(_, 0) ->
3     io:format("Process arity 2 'say_hello' finished~n", []),
4     precipient ! finished;
5   say_hello(What, Times) ->
6     io:format("2: ~p~n", [What]),
7     precipient ! What,
8     say_hello(What, Times - 1).
```

This code works with pattern matching. Line 2

```
say_hello(_, 0) ->
```

---

[4]https://github.com/erlang/otp/blob/maint/erts/emulator/beam/erl_term.h#L571
[5]http://erlang.org/doc/apps/erts/erl_ext_dist.html#id93725

defines the function say_hello with two arguments. The first argument is irrelevant, so you just write a catch-all argument (the underscore). The second argument is the counter and if this argument is "0" then you just write some text and send a _finished atom to the recipient process. After that, the say_hello process will terminate.

Note the ; at the end of line 4. This indicates that the function definition is not done yet. As a side note, statements are separated by a comma, which needs a bit getting used to coming from other, especially imperative, languages.

The second form of say_hello takes two arguments as well; it would not work with a different number of arguments similar to C, Java, and others where the name of the function together with the arguments' names and types form the *signature* of the function. In the second definition of say_hello, you are interested in both arguments:

- What defines what you want to send to the recipient. It has an uppercase first letter, so it is a *variable*.

- Times is also a variable. It is the counter that was initiated in the spawn call of the process *precipient*.

The important line is this:

```
say_hello(What, Times - 1).
```

Here you establish the loop with a decremented counter. This function will loop until Times reaches "0" and then the first function definition will match and tell the recipient process to terminate by sending the atom *finished*. After that, the say_hello process will terminate. Now you know why you were not interested in the first argument previously; it truly is irrelevant.

When you run the function sayhello:start() you get the output shown in Example 9-9.

Example 9-9.

```
1    1> sayhello:start().
2    Recipient received nomessagedefined
3    2: "Hello"
4    <0.36.0>
5    2: "Hello"
6    Recipient received Hello
7    2: "Hello"
8    Recipient received Hello
9    2: "Hello"
10   Recipient received Hello
11   Process arity 2 'say_hello' finished
12   Recipient received Hello
13   Recipient process finished
```

So what happens on the receiver process? The function *recipient* is all that is needed; see Example 9-10.

Example 9-10.

```
1    %% recipient of say_hello-messages
2    recipient() ->
3      receive
4        finished ->
5          io:format("Recipient process finished~n", []);
```

```
6        log ->
7          io:format("Recipient received log message~n", []),
8          recipient();
9       What ->
10         io:format("Recipient received ~s~n", [What]),
11         recipient()
12   end.
```

The function defines a `receive` block. This expression defines code that is executed when a message via the operator "!" is sent. This example does not show the *after* expression, which can be used to implement timeouts.

The receive block works with patterns. The first two patterns are atoms, the third pattern is the value What (note the different case of the first character). The code just outputs some string to show what happened. The interesting line is in Example 9-11.

Example 9-11.

```
recipient();
```

It establishes the loop, so after printing out some information in case of the atom *log* or the value What sent, the function will continue. In case of the atom *finished* received it will simply terminate. This implementation is tail-recursive and does not grow the stack; see the *Recursion* section.

It is useful to look at the same function in Elixir; see Example 9-12.

Example 9-12.

```
1    # recipient of say_hello-messages
2    def recipient do
3      receive do
4        :finished  ->
5          IO.puts "Recipient process finished"
6        :log ->
7          IO.puts "Recipient received log message"
8          recipient
9        what  ->
10         IO.puts "Recipient received #{what}"
11         recipient
12     end
13   end
```

Apart from syntax differences, they are the same. Elixir adds string interpolation, which is used in line 10:

```
"Recipient received #{what}"
```

Running on Two Machines

When you run the Erlang version in bash or the command line, you get the following output for the recipient and the client. First, the recipient needs to be started; see Example 9-13.

Example 9-13.

```
1   $ erl -sname precipient -setcookie scookie
2   Erlang/OTP 18 [erts-7.1] [source] [64-bit] [smp:8:8] [async-threads:10] [hipe]
3   [\kernel-poll:false] [dtrace]
4
5   Eshell V7.1 (abort with ^G)
6   (precipient@Wolfgangs-MacBook-Pro)1> sayhello:start_recipient().
7   true
8   Recipient received log message
9   Recipient received Hello
10  Recipient received Hello
11  Recipient process  finished
```

In line 1, you start the Erlang VM and set the name of the node (*precipient*) and the magic cookie (*scookie*). Once the recipient is started in line 6 (sayhello:start_recipient()) it will wait for messages and process them. The magic cookie lets all nodes with the same cookie value talk to each other. If the cookie values are different, the calls will be blocked.

The client is started in a similar way with the same magic cookie and a different node name (*psayhello*); see Example 9-14.

Example 9-14.

```
1   $ erl -sname psayhello -setcookie scookie
2   Erlang/OTP 18 [erts-7.1] [source] [64-bit] [smp:8:8] [async-threads:10] [hipe]
3   [\kernel-poll:false] [dtrace]
4
5   Eshell V7.1 (abort with ^G)
6   (psayhello@Wolfgangs-MacBook-Pro)1> sayhello:start_sayhello('precipient@Wolfgang\
7   s-MacBook-Pro').
8   3: "Hello"
9   3: "Hello"
10  Process arity 3 'say_hello' finished
```

The sender sends the greetings and then terminates.
The Elixir version behaves in the same way; see Examples 9-15 and 9-16.

Example 9-15.

```
1   $ iex --sname precipient --cookie scookie
2   Erlang/OTP 18 [erts-7.1] [source] [64-bit] [smp:8:8] [async-threads:10] [hipe]
3   [\kernel-poll:false] [dtrace]
4
5   Interactive Elixir (1.1.1) - press Ctrl+C to exit (type h() ENTER  for help)
6   iex(precipient@Wolfgangs-MacBook-Pro)1> SayHello.start_recipient
7   :yes
8   Recipient received log message
9   Recipient received Hello
10  Recipient received Hello
11  Recipient process  finished
```

Example 9-16.

```
1   $ iex --sname pinit --cookie scookie
2   Erlang/OTP 18 [erts-7.1] [source] [64-bit] [smp:8:8] [async-threads:10] [hipe]
3   [\kernel-poll:false] [dtrace]
4
5   Interactive Elixir (1.1.1) - press Ctrl+C to exit (type h() ENTER  for help)
6   iex(pinit@Wolfgangs-MacBook-Pro)1> Node.connect :"precipient@Wolfgangs-MacBook-P\
7   ro"
8   true
9   iex(pinit@Wolfgangs-MacBook-Pro)2> SayHello.start_sayhello
10  Hello
11  Hello
12  :log
13  Process 'say_hello' finished
```

Having two processes on one machine maybe sufficient for testing, but the Erlang VM shows its strength when building distributed and concurrent applications. The *Say Hello* example does not do much, but it implements a basic framework for distributed processes.

Later chapters will go deeper into options for calling processes on a different machine. In the example, you use a global namespace. The lines

```
register(precipient, spawn(sayhello, recipient, [])).
```

in Erlang and

```
:global.register_name(:precipient, precipient)
```

in Elixir register a *name* in the global registry, which is nothing more than a data store that is replicated to all machines in your system running Erlang VMs. *Global* means your system; the registry is private to your network, which can be on your premises or partly or wholly in the cloud. The registered names must be unique and are atoms for easier retrieval.

You can start shells with

```
erl -sname precipient -setcookie scookie
```

for Erlang or

```
iex --sname precipient --cookie scookie
```

for Elixir.

The argument -sname defines the name of the machine, called node in Erlang and Elixir. In your case, you have named the node *precipient* for the recipient node. You could also define a fully qualified name with the argument *name*, while *sname* stands for *short name*. It is also possible to say *-sname precipient@ localhost*, which seems to define a fully qualified name, but it is actually a fake short name.

⚷ Kill node   When you experiment with nodes, you will likely come into the situation that a node is still running and you need to kill it. This seems to be an easy task, but you will need the (operating system) process id.

On the Mac epmd, lsof, and kill can be used to achieve this.

You can find a bash script called kill_node_erlang.sh in the book companion repository in the folder Scripts/Mac. This script is based on another script on GitHub[6].

All registered nodes can be found with the Erlang Port Mapper Daemon[7] by executing the command shown in Example 9-17.

Example 9-17.

```
epmd -names
```

In a shell, the built-in function nodes() can be used to discover nodes that are visible to the process. After running the above commands to open shells, you will see the return of nodes() as *[]*, the empty list. What happened? Firstly, the argument -setcookie or –cookie set a *secret cookie*, in your case *scookie*. You will find out more about security in Erlang/OTP later, but this cookie is necessary so that nodes can see each other. I'm assuming that no firewalls or other port restrictions are in place at this time.

Secondly, even if the secret cookie is in place, the nodes have not communicated with each other, so they don't know about each other. In the Erlang shell, you can execute the code in Example 9-18 if your name is *precipient@localhost* and you will receive either a *pong* for a successful connection or a *pang* for an unsuccessful connection.

Example 9-18.

```
net_adm:ping('precipient@localhost').
```

In case of success, both nodes will show the connected nodes as output of *nodes()*.
The Elixir code shows in the comment that the command

```
Node.connect :"precipient@machinename"
```

is used to connect to the other node.

Once you have a connection between nodes you can send messages to those nodes. In your example you use

```
{precipient, Node} ! What
```

in Erlang or

```
send :global.whereis_name(:precipient), what
```

in Elixir.

---

[6]https://gist.github.com/robertoaloi/8884096
[7]https://erlang.org/doc/man/epmd.html

The Erlang version has the node information as an argument; the Elixir version uses another option to query the global names data store directly. Remember, this data store is on all nodes and is automatically replicated.

Again, both language versions just differ in syntax. Two more notes:

- The recipient process must be started first when more machines are used, because the send process needs to know where to send messages.

- In production, nodes will be started automatically. The cookie and name information can be configured in the release files.

And now a quick test. In the Erlang implementation, the `start()` function sends the message shown in Example 9-19.

Example 9-19.

```
precipient ! nomessagedefined
```

What will happen in the receiver function and why?

Project Structure

The structure of the Digital Asset Repository (DAR) project (see Chapter 4 for an introduction to DAR) is shown in Figure 9-2.

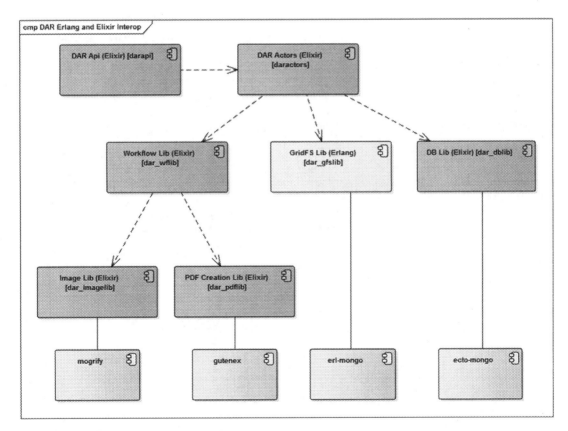

Figure 9-2. *DAR components*

The components have the following purposes:

- *darapi*: HTTP server process that implements the public API.

- *daractors*: A process similar to a business server that handles and distributes messages from the API.

- *dar_wflib*: A workflow process implemented as finite state machine.

- *dar_imagelib*: A library handling images processing like watermarks.

- *dar_dblib*: A library providing access to data stores like MongoDB.

- *dar_gfslib*: A library providing access to MongoDB's GridFS.

ⓘ Elixir umbrella projects   If you run the creation of a new project with the option `-umbrella`, you get a file structure and a configuration to have more than one application in the project. `Mix.exs` has a new key/value pair in the `project` function: `apps_path: "apps"`. It gives a hint that all the applications are in the folder specified and Mix assumes an umbrella project.

Compiling and testing can be done from the root directory of the project as well as starting all the applications in the project with `iex -S mix`.

You can mix Elixir and Erlang. The decision of which language to use was caused by availability of third-party libraries. For example, GridFS can be easily accessed with `erl-mongo`, but the Elixir library `ecto- mongo` makes it easier to manipulate documents in MongoDB and other data stores. The project set out with more Erlang modules, but with time most modules were implemented in Elixir.

Mixing Erlang and Elixir Modules

Mixing Erlang and Elixir modules is not a problem because eventually the source code will be compiled into byte code the BEAM understands. This chapter refers to the former structure of the project, which had more Erlang modules. Although this has changed, the old code can still be found in the accompanying GitHub repository. The following explanations are based on that code.

What happens if you want to have a library accessible by Elixir and Erlang modules? An example is *dar_model*. It is written in Erlang and can be configured in `mix.exs` as a dependency; see Example 9-20.

Example 9-20.

```
1  defp deps do
2    [
3      {:mongodb_ecto, "~> 0.1"},
4      {:dar_model, path: "~/Projects/creative-common-dar/Erlang/Libs/dar_model"}
5    ]
6  end
```

The deps function defines a list of dependencies, one of them a path dependency to a local folder with an Erlang project. When you run `mix compile`, the Erlang project will be automatically compiled. Internally, `mix` is using the installed Rebar version to do that, so the `.beam` file will be updated in the Erlang project.

Alternatively, you could put the Erlang code into the *src folder of the Elixir project and mix would compile this as well.

The other way round, compiling Elixir modules from an Erlang project, is not so easy. For the older Rebar a plug-in[8] exists, but not for Rebar3. I tried a few ways to achieve this task, but failed.

Rebar3 is, as you have seen, very strict with a project's structure. Dependencies from a git repository or a package repository are straightforward. Local Erlang repositories need to be integrated with what I would call a hack. A folder named checkouts in the projects can have a symbolic link (*symlink*) that points to the source code folder of the project and then it will be compiled with the dependent project. For example, dar_gfslib has a link to dar_model, and rebar.config defines this project as dependency; see Example 9-21.

Example 9-21.

```
1   {deps, [
2       {erlmongo, {git, "https://github.com/SergejJurecko/erlmongo.git"}},
3       dar_model
4   ]}.
```

So how do you call Elixir-based modules from Erlang code? You can use RPC calls. In *daractors* you can find lines like those in Example 9-22.

Example 9-22.

```
J  = rpc:call(
  'dblib@localhost',
  'Elixir.DarDblib',
  write_meta_to_collection,
  [M]).
```

These lines send the argument M to the function write_meta_to_collection in the module *Elixir.DarDblib*. Note that the module name must be prefixed with *Elixir* and surrounded with single quotes.

An RPC call to an Erlang module from Elixir sends the module and function names as atoms; see Example 9-23.

Example 9-23.

```
:rpc.call(
  :"dargfslib@Wolfgangs-MacBook-Pro",
  :dar_gfslib_process_files,
  :read_from_gfs,['filetestwrite','dar'])
```

RPC in Erlang has a scaling problem due to its implementation, so the community has developed a *gen_rpc* server[9] to allow better scaling. This implementation can be used in Erlang and Elixir, and offers a similar API to the original RPC module in Erlang.

Libraries

The following libraries most probably cover what you need for a first application built with Erlang and Elixir. Sprinkled in are a few not-so-expected libraries or applications to show the breadth of the system. All the libraries and applications described are open source. I also included some that are not working very well with Rebar3.

---

[8]https://github.com/yrashk/rebar_elixir_plugin
[9]https://github.com/priestjim/gen_rpc

Database Access: Ecto, Erlmongo, and Others

Every application or service needs to have some sort of data store. Erlang has Mnesia[10] as a capable database that is free for commercial use. Companies that start out with Erlang or Elixir will have the need to access legacy and mostly relational databases from Oracle, IBM, or Microsoft.

Erlang supports the ODBC interface[11], but as the manual says *"currently it is only regularly tested for sqlserver and postgres."*

Libraries like Erlmongo[12], which you use in your implementation, specialize in particular databases, in this case MongoDB. You will see more from Erlmongo later.

Elixir's creator and the community have taken up the task to develop a modern database access layer called *Ecto*. In fact, it is a domain-specific language for interacting with databases. At the moment, the following databases are supported with adapters:

- MongoDB

- MSSQL

- MySQL

- PostgreSQL

- SQLite3

Ecto, now in version 2, is the standard way for Elixir applications to access databases and, with further development of tools like Rebar3 that support integrating Elixir packages, Erlang modules will be able to use this database layer as well.

Riak KV

Riak[13] is a key-value database with the option of a commercial *enterprise license*. It has vast documentation and can be installed on various Linux distributions.

This is not the database for a small project. The effort to set it up makes sense if the project needs a distributed and load balanced data store. It is geared towards high capacity as the use case descriptions on their web site explain.

I included Riak in this overview to show a product that goes beyond simple libraries. It is also a good idea to have a look at the source code to get a feeling how large projects like this are organized and implemented.

JSON

Jiffy[14] is a JSON (JavaScript Object Notation) library for Erlang. JSON is a lightweight data-interchange format that is easy for humans to read and write and easy for machines to parse and generate. The interesting aspect of Jiffy is that it is a *NIF (native implemented function)*. That means it is implemented in C and is called from Erlang at runtime.

Apart from that interesting aspect, I had problems with it. First, it needs an additional configuration in Rebar3 to make it compile; see Example 9-24.

---

[10]http://erlang.org/doc/man/mnesia.html
[11]http://erlang.org/doc/apps/odbc/databases.html
[12]https://github.com/SergejJurecko/erlmongo
[13]http://basho.com/products/#riak
[14]https://github.com/davisp/jiffy

Example 9-24.

```
1    {overrides,
2      [{override, jiffy, [
3        {plugins, [pc]},
4        {artifacts, ["priv/jiffy.so"]},
5        {provider_hooks, [
6          {post,
7            [
8              {compile, {pc, compile}},
9              {clean, {pc, clean}}
10           ]
11         }]
12       }
13     ]}
14   ]}.
```

The creator of the library is working on Rebar3 compatibility, so it may be working without the workaround

Then, how could I decode a real world JSON file? It turns out that the file shown in Example 9-25 needs to be called as in Example 9-26.

Example 9-25.

```
1    {
2      "Title": "The boy that did not want to speak",
3      "Meta": {
4        "Pages":   "12"
5      }
6    }
7
8    {"Title": "The boy that did not want to speak","Meta": {"Pages": "12"}}
```

Example 9-26.

```
1    1> jiffy:decode(<<"{\"Title\": \"The boy that did not want to speak\",\"Meta\": \
2    {\"Pages\": \"12\"}}">>).
3    {[{<<"Title">>,<<"The boy that did not want to speak">>},
4      {<<"Meta">>,{[{<<"Pages">>,<<"12">>}]}}]}
```

Of course, all quotes need to be escaped and the whole string wrapped in a binary list. The same applies to another library: jsone[15]. It is the intrinsic string problem of Erlang that does not come up most of the time, but trying to use it for web pages or services sees it bubble up to the surface.

The Erlang web server *Cowboy* takes care of this problem in a way that JSON strings in the request body are binary lists that can be fed directly into JOSN libraries' *decode* functions.

Poison[16] is a JSON library for Elixir and it does not have the aforementioned problem. After adding it to the dependencies in mix.exs Poison can be called as shown in Example 9-27.

---

[15]https://github.com/sile/jsone
[16]https://github.com/devinus/poison

Example 9-27.

```
1  iex(1)> Poison.decode!(~s({"Title": "The boy that did not want to speak","Meta":\
2    {"Pages": "12"}}))
3  %{"Meta" => %{"Pages" => "12"}, "Title" => "The boy that did not want to speak"}
```

You can wrap the JSON into a string with the sigil ~s and it gets transformed into a struct with a nested struct as expected. The sigil is useful for situations like this when you want to express a string with quotes as a string without having to escape the quotes.

These are only some examples. There are at least 14 other JSON libraries for Elixir available.

Logging: Lager

Lager[17] is a logging library for Erlang, but there exists a wrapper for Elixir[18]. It can be configured in many ways to have logging information displayed or saved in the way a project needs it.

One drawback is that Lager does not play nicely with Rebar3 at the moment; at least I could not figure out a way to make Lager understand the needed configuration. Since the Erlang implementation of the API service was replaced with an Elixir/Phoenix version, I did not put too much time into it. Nevertheless, the default configuration works nicely, Rebar3 or not.

First, the Lager dependency needs to be added to rebar.config in the *deps* section, as shown in Example 9-28.

Example 9-28.

```
{lager, {git, "git://github.com/basho/lager.git", {tag, "2.2.2"}}}
```

The module can be started during boot up automatically if it is in the *relx* definition; see Example 9-29.

Example 9-29.

```
1   {relx, [{release, { darapi, "0.1.0" },
2            [
3              lager,
4              cowboy,
5              jsone,
6              uuid,
7              darapi,
8              sasl,
9              daractors]},
10
11           {sys_config, "./config/sys.config"},
12           {vm_args, "./config/vm.args"},
13
14           {dev_mode, true},
15           {include_erts, false},
16
17           {extended_start_script, true}]
18   }.
```

---

[17]https://github.com/basho/lager
[18]https://github.com/khia/exlager

It can also be started from code, as shown in Example 9-30.

Example 9-30.

```
lager:start()
```

In any case, a compiler directive needs to be either globally defined or in the module. Without it, Lager calls will fail: see Example 9-31.

Example 9-31.

```
-compile([{parse_transform, lager_transform}]).
```

Once you have Lager available, you can simply tell it to log something, as in Example 9-32.

Example 9-32.

```
1   lager:info("from_json: Method~p~n", [lager:pr(Method, ?MODULE)])
2   lager:error("from_json: Method~p~n", [lager:pr(Method, ?MODULE)])
```

The messages together with a header will be, in the default configuration, placed into files in a folder log, which is created by Lager if it does not exist. Info messages go into console.txt and error messages into error.txt.

These lines in the example above would result in the entries in the log files shown in Example 9-33.

Example 9-33.

```
2016-05-26 08:57:10.330 [info] <0.335.0>@darapi_handler_assets:from_json:61 from\
_json: Method<<"POST">>
2016-05-26 08:57:10.330 [error] <0.335.0>@darapi_handler_assets:from_json:62 fro\
m_json: Method<<"POST">>
```

There will also be an output in the console by default. There are ways to redirect logging to databases, have colored console output, set the severity level for logging, or catch Erlang errors to log them.

Elixir applications can use Lager via a wrapper as well, although there exists a logger in the Elixir system that pretty much does what Lager basically does.

If you want to use Lager, you will have to define the lager and the wrapper dependency in mix.exs and also start them at boot up; see Example 9-34.

Example 9-34.

```
def application do
  [
    mod: {DarDblib.App, []},
    applications: [:logger, :exlager]
  ]
end

defp deps do
  [
    {:lager, git: "https://github.com/basho/lager.git"},
    {:exlager ,git: "https://github.com/khia/exlager.git"}
  ]
end
```

After that, you can log messages with different severity, as in Example 9-35.

Example 9-35.

```
1  Lager.debug "Debug message"
2  Lager.info "Info message"
3  Lager.notice "Notice message"
4  Lager.warning "Warning  message"
5  Lager.error "Error message"
6  Lager.critical "Critical  message"
7  Lager.alert "Alert  message"
8  Lager.emergency "Emergency message"
```

As in Erlang, all messages will be written to the console and to files in the log folder that is created by Lager if it does not exist.

Some configuration like the truncation size of files and severity level can be set either in code or as compiler options.

Timex

Timex[19] is a library for Elixir that handles the always daunting task to handle local time, timestamps, and dates in code. It can handle time zones, custom formatting, and parsing, and it is documented very well.

As always, add the dependency to mix.exs and then optionally add the line shown in Example 9-36.

Example 9-36.

```
{:timex, "~> 2.1.5"}
```

This line calls the *using* macro in the *Timex* module and adds aliases for several types, so for example *Timex.DateTime* can be simply accessed as *DateTime*. See Example 9-37.

Example 9-37.

```
1   iex(1)> timezone1 = Timex.timezone("Africa/Nairobi", Timex.DateTime.today)
2   #<Timezone(Africa/Nairobi - EAT (+03:00))>
3   iex(2)> Timex.DateTime.now
4   #<DateTime(2016-05-26T08:54:23Z)>
5   iex(3)> tu = Timezone.convert Timex.DateTime.now, timezone1
6   #<DateTime(2016-05-26T11:54:52 Africa/Nairobi (+03:00:00))>
7   iex(4)> tu |> Timex.format!("{ISO:Extended}")
8   "2016-05-26T11:54:52.785+03:00"
9   iex(5)> tu |> Timex.format!("{ANSIC}")
10  "Thu May 26 11:54:52 2016"
```

On line 1, you create a time zone for Nairobi. The library uses the names in this list[20], so you define *Africa/Nairobi* as time zone name.

---

[19]https://github.com/bitwalker/timex
[20]https://en.wikipedia.org/wiki/List_of_tz_database_time_zones

Line 3 is the command to get the current date and time formatted as universal date time. You convert this into the Nairobi time zone. Lines 7 and 9 format the date and time in different formats. There are more than 20 formats to choose from and if this is not covering your case it is possible to define custom formats.

A nice addition is that Timex also works together with Ecto to provide timestamps where needed.

Overall, Timex is a very good library to cover any requirement for working with dates and time in Elixir applications.

In version 1.3, Elixir has added the module *Calendar*. Its goal is to provide interoperability and it provides basic functionality. It is similar to the community library Calendar[21], which can use the built-in calendar types in Elixir 1.3, but offers more features. An example similar to the one above looks like Example 9-38.

Example 9-38.

```
1  iex(1)> nbo = Calendar.DateTime.now! "Africa/Nairobi"
2  %DateTime{calendar: Calendar.ISO, day: 23, hour: 12, microsecond: {149378, 6},
3   minute: 31, month: 7, second: 54, std_offset: 0, time_zone: "Africa/Nairobi",
4  utc_offset: 10800, year: 2016, zone_abbr: "EAT"}
5  iex(2)> nbo |> Calendar.DateTime.shift_zone!("Europe/Vienna")
6            |> Calendar.DateTime.Format.iso8601
7  "2016-07-23T11:31:54.149378+02:00"
```

UUID

Many times it is possible to create unique id values before data is written to a data store. The library *uuid*[22] can take care of that.

After adding the dependency (either via git or local via *_checkouts*), you can use the library like Example 9-39.

Example 9-39.

```
1  new_uuid(Pid)  ->
2    U = uuid:new(Pid),
3    {UU,_} = uuid:get_v1(U),
4    uuid:uuid_to_string(UU,standard).
```

The function takes a PID because the library *uuid* uses it for randomization. When you call the function you get a uuid, as shown in Example 9-40.

Example 9-40.

```
1  1> darapi_helpers:new_uuid(self()).
2  "f538acae-232a-11e6-93a9-90e6000000ab"
```

The uuid can be formatted in different ways; I show the default (*standard*) here.

This short overview just gives you a glimpse into what is available. Some other libraries are used in your implementation and are explained further in Chapter 10 and Chapter 11, especially web libraries. For other libraries, you may find information in Appendix B.

---

[21]https://github.com/lau/calendar
[22]https://github.com/okeuday/uuid

CHAPTER 10

■ ■ ■

Public Interface

This chapter describes the server part of the project. The API of the solution is a simple web service mostly adhering to the REST principles of a uniform interface with stateless interactions and cacheable results. See Figure 10-1.

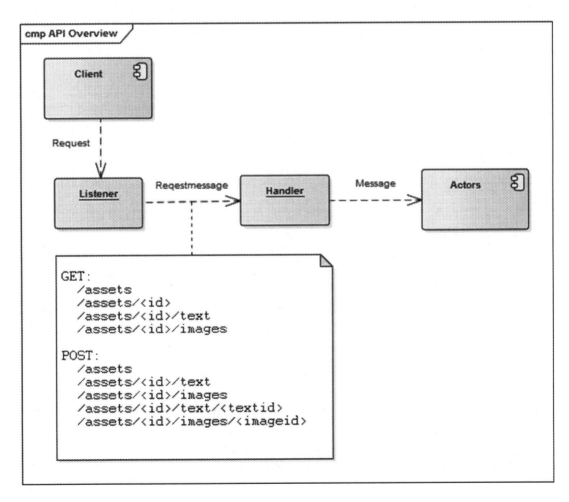

Figure 10-1. *API overview*

W. Loder, *Erlang and Elixir for Imperative Programmers*, DOI 10.1007/978-1-4842-2394-9_10

The blue objects in Figure 10-1 represent the API server with a *listener* and a request *handler*. The client (web, mobile and similar) sends a request to the server to either get or retrieve an asset.

In this case, the server listens to *GET* and *POST* http requests:

GET:

- `/assets` - Get a list of assets

- `/assets/<id>` - Get asset with id <id>

- `/assets/<id>/text` - Get text only for asset <id>

- `/assets/<id>/images` - Get image list only for asset <id>

POST:

- `/assets` - Add a new asset

- `/assets/<id>/text` - Add a text for asset <id>

- `/assets/<id>/images` - Add an image for asset <id>

- `/assets/<id>/text/<textid>` - Change text <textid> for asset <id>

- `/assets/<id>/images/<imageid>` - Change image <imageid> for asset <id>

All urls can have additional request commands in the query string, as in Example 10-1.

Example 10-1.

`/assets?page=3&pagesize=20`

This indicates that *page 3* of the list with a *page size* of 20 should be sent by the server. Other commands support filtering and sorting.

The server sends the usual http status code responses:

- *200 OK* - Get requests were processed successfully

- *201 Created* - Post requests were processed successfully

- *202 Accepted* - Requests were accepted but not yet processed

- *204 No Content* - Requests don't have content

- *400 Bad Request* - Commands in the query string are not supported

- *403 Forbidden* - Request not allowed

- *404 Not Found* - Request could not be processed because of a non-existing id

- *409 Conflict* - Request content does not validate

- *500 Internal Server Error* - Any error or exception on the server side not handled

The handler will create a system internal message and send it to the actors which process the messages as needed. The system is asynchronous, so client-server connections need to be handled with asynchronous mechanisms like web sockets or polling.

There are Web and REST frameworks available to make the implementation of such a service easier, but first let's make it hard, and try to implement simple servers with the means Erlang/OTP and Elixir provide. This will help you to understand the implementation with frameworks later.

Low Level

The standard library provides a way to program a HTTP server. The Erlang code in Example 10-2 does not do much, but it is working as a web server on the arbitrarily chosen port 4242.

Example 10-2.

```
1   %%%-------------------------------------------------------------------
2   %%% @author  Wolfgang  Loder
3   %%% @doc
4   %%% inets:start().
5   %%% browse http://localhost:4242/www/simplewebserver/service
6   %%%  @end
7   %%%-------------------------------------------------------------------
8   -module(simplewebserver).
9
10  -export([start/0,service/3]).
11
12  start()  ->
13    inets:start(httpd, [
14      {modules, [
15        mod_alias,
16        mod_auth,
17        mod_esi,
18        mod_actions,
19        mod_cgi,
20        mod_dir,
21        mod_get,
22        mod_head,
23        mod_log,
24        mod_disk_log
25      ]},
26    {port,4242},
27    {server_name,"simplewebserver"},
28    {server_root,"."},
29    {document_root,"."},
30    {erl_script_alias, {"/www", [simplewebserver,io]}},
31    {error_log, "error.log"},
32    {security_log, "security.log"},
33    {transfer_log, "transfer.log"},
34    {mime_types,[
35      {"html","text/html"},
36      {"css","text/css"},
37      {"js","application/x-javascript"}
38    ]}
39  ])
40
41  service(SessionID, _Env, _Input) ->
42    mod_esi:deliver(SessionID, [
43      "Content-Type: text/html\r\n\r\n",
44      "<html><body>Hello, World!</body></html>"
45    ])
```

The module *inets* is implemented according to OTP patterns; you will see examples in the next chapter. It is a little bit difficult to configure, as you can see in the argument of *inets:start*, and you would not write a web application with it. But as a quick and dirty way to set up a working HTTP server, it is sufficient.

If you don't start the *simplewebserver* module with Rebar3 but with erl, then you need to start inets first. The URL the server runs on is in the header of the example file above. It is a combination of the erl_script_alias value, the module, and the function name service. It can be configured in different ways, but whenever I changed something, the server threw an error, so be warned if you want to play with the code.

Example 10-3 is a simple UDP server.

Example 10-3.

```
1    -module(rawudp).
2
3    -export([start/1, client/2]).
4
5    start(Port)  ->
6       {ok, Socket} = gen_udp:open(Port, [binary, {active, false}]),
7         io:format("server  opened  socket:~p~n",[Socket]),
8         loop(Socket).
9
10   loop(Socket)  ->
11     inet:setopts(Socket, [{active, once}]),
12     receive
13         {udp, Socket, Host, Port, Bin} ->
14             io:format("server received:~p~n",[Bin]),
15             gen_udp:send(Socket, Host, Port, <<"From Server:", Bin/binary>>),
16             case Bin of
17                <<"stop">> -> gen_udp:close(Socket);
18                 _ -> loop(Socket)
19             end
20     end.
21
22   client(N, Port) ->
23       {ok, Socket} = gen_udp:open(0, [binary]),
24       io:format("client opened socket=~p~n",[Socket]),
25       ok = gen_udp:send(Socket, "localhost", Port,  N),
26       Value = receive
27                   {udp, Socket, _, _, Bin} ->
28                       io:format("client received:~p~n",[Bin])
29               after 1000 ->
30                       0
31               end,
32       gen_udp:close(Socket),
33       Value.
```

The UDP server is called *gen_udp* and is part of the kernel together with a TCP and a SCTP server.

The example is simple. Start the server with start(4242) and it will open the port 4242 for communication. The client is started with, for example, client("Hi server, 4242) and it will send the first argument to port 4242. Whatever the server receives is echoed back to the client; see Examples 10-4 and 10-5.

Example 10-4.

```
1   2> rawudp:start(4242).
2   server opened socket:#Port<0.52569>
3   server received:<<1>>
4   server received:<<"hi  server">>
5   server received:<<"stop">>
6   ok
7   3>
```

Example 10-5.

```
1   2> rawudp:client("hi server",4242).
2   client opened socket=#Port<0.25273>
3   client received:<<"From Server:hi server">>
4   ok
5   3> rawudp:client("stop",4242).
6   client opened socket=#Port<0.25274>
7   client received:<<"From Server:stop">>
8   ok
9   4>
```

When the client sends "stop" as the first argument, the server stops and releases the port. You can use *gen_udp* in Elixir as well; see Example 10-6.

Example 10-6.

```elixir
1   defmodule RawUdpServer do
2     use GenServer
3     require Logger
4
5     def start_link(opts \\ []) do
6       GenServer.start_link(__MODULE__, :ok, opts)
7     end
8
9     def init (:ok) do
10      {:ok, _socket} = :gen_udp.open(4242)
11    end
12
13    def handle_info({:udp, _socket, _ip, _port, data}, state) do
14      Logger.info "Received a message: " <> inspect(data)
15      {:noreply, state}
16    end
17  end
```

Ignore for now that *RawUdpServer* is implemented as *gen_server*. Line 10 is opening a *gen_udp* server on port 4242. All messages sent are handled in handle_info and then logged to the console. Since you are using an Erlang module from Elixir, you need to use the atom *:gen_udp* to call the functions.

You can use the client from Example 10-3 and for the call, as shown in Example 10-7.

Example 10-7.

rawudp:client("hi server",4242).

You will get the response shown in Example 10-8 after having started the server with `RawUdpServer.start_link`.

Example 10-8.

```
1   iex(1)> RawUdpServer.start_link
2   {:ok, #PID<0.59.0>}
3   iex(2)>
4   09:16:02.088 [info] Received a message: 'hi server'
```

There are other low-level servers like *gen_tcp* available. They may be useful for some scenarios, but most of the time you will use implementations on a higher level like *Cowboy* or *Phoenix*, which you will examine later in this chapter.

OTP Servers

OTP is the heart of the Erlang system. It provides concepts and generic implementations for often used designs; without it, the Erlang system would not be so easy to use. Most of the time you use OTP concepts except for the most simple applications, but it is possible to develop without those concepts.

Erlang and Elixir have their own standard libraries and on top of these build more generic concepts. There are six default generic implementations, and all of them can be used in Erlang and Elixir:

- Generic Server

- Generic FSM

- Generic State Machine

- Generic Event Handler

- Supervisor

- Application

The first five are called *behaviours* and are part of the Erlang *stdlib*; *application* is defined in *kernel*. Elixir has a new generic server that is not available in Erlang/OTP: GenStage.

Generic Server[1]

Generic Server is the commonly used behaviour for any kind of server. In the OO world, this would be the base class for other servers, but in Erlang, only the concept is inherited, not the implementation.

You encountered a *gen_server* implementation in the last chapter when I discussed the example *RawUdpServer*. It shows some of the functions that can be implemented to create a generic server (see Example 10-6). In Elixir, not all callbacks need to be used; if they are not implemented, then default implementations are called. In Erlang, the minimum implementation looks like Example 10-9.

---

[1]https://github.com/erlang/otp/blob/maint/lib/stdlib/src/gen_server.erl

Example 10-9.

```
1   -module(erlangexamples_server).
2   -behaviour(gen_server).
3
4   -record(state, { }).
5   -export([ start_link/0,
6             init/1,
7             handle_call/3,
8             handle_cast/2,
9             handle_info/2,
10            terminate/2,
11            code_change/3]).
12  -define(SERVER, ?MODULE).
13
14  start_link()  ->
15      gen_server:start_link({local, erlangexamples_server}, erlangexamples_server,\
16  [], []).
17
18  init([]) ->
19      {ok, #state{}}.
20
21  handle_call({F, A}, _From, State) ->
22    Reply = process_request({F,A}),
23    {reply, Reply, State};
24  handle_call(_Request, _From, State) ->
25    Reply = done,
26    {reply, Reply, State}.
27
28  handle_cast(_Msg, State) ->
29      {noreply, State}.
30
31  handle_info(_Info, State) ->
32      {noreply, [1]}.
33
34  terminate(_Reason, _State) ->
35      ok.
36
37  code_change(_OldVsn, State, _Extra) ->
38      {ok, State}.
```

Generic Server callbacks:

- handle_call - This function handles synchronous calls that expect a return value.

- handle_cast - This function handles asynchronous calls without return value.

- handle_info - All messages except *call* and *cast* are handled by this function.

- init - This function is called after the gen_server is started to allow initialization work done.

- terminate - This function is called when the gen_server is about to terminate to allow any cleanup necessary.

- code_change - This function has to do with hot code swapping and allows to update the internal state of the gen_server during an update.

- format_status - It is not needed to implement this callback. If so, it allows you to format, for example, the internal state in a compact form to display in case errors or other status displays.

There are two ways to start a gen_server:

- start_link - This is one function to start the gen_server. It can be called directly or more likely by a supervisor.

- start - Another function to start the gen_server, provides the same arguments than start_link.

The difference between the functions is that start_link creates a bi-directional link between the caller and the gen_server, and is used by a supervisor. In this case, the gen_server will be stopped automatically by the supervisor or restarted if the gen_server fails. Otherwise, it needs to be stopped by the caller by calling the gen_server function stop.

Both start functions allow you to name a gen_server process.

Example 10-10.

GenServer.start_link(MODULE , :ok, name: name)

Example 10-10 defines the option key *name* with a locally registered name.

Example 10-11.

GenServer.start_link(MODULE , :ok, name: {:global, name})

Example 10-11 defines a globally registered name.

The advantage of using the gen_server is that the code is structured and a developer can see clearly what an implementer has intended to do. Server and client code can be in one module or separated if this makes it easier to understand the implementation.

Generic FSM[2] and Generic State Machine[3]

The generic state machine behaviour *gen_fsm* was replaced by another behaviour called *gen_statem*. The difference is that the latter has less restrictions regarding data types and events. It is recommended that new applications use *gen_statem*, so I am not describing *gen_fsm* in this chapter.

ℹ **Requirements**   Please note that you need at least Erlang/OTP 19.0 and Elixir 1.3 to use *gen_statem*.

The DAR workflow is implemented as a state machine. In Elixir, you can use *GenStateMachine*[4] as a wrapper for *gen_statem*, which adds Elixir features like default arguments. Of course, it is possible to use the Erlang callbacks directly, as in Example 10-12.

---

[2]https://github.com/erlang/otp/blob/maint/lib/stdlib/src/gen_fsm.erl
[3]https://github.com/erlang/otp/blob/maint-19/lib/stdlib/src/gen_statem.erl
[4]https://github.com/antipax/gen_state_machine

Example 10-12.

```
:gen_statem.start_link(name, module, args, options)
```

All Erlang *gen_statem* functions are available via *:gen_statem*.

The new state machine behaviour has two callback modes: *state_functions* is similar to the old *gen_fsm*, and *handle_event_function* is the less restrictive mode regarding data types. The second mode is the default mode in *GenStateMachine*, but the callback mode can be set in code if necessary.

As with all OTP generic servers, you must implement certain callbacks to make the behaviour working. This implementation uses Elixir, so only functions you need are coded; see Example 10-13.

Example 10-13.

```
defmodule DARWf do
  use GenStateMachine

  # Client
  def start_link(m) do
    GenStateMachine.start_link(DARWf, {DARState.idle, m}, name: DARWf)
end

  # ... truncated

  # Server (callbacks)
  def handle_event({:call, from}, :requestreceived, state, msg) do
    case DARWorkflowOperations.validate_request msg do
      {:ok, res} ->
        {:next_state, DARState.requestvalidated,
          %{msg | :state => DARState.requestvalidated, :actiongroups => res},
          {:reply, from, %{msg | :state => DARState.requestvalidated, :actiong\
roups => res}}}
      {_, err} ->
        {:next_state, DARState.errorstate,
          %{msg | :state => DARState.errorstate, :comment => err},
          {:reply, from, %{msg | :state => DARState.errorstate, :comment => er\
          r}}}

    end
  end

# ... truncated

  def handle_event(event_type, event_content, state, data) do
    # Call the default implementation from GenStateMachine
    super(event_type, event_content, state, data)
  end
end
```

The example only shows the implementation of most important messages; the full code will be discussed in the next chapter.

Using the callback mode *handle_event_function* there needs to be the *handle_event* callback to be implemented. Other callbacks as described in the section about *gen_server* are

- init

- terminate

- code_change

Those callbacks are implemented by *GenStateMachine* as well as a generic *handle_event* callback that can be used as a *catch-all* function. The server is called with *start_link* like *gen_server*. The initial state can be set and optionally a local or global name registered, as in Example 10-14.

Example 10-14.

```
GenStateMachine.start_link(DARWf, {DARState.idle, nil}, name: DARWf)
```

Generic Event Handler[5]

This generic server is likely the least used server in projects, although it is used in OTP for handling error logs and alarms. It may be one of the most underrated generic servers as well.

An event handler implementation has three parts:

- *Event Manager* - This is a process that manages all event handlers.

- *Event Handler* - This is a callback module to handle events.

- *Events* - Any Erlang term can be an event.

Callback modules can be registered with and unregistered from the event manager dynamically. The event handler itself implements the *gen_event behaviour* and has to implement the same callbacks as a *gen_server*. Again, in Elixir all callbacks have default implementations and do not need to be implemented if not needed.

Let's look at an example. First, the Erlang version in Example 10-15.

Example 10-15.

```
1   -module(eventhandler).
2   -behaviour(gen_event).
3   -export([
4     init/1, terminate/2, handle_info/2,
5     handle_call/2, code_change/3, handle_event/2
6   ]).
7   -record(state, {course = "undefined"}).
8
9   init([]) ->
10     {ok, #state{} }.
11
12   handle_info(_Info, State)  ->
13     {ok, State}.
14
```

---

[5]https://github.com/erlang/otp/blob/maint/lib/stdlib/src/gen_event.erl

```
15    handle_call(_Request, State)  ->
16      {ok, not_implemented, State}.
17
18    handle_event(Event,  S) ->
19      io:format("Old State: ~p~n", [S]),
20      io:format("Event: ~s~n", [Event]),
21      {ok,  S#state{course=Event}}.
22
23    code_change(_OldVsn, State, _Extra) ->
24      {ok, State}.
25
26    terminate(_Arg,  S)  ->
27      io:format("State: ~p~n", [S]),
28      io:format("Terminate ~n"),
29      ok.
```

When you run the example, you get the output in Example 10-16.

Example 10-16.

```
1     1> {ok, Pid} = gen_event:start().
2     {ok,<0.130.0>}
3     2> gen_event:add_handler(Pid, eventhandler, []).
4       ok
5     3> gen_event:notify(Pid, "first").
6      Old State: {state,"undefined"}
7       Event: first
8     4> gen_event:notify(Pid, "main").
9      Old State: {state,"first"}
10      Event: main
11    5> gen_event:notify(Pid, "dessert").
12     Old State: {state,"main"}
13      Event: dessert
14    6> gen_event:delete_handler(Pid, eventhandler, ok).
15     State: {state,"dessert"}
16      Terminate
17    7> gen_event:notify(Pid, []).
18      ok
19    8> gen_event:stop(Pid).
20      ok
21    9> gen_event:notify(Pid, []).
22      ok
23    10> gen_event:sync_notify(Pid, []).
24     ** exception exit: noproc
25        in function gen:do_call/4 (gen.erl, line 177)
26        in call from gen_event:rpc/2 (gen_event.erl, line 197)
```

The same features implemented in Elixir show less code due to default implementations and the output of the Elixir version is the same, only the syntax differs. See Example 10-17.

Example 10-17.

```
1   iex(1)> {:ok, pid} = GenEvent.start_link([])
2   {:ok, #PID<0.187.0>}
3   iex(2)> GenEvent.add_handler(pid, GenEventExample, [])
4   :ok
5   iex(3)> GenEvent.notify(pid, "first")
6   Event: first
7   :ok
8   Old State: []
9   iex(4)> GenEvent.notify(pid, "main")
10  Event: main
11  :ok
12  Old State: "first"
13  iex(5)> GenEvent.notify(pid, "dessert")
14  Event: dessert
15  :ok
16  Old State: "main"
17  iex(6)>  GenEvent.remove_handler(pid,GenEventExample,:ok)
18  :ok
19  iex(7)> GenEvent.notify(pid, "")
20  :ok
21  iex(8)> GenEvent.stop pid
22  :ok
23  iex(9)> GenEvent.notify(pid, "")
24  :ok
25  iex(10)> GenEvent.sync_notify(pid, "")
26  ** (exit) no process
27      (stdlib) gen.erl:177: :gen.do_call/4
28      (elixir) lib/gen_event.ex:635: GenEvent.rpc/2
```

In lines 1 and 3, you create the event manager and add your event handler to the manager process. Then you call the notify function on the manager, which in turn will call the handle_event function of the handler. If you had added more than one handler, all of them would have been called. Your handlers update the internal state and just print the sent event term to the console.

With a call to delete_handler (Erlang) or remove_handler (Elixir) you deregister the event handler from the manager. Interesting is that subsequent calls to the manager's notify functions don't return any notification that there is actually no handler attached. Even after you stop the manager (for example, in line 21 in the Elixir example) you do not get an error when calling notify. The reason is that the function is asynchronous and just returns after being called. The *ok* is more an acknowledgment that the function was called. Only the synchronous sync_notify function returns an error as expected.

There is one problem with gen_event: all handlers are running in the process of the event manager. This means that concurrency features are not available and gen_server is more useful for ad hoc event managing than for long-running processes. Elixir's GenStage (see the description later in this chapter) could be used to implement these long-running event processes.

Supervisor[6]

Two of the most important concepts in Erlang/OTP are fault tolerance and supervisors.

When you create applications you want to put them into a supervisor tree to make sure that application nodes will be restarted in case of failures. A simple supervisor is shown in Example 10-18.

Example 10-18.

```
1   defmodule DARDataStore do
2     use Supervisor
3
4     def start_link(name) do
5       Supervisor.start_link(__MODULE__, [], name: {:global, name})
6     end
7
8     def init(_opts) do
9       children = [
10        worker(DARMetaData, [DARMetaData]),
11        worker(DARGfs, [DARGfs])
12      ]
13      supervise children, strategy: :one_for_one
14    end
15  end
```

A *supervisor* is a *behaviour* and this example implements all of the functions a supervisor needs. The function start_link starts the supervisor server and gives it a global name. The *name* value is supplied by the caller in the argument. See Example 10-19.

Example 10-19.

```
1   Supervisor.start_link(__MODULE__, [], name: {:global, name})
```

The function init defines the children the supervisor should monitor; see example 10-20.

Example 10-20.

```
1   children = [
2     worker(DARMetaData, [DARMetaData]),
3     worker(DARGfs, [DARGfs])
4   ]
5   supervise children, strategy: :one_for_one
```

In line 5, you define the supervisor strategy. There are several of them. The most important ones are

- *one_for_one* - The child that fails will be restarted.

- *one_for_all* - All children defined will be restarted.

It depends on the implemented feature which supervisor strategy should be used. In your example the children are independent from each other, so one failing does not affect the others.

---

[6]https://github.com/erlang/otp/blob/maint/lib/stdlib/src/supervisor.erl

Application[7]

The *behaviour Application* is defining the basic structure for running code in Erlang and Elixir, almost comparable to an executable. Rebar3 and Mix will both create skeletons of applications. Example 10-21 shows the code from *erlangexamples*; later you will have a look at *elixirexamples*.

Example 10-21.

```
1    -module(erlangexamples_app).
2    -behaviour(application).
3
4    -export([ start/2,
5              stop/1
6            ]).
7
8    start(_StartType, _StartArgs) ->
9        erlangexamples_sup:start_link().
10
11   stop(_State) ->
12       ok.
```

Rebar3 creates a supervisor by default and calls it in the function start. This is a minimal implementation, the *Application* module exports many more functions, for example *which_applications*, which can be used in a shell in Erlang. See Example 10-22.

Example 10-22.

```
application:which_applications().
```

See Example 10-23 for Elixir code to show all running applications.

Example 10-23.

```
:application.which_applications
```

To show all loaded applications, use the function loaded_applications.

Other functions can manipulate the environment, load applications and even permissions. One interesting callback is *config_change*, which allows you to change values of existing parameters, add new parameters with default values, or delete parameters during code changes. There are certainly enough options to make an application totally unusable if you're not careful.

Mix creates applications without implicitly stating the *behaviour*, but application settings like *name* can be changed in the mix.exs file. Regardless of the method of creation and language, during compilation an .app file will be created. It is application specification and is used by the VM during startup or creation of startup scripts. See Example 10-24.

Example 10-24.

```
1    {application,elixirexamples,
2                [{registered,[]},
3                 {description,"elixirexamples"},
```

---

[7]https://github.com/erlang/otp/blob/maint/lib/kernel/src/application.erl

```
 4              {vsn,"1.0.0"},
 5              {modules,['Elixir.Assignment','Elixir.BeefStewB',
 6                       'Elixir.BeefStewM','Elixir.CalendarExamples',
 7                       'Elixir.ClosuresExample','Elixir.Conditionals',
 8                       'Elixir.ContinuationPassing','Elixir.Currying',
 9                       'Elixir.Documentrecord','Elixir.HigherOrderFunctions',
10                       'Elixir.Json','Elixir.KeywordLists',
11                       'Elixir.ListExample','Elixir.Macros','Elixir.Maps',
12                       'Elixir.Printer','Elixir.Protocols',
13                       'Elixir.Protocols.Stew','Elixir.Protocols.Stew.Any',
14                       'Elixir.Protocols.Stew.Stewtype','Elixir.RawUdp',
15                       'Elixir.RawUdpServer','Elixir.RawUdpSupervisor',
16                       'Elixir.RecipeMixins','Elixir.Records',
17                       'Elixir.Specifications','Elixir.StewProtocol',
18                       'Elixir.Stewtype','Elixir.TimexExamples',
19                       'Elixir.VegStewB','Elixir.VegStewM']},
20              {applications,[kernel,stdlib,elixir,logger,timex]}]}.
```

This is the specification for the *elixirexamples* application and the important keys are the following:

- *modules* defines all the modules in the application. In your example they are all Elixir modules and therefore have the prefix "Elixir.".

- *applications* lists all applications that have to be loaded before the application specified. This list correlates to the definition in mix.exs and adds important ones like Elixir by default. See Example 10-25.

Example 10-25.

```
1  def application do
2    [
3            applications: [:logger, :timex]
4    ]
5  end
```

If you use a supervised application in Elixir, you have to implement the *start* callback as in Erlang; see Example 10-26.

Example 10-26.

```
 1  defmodule DarApi do
 2    use Application
 3
 4    def start(_type, _args) do
 5      import Supervisor.Spec
 6      children = [
 7        supervisor(DarApi.Repo, []),
 8      ]
 9      opts = [strategy: :one_for_one, name: DarApi.Supervisor]
10      Supervisor.start_link(children,  opts)
11    end
12  end
```

Other callbacks don't need to be implemented; you can use the default implementations.

Application is the basis for projects in Erlang and Elixir. For example, Kernel and Stdlib are applications: the first one with processes, the second one without. Whatever you create, most of the time you will have an application behaviour implemented in your project.

GenStage[8]

In 2016, Elixir released a pre-version of *GenStage*, a *generic behaviour* in the spirit of OTP, but without direct relation to an Erlang implementation. Basically, it is an abstraction of producing and consuming data. *Data* could come from a file, a web service, a database, or simply from a direct call.

GenStage provides concurrency and supervisors to go beyond what is possible in the *gen_event behaviour* that is related to GenStage. In addition, a *Flow* module is implemented on top of GenStage to ease the work with collections.

The following examples use GenStage version 0.5 (August 2016) and all modules are in the namespace *Experimental*. Be aware that the following code examples may stop working with a different version.

A GenStage server is in fact a GenServer and provides default implementations of all the default callbacks, but has two more callbacks defined:

- *handle_demand* - A producer has to implement this callback to reply to demands from consumers.

- *handle_events* - A consumer has to implement this callback to handle received events from the producer.

An *event* is a valid Elixir term, so can be basically any data that fits the use case.

Example 10-27 is taken directly from the documentation and only slightly changed. It behaves like a GenEvent server, but additional features can be implemented. The Manager is a *producer* and has a dispatch_events function that handles a queue of events until demanded, that means until a *consumer* subscribes to the producer and *demands* an event to be delivered.

Example 10-27.

```
1    alias Experimental.GenStage
2
3    defmodule EventManager do
4      use GenStage
5
6      def start_link() do
7        GenStage.start_link(__MODULE__ , :ok, name: __MODULE__)
8      end
9
10     def async_notify(event, timeout \\ 5000) do
11       GenStage.call(__MODULE__, {:notify, event}, timeout)
12     end
13
14   def sync_notify(event, timeout \\ 5000) do
15     GenStage.call(__MODULE__, {:notify, event}, timeout)
16   end
17
```

---

[8]https://github.com/elixir-lang/gen_stage

```
18    def init(:ok) do
19        {:producer, {:queue.new, 0}, dispatcher: GenStage.BroadcastDispatcher}
20    end
21
22    def handle_call({:notify, event}, from, {queue, demand}) do
23      dispatch_events(:queue.in({from, event}, queue), demand, [])
24    end
25
26    def handle_demand(incoming_demand, {queue, demand}) do
27      dispatch_events(queue, incoming_demand + demand, [])
28    end
29
30    defp dispatch_events(queue, demand, events) do
31      with d when d > 0 <- demand,
32           {item, queue} = :queue.out(queue),
33           {:value, {from, event}} <- item do
34        GenStage.reply(from, :ok)
35        dispatch_events(queue, demand - 1, [event | events])
36      else
37        _ -> {:noreply, Enum.reverse(events), {queue, demand}}
38      end
39    end
40  end
```

The handler is a *consumer* and subscribes in the function *init* to the manager. See Example 10-28.

Example 10-28.

```
1    alias Experimental.GenStage
2
3    defmodule EventHandler do
4      use GenStage
5
6      def start_link() do
7        GenStage.start_link(__MODULE__, :ok)
8      end
9
10     def init(:ok) do
11       {:consumer, :ok, subscribe_to: [EventManager]}
12     end
13
14     def handle_events(event, _from, state) do
15       IO.inspect event
16       {:noreply, [], event}
17     end
18   end
```

When you run both manager and handler we get the output in Example 10-29.

Example 10-29.

```
1   iex(1)> alias Experimental.GenStage
2   Experimental.GenStage
3   iex(2)> {:ok, manager} = EventManager.start_link
4   {:ok, #PID<0.214.0>}
5   iex(3)> {:ok, handler} = EventHandler.start_link
6   {:ok, #PID<0.210.0>}
7   iex(5)> GenStage.sync_notify manager,"first course"
8   :ok
9   ["first course"]
```

On line 7 you call a GenStage function to send an event to the manager to trigger the processing of the event and broadcasting it to the subscribers.

Apart from consumers and producers, there is also a role that is both producer and consumer. For the next example, let's assume you have an Italian restaurant with a kitchen, people working in service, and patrons waiting for their pizza, pasta, or salad. The kitchen is the producer, the service is a consumer (from the kitchen), and a producer (serving the patron). See Example 10-30.

Example 10-30.

```
1   alias Experimental.GenStage
2
3   defmodule Kitchen do
4     use GenStage
5
6     def init({maxpizza,maxpasta,maxsalad}) do
7       {:producer, {maxpizza,maxpasta,maxsalad}}
8     end
9
10    def handle_demand(demand, {maxpizza,maxpasta,maxsalad}) do
11      {event,state} = case demand do
12        :pizza  -> {:servepizza,{maxpizza-1,maxpasta,maxsalad}}
13        :pasta -> {:servepasta,{maxpizza,maxpasta-1,maxsalad}}
14        :salad -> {:servesalad,{maxpizza,maxpasta,maxsalad-1}}
15        _ -> {:nothingtoserve, {maxpizza,maxpasta,maxsalad}}
16      end
17      {:noreply, [event], state}
18    end
19  end
20
21  defmodule Service do
22    use GenStage
23
24    def init(state \\ :idle) do
25      {:producer_consumer, state}
26    end
27
28    def handle_events(event, _from, state) do
29      event = case event do
30        :servepizza  -> :pizzaserved
31        :servepasta -> :pastaserved
```

```
32          :servesalad -> :saladserved
33             _    ->   :nothingserved
34        end
35        {:noreply, [event], state}
36     end
37  end
```

The patron is a consumer only and, after being initialized with an order, is just sitting and waiting. See Example 10-31.

Example 10-31.

```
1    alias Experimental.GenStage
2
3    defmodule Patron do
4      use GenStage
5
6      def init(order) do
7        {:consumer, order}
8      end
9
10     def handle_events(event, _from, order) do
11       IO.inspect(event)
12       IO.inspect(order)
13       Process.sleep(1000)
14       {:noreply, [], order}
15     end
16   end
```

Running this code produces the output in Example 10-32.

Example 10-32.

```
1    iex(1)> alias Experimental.GenStage
2       Experimental.GenStage
3    iex(2)> {:ok, kitchen} = GenStage.start_link(Kitchen, {10,10,10})
4       {:ok, #PID<0.220.0>}
5    iex(3)> {:ok, service1} = GenStage.start_link(Service, :idle)
6       {:ok, #PID<0.222.0>}
7    iex(4)> {:ok, patron1} = GenStage.start_link(Patron, 1000)
8       {:ok, #PID<0.224.0>}
9    iex(5)>  GenStage.sync_subscribe(service1, to: kitchen)
10      {:ok, #Reference<0.0.4.1299>}
11   iex(6)> GenStage.sync_subscribe(patron1, to: service1)
12      {:ok, #Reference<0.0.4.1305>}
13      [:nothingtoserve]
```

You subscribe at runtime to kitchen and service with synchronous links. The names *service1* and *patron1* indicate that you can have more than one. The kitchen will always be only one, but you can have more services and (hopefully for the restaurant) more patrons.

GenStage is still in the early "stages" of development, so features described here may and probably will change. You will also see which use cases you can use GenStage for in future.

Erlang and Cowboy

When Erlang was designed it needed to cater to low level network communication. Several generic servers (some of which you have seen in examples above) let us implement those low level communications requirements. In the last 10-15 years, the HTTP protocol, which sits on a higher layer in the OSI model[9], has been important for networked implementations.

Erlang has seen and is still seeing the development of web server implementations like Elli[10] or Chatterbox[11], but the most prominent is certainly Cowboy[12].

The first version of *DarApi* was implemented with Erlang and Cowboy. The first step, as always, is to define the dependency in rebar.config. See Example 10-33.

Example 10-33.

```
1    {erl_opts, [debug_info]}.
2    {deps, [
3      {cowboy, {git, "git://github.com/ninenines/cowboy.git", {tag, "1.0.4"}}},
4      {lager, {git, "git://github.com/basho/lager.git", {tag, "2.2.2"}}},
5      uuid,
6      jsone,
7      daractors
8    ]}
9
10   {relx, [{release, { darapi, "0.1.0" },
11          [
12            lager,
13            cowboy,
14            jsone,
15            uuid,
16            darapi,
17            sasl,
18            daractors]},
19          {sys_config, "./config/sys.config"},
20          {vm_args, "./config/vm.args"},
21          {dev_mode, true},
22          {include_erts, false},
23          {extended_start_script, true}]
24   }.
25
26   {profiles, [{prod, [{relx, [{dev_mode, false},
27                               {include_erts, true}]}]}
28            }]
29   }.
```

You define version 1.0.4 as dependency. There is work done on a new version 2, but that is a preview and I had some trouble making it work. Some function signatures changed and also almost all examples are for version 1.

---

[9]https://en.wikipedia.org/wiki/OSI_model
[10]https://github.com/knutin/elli
[11]https://github.com/joedevivo/chatterbox
[12]https://github.com/ninenines/cowboy

On lines 12ff, you define which modules need to be loaded. The web server implementation *DarApi* is using *Lager* for logging Cowboy and other modules, so you need to load them before you can access them.

The API server is implemented as an application that calls Cowboy and has a supervisor. Example 10-34 shows the module *darapi_app*.

Example 10-34.

```
1   -module(darapi_app).
2   -behaviour(application).
3   -export([start/2
4            ,stop/1]).
5   -define(
6     ROUTES,
7     [
8        {"/api/assets", darapi_handler_assets, []},
9        {"/api/assets/:id/text", darapi_handler_assets, []},
10       {"/api/assets/:id/images", darapi_handler_assets, []},
11       {"/api/assets/:id/images/:imgid", darapi_handler_assets, []},
12       {"/api/assets/:id", darapi_handler_assets, []},
13       {"/test", darapi_handler_testpage, []},
14       {'_', darapi_handler_home, []}
15     ]
16  ).
17
18  start(_Type, _Args) ->
19    Dispatch = cowboy_router:compile([{'_', ?ROUTES}]),
20    {ok, _} = cowboy:start_http(
21               http,
22               100,
23               [{port,  8402}],
24               [{env,  [{dispatch,  Dispatch}]}]
25             ),
26  darapi_sup:start_link().
27
28  stop(_State) ->
29      ok.
```

Lines 5-16 define a macro for routing. The routes are a list of tuples that define the route and a handler for the route. This example has several routes for the api, one for a test page and a catch-all route.

A route is a tuple with three elements; see Example 10-35.

Example 10-35.

```
{"/api/assets/:id/text", darapi_handler_assets, []}
```

- The first element is a string with the route URL. The segment ":id" means that a binding to a variable will occur at runtime and the value can be retrieved.

- The second element is the name of the handler for this route expressed as an atom.

- The third element is an option list. You will look at this later.

Before you can start the server, you must prepare the routes; see Example 10-36.

Example 10-36.

```
Dispatch = cowboy_router:compile([{'_', ?ROUTES}])
```

The *compilation* is a creation of a list with routes in an internal format; see Example 10-37.

Example 10-37.

```
1   % {"/test", darapi_handler_testpage, []}
2   {[<<"test">>],[],darapi_handler_testpage,[{test,true}]}
```

Then you can start the server; see Example 10-38.

Example 10-38.

```
1   {ok, _} = cowboy:start_http(
2               http,
3               100,
4               [{port,  8402}],
5               [{env,  [{dispatch,  Dispatch}]}]
6           )
```

Line 3 defines the maximum requests on a connection. The previously compiled routes are injected into the server environment on line 5. The port on line 4 could, of course, come from an environment variable or any other configuration. Once this statement returns successfully, you can call the URL from a browser on port 8402.

The catch-all route goes to the handler *darapi_handler_home*; see Example 10-39.

Example 10-39.

```
1    -module(darapi_handler_home).
2
3    -export([init/3]).
4    -export([handle/2]).
5    -export([terminate/3]).
6
7    init(_Type, Req, []) ->
8            {ok, Req, undefined}.
9
10   handle(Req, State) ->
11     {ok, Body} = homepage_dtl:render([]),
12     Headers = [{<<"content-type">>, <<"text/html">>}],
13     {ok, Reply} = cowboy_req:reply(200, Headers, Body, Req),
14     {ok, Reply, State}.
15
16   terminate(_Reason, _Req, _State)  ->
17     ok.
```

The init function is called at initialization time and is not doing anything in this example. The handle function is more interesting. In general, it defines the page header and body, sets the HTTP return code, and calls the Cowboy function reply.

Also interesting is line 11, which uses a template system called Erlydtl[13] to get the markdown for the body; see Example 10-40.

Example 10-40.

```
{ok, Body} = homepage_dtl:render([])
```

The templates live in the folder `templates` as files with a suffix `.dtl`. The markup for the home page is simple and is just pure HTML; see Example 10-41.

Example 10-41.

```
1   <html>
2     <body>
3       DAR   API
4     </body>
5   </html>
```

The templates used by Erlydtl use the Django template syntax[14] and can bind variables at runtime. The template for the test page uses this feature; see Example 10-42.

Example 10-42.

```
1   <html>
2     <body>
3       Test: {{ test }}
4     </body>
5   </html>
```

Here *{{ test }}* means that the template expects a variable *test* when it is rendered. In this case, the rendering line is shown in Example 10-43.

Example 10-43.

```
{ok, B} = testpage_dtl:render([{test, io_lib:format("~p", [Test])}])
```

The render function takes a list of tuples which are key-value pairs of the variable name atom and the value. The term *Test* in the example is an atom to indicate which test to run.

Templates need to be compiled before use. This is where the module name *testpage_dtl* comes from. The compilation can either happen in a makefile or in code. The line in Example 10-44 compiles the test page template.

Example 10-44.

```
erlydtl:compile_file("templates/testpage.dtl", testpage_dtl).
```

It takes the file `templates/testpage.dtl` and is told to create `testpage_dtl`.

---

[13]https://github.com/erlydtl/erlydtl
[14]https://docs.djangoproject.com/en/1.9/topics/templates/#the-django-template-language

Templates combine static markup with variables that are processed at runtime. These variables can be passed from the handler and can originate from user input or other sources like data stores.

In Cowboy, you can get dynamic input, as in other web servers, from the request, but you can also send hard-coded options to the handler from the route definitions.

Route Options

In Example 10-45, the line in the route definition sets an option for the test page handler. The key is the atom *testmode* and the value another atom with the name *get_apiassets*.

Example 10-45.

```
{"/test", darapi_handler_testpage, [{testmode,get_apiassets}]}
```

The function init gets the option passed in as the third argument. See Example 10-46.

Example 10-46.

```
1   -record(state, {
2         testmode :: get_apiassets | post_apiassets
3   }).
4
5   init(_Type, Req, Opts) ->
6     {_, Testmode} = lists:keyfind(testmode, 1, Opts),
7     {ok, Req, #state{testmode=Testmode}}.
8
9   handle(Req, State=#state{testmode=Testmode}) ->
10    lager:info("test_response state: ~p~n", [lager:pr(Testmode, ?MODULE)]),
11    Body = test_response(Testmode),
12    {ok, Reply, State}.
```

You define the record *state* with one field named *testmode*. In init you first get the value for *testmode* from the *Opts* list and then create a state record. *State* is passed to handler calls and can then be used. In this example, the testmode variable is passed to the function test_response, which creates markdown according to the value of *testmode*.

This key-value pair is given at compile time. You can change it with one of the following methods to define variables at runtime.

Query Strings

Query strings can be used to pass variables to the server. For example, you can call the server with the URL shown in Example 10-47.

Example 10-47.

```
/test?testmode=post_apiassets
```

The query string key *testmode* will overwrite the default value. With *cowboy_req:qs_val* you can retrieve the value of one key. If the key does not exist, it returns *undefined*.

You must change the handle code to be able to process different values; see Example 10-48.

Example 10-48.

```
1  {Tqs, _} = cowboy_req:qs_val(<<"testmode">>, Req),
2  Body  =
3    case Tqs of
4      undefined -> test_response(Testmode);
5      <<>> -> test_response(Testmode);
6      _ -> test_response(list_to_atom(binary_to_list(Tqs)))
7  end.
```

Depending on the query string value, the function test_response is called with different arguments. You can retrieve all query strings in a list, as in Example 10-49.

Example 10-49.

```
1  %  /test?testmode=get_apiassets&paged=true&page=2
2  {AllValues, _} = cowboy_req:qs_vals(Req).
3  %  [
4  %  {<<"testmode">>,<<"get_apiassets">>},
5  %  {<<"paged">>,<<"true">>},
6  %  {<<"page">>,<<"2">>}
7  %  ]
```

The query string on line 1 will return the list on lines 3-7 when you call the function cowboy_req:qs_-vals. All elements, key or values, in the list are binary lists, so it will be necessary to convert them into something more meaningful. See Example 10-50.

Example 10-50.

```
1  1> jsone:encode([{<<"testmode">>,<<"get_apiassets">>},
2                   {<<"paged">>,<<"true">>},
3                   {<<"page">>,<<"2">>}]).
4
5  <<"{\"testmode\":\"get_apiassets\",\"paged\":\"true\",\"page\":\"2\"}">>
```

you convert the returned list of query string key-value tuples into JSON and then you can send it to other functions that can handle JSON directly.

Body Data

Data sent in the body of a request with content type *application/x-www-form-urlencoded* can be read with *body_qs*, as shown in Example 10-51.

Example 10-51.

```
1  {ok, B, Req2} = cowboy_req:body_qs(Req),
2  {_, K} = lists:keyfind(k, 1, B).
```

Line 2 tries to find the key *k* in the tuples of the returned body values *B*. The value will be in K.

HTTP Verbs

You have defined routes and handlers, and you know how to retrieve data from query strings or bodies. What is left is to define the code for different HTTP verbs sent.

One way is to check the requested method in the handler; see Example 10-52.

Example 10-52.

```
1    {Method, Req2} = cowboy_req:method(Req),
2        case Method of
3            <<"POST">> ->
4                % ...
5            <<"GET">> ->
6                % ...
7            _ ->
8                % ...
9        end.
```

The better solution for REST services is to use Cowboy functions to define methods; see Example 10-53.

Example 10-53.

```
1     allowed_methods(Req, State) ->
2        {[<<"GET">>, <<"POST">>], Req, State}.
3
4     content_types_accepted(Req, State) ->
5         {[{{<<"application">>, <<"json">>, []}, post_handler}], Req, State}.
6
7     content_types_provided(Req, State)  ->
8             {[
9                     {<<"application/json">>, get_handler}
10            ], Req, State}.
```

This code defines that the handler accepts JSON requests and also delivers JSON. To do this it defines a *post_handler* and a *get_handler* (both not in the listing).

Cowboy has not only an impact on Erlang, but also on Elixir as the basis of the web framework Phoenix. Fortunately, the latter makes it a bit easier to implement routes and handlers.

Elixir and Phoenix

Phoenix[15] is a web framework for Elixir that is not only widely used in the community but also brings interested developers to the community. As with Elixir itself, it is evolving over time, bringing new features into the framework. Phoenix is a modern web framework that makes building APIs and web applications easy. It is built with Elixir and has been commonly used to support handling very large numbers[16] of simultaneous users.

Once Phoenix is installed on your machine, you have a new task in Mix to create a Phoenix application skeleton. The help page for the task displays the options; see Example 10-54.

---

[15]www.phoenixframework.org/
[16]www.phoenixframework.org/blog/the-road-to-2-million-websocket-connections

Example 10-54.

```
1   mix help phoenix.new
2
3   Options
4
5     &#x007F; --app - the name of the OTP application
6     &#x007F; --module - the name of the base module in the generated skeleton
7     &#x007F; --database - specify the database adapter for ecto. Values can be
8       postgres, mysql, mssql, sqlite or mongodb. Defaults to postgres
9     &#x007F; --no-brunch - do not generate brunch files for static asset building.
10      When choosing this option, you will need to manually handle JavaScript
11      dependencies if building HTML apps
12    &#x007F; --no-ecto - do not generate ecto files for the model layer
13    &#x007F; --no-html - do not generate HTML views.
14    &#x007F; --binary-id - use binary_id as primary key type in ecto models
```

ℹ **Installing the Phoenix archive**   Before Mix knows Phoenix tasks, you need to install Phoenix into the Mix Archives: `mix    archive.install` https://github.com/phoenixframework/archives/raw/master/ `phoenix_- new.ez`

The files will be installed in a folder /.mix/`archives` or similar, depending on your operating system.

You can create a new application with the following command, passing a name and the option *binary_id* to create Guids for your database tables; see Example 10-55.

Example 10-55.

```
1   mix phoenix.new phoenixskeleton --binary-id
```

The output shows what was created (it's a lengthy list, not printed here) and what to do now; see Example 10-56.

Example 10-56.

```
1   We  are all set! Run  your Phoenix  application:
2
3       $ cd phoenixskeleton
4       $ mix  phoenix.server
5
6   You can also run your app inside IEx (Interactive Elixir) as:
7
8       $ iex -S mix phoenix.server
9
10  Before moving on, configure your database in config/dev.exs and run:
11
12      $ mix  ecto.create
```

ℹ️ Ecto and database adapters At the time of writing, not all adapters were up-to-date to work with the latest Ecto version.

The task *phoenix.new* will create the skeleton for any database adapter, but you should have a look at the Ecto GitHub page to check which adapters are working with the latest version.

The process of creating a new Phoenix application is straightforward and well explained, so let's switch to *DARApi* that uses Phoenix to see examples of an application that goes beyond the skeleton.

Phoenix is based on a supervised application that uses Cowboy as the web server and plug[17] for composing modules. It supports web sockets by default and generalizes them with *channels* and a publisher-subscriber module *Phoenix.PubSub*, which can be used to talk to third-party services or Elixir GenServers.

The code in Example 10-57 shows the DarApi application module.

Example 10-57.

```
1   defmodule DarApi do
2     use Application
3
4     def start(_type, _args) do
5       import Supervisor.Spec
6       children = [
7         supervisor(DarApi.Endpoint, []),
8         worker(DARRouter,[DARRouter])
9       ]
10      opts = [strategy: :one_for_one, name: DarApi.Supervisor]
11      Supervisor.start_link(children,  opts)
12    end
13
14    def config_change(changed, _new, removed) do
15      DarApi.Endpoint.config_change(changed,    removed)
16      :ok
17    end
18  end
```

The start function defines children to be supervised and starts the supervisor. In Phoenix, it is a supervisor tree, because the endpoint supervisor is defined as a child. Normally you may find a *repo* supervisor child defined here, but you are not using the database directly from the web server. You add a worker child to the definition, the *DARRouter*, that handles incoming messages and invokes the workflow. The rest of the code starts the supervisor with default options.

When your endpoint receives a request, it needs to know if the request is valid and if the URL is defined as valid. For this purpose, it uses DarApi.Router defined in router.ex; see Example 10-58.

---

[17]https://github.com/elixir-lang/plug

Example 10-58.

```
 1   defmodule DarApi.Router do
 2     use DarApi.Web, :router
 3
 4     pipeline :browser do
 5        plug :accepts, ["html"]
 6        plug :fetch_session
 7        plug :fetch_flash
 8        plug :protect_from_forgery
 9        plug :put_secure_browser_headers
10     end
11
12     pipeline :api do
13       plug :accepts, ["json"]
14     end
15
16     scope "/", DarApi do
17       pipe_through :browser # Use the default browser stack
18       get "/", PageController, :index
19     end
20
21     scope "/api", DarApi do
22       pipe_through :api
23       resources "/assets", ApiController, except: [:new, :edit, :update, :delete]
24       get "/assets/:id/text", ApiController, :get_text_for_id
25       get "/assets/:id/images", ApiController, :get_images_for_id
26       post "/assets/:id/text/:textid", ApiController, :update_text_for_id
27       post "/assets/:id/image/:imageid", ApiController, :update_image_for_id
28       post  "/assets/:id/text", ApiController, :post_text_for_id
29       post  "/assets/:id/image", ApiController, :post_image_for_id
30       get "/assets/:id/document", ApiController, :get_document_for_id
31     end
32   end
```

This code shows the usage of *plug*. It gets the current connection from Cowboy and calls the functions or modules specified with the connection and any parameters. In the example, the pipeline *browser* defines to call accepts with "html" as parameter, then calls fetch_session with no parameters and so on.

Before the endpoint handles a request, it will look for a valid route. The example defines two scopes, similar to base URLs, for the root, /, and for /api. The scope tells which pipeline should be used and which HTTP verbs are bound to which URL and controller. See Figure 10-2.

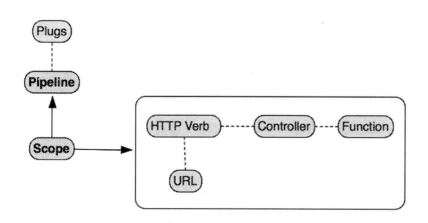

Figure 10-2. *Phoenix router*

In this example, the root URL (scope /) has just one page, index, to display, using the *browser* pipeline. The scope /api uses the *api* pipeline and defines several routes as described at the beginning of this chapter. The routes are self-explanatory except the first one with the special verb *resource*. To see what routes will be created at runtime, you can use one of the helper tasks in Mix; see Example 10-59.

Example 10-59.

```
1  $ mix phoenix.routes
2  page_path  GET   /                              DarApi.PageController :index
3   api_path  GET   /api/assets                    DarApi.ApiController  :index
4   api_path  GET   /api/assets/:id                DarApi.ApiController :show
5   api_path  POST  /api/assets                    DarApi.ApiController :create
6   api_path  GET   /api/assets/:id/text           DarApi.ApiController
7                                                    :get_text_for_id
8   api_path  GET   /api/assets/:id/images         DarApi.ApiController
9                                                    :get_images_for_id
10  api_path  POST  /api/assets/:id/text/:textid   DarApi.ApiController
11                                                   :update_text_for_id
12  api_path  POST  /api/assets/:id/image/:imageid DarApi.ApiController
13                                                   :update_image_for_id
14  api_path  POST  /api/assets/:id/text           DarApi.ApiController
15                                                   :post_text_for_id
16  api_path  POST  /api/assets/:id/image          DarApi.ApiController
17                                                   :post_image_for_id
18  api_path  GET   /api/assets/:id/document       DarApi.ApiController
19                                                   :get_document_for_id
```

Lines 3 to 5 show REST routes for the route you defined with *resource*. Two *GET* routes for showing all assets and one asset filtered by *id*, one *POST* route for creating an asset. The line except: [:new,:edit, :update, :delete] in the route definitions prevents the creation of *PUT, PATCH, DELETE* routes and routes with *edit* and *new* in the URL.

Once a route is validated, the corresponding controller will be called. The controller for the index page is, according to your router definition, *PageController*. See Example 10-60.

Example 10-60.

```
1   defmodule DarApi.PageController do
2     use DarApi.Web, :controller
3
4     def index(conn, _params) do
5       render conn, "index.html"
6     end
7   end
```

This is the minimal code to display a page with just static text, shown in Figure 10-3.

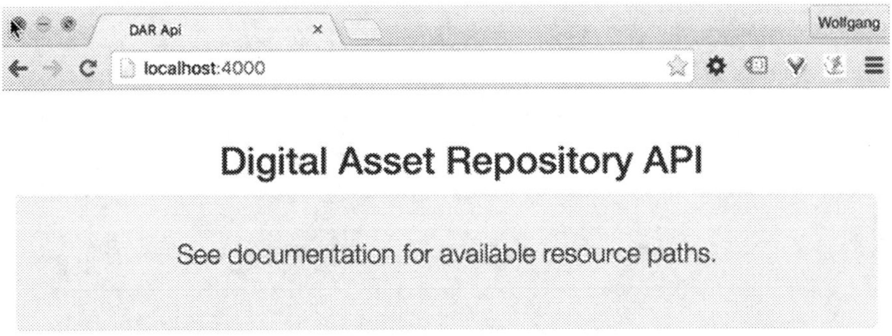

Figure 10-3. *Index page*

When the controller's function index (the *:index* atom in the route definition) is called, it just calls render with the name of the page, index.html, as parameter in addition to the connection parameter. The rendering function looks into the templates folder, which was created by the Phoenix.new task, and looks for the template index.html.eex in the folder *page*, which is the folder name for the *pagecontroller* without "controller". See Example 10-61.

Example 10-61.

```
1   <div  class="jumbotron">
2     <p>
3         See documentation for available resource paths.
4     </p>
5   </div>
```

This is all the markup for the index page; the rest of the page is taken from an app.html.eex file in the folder templates/layout. The important markup of that file is shown in Example 10-62.

Example 10-62.

```
1   <main role="main">
2     <%= render @view_module, @view_template, assigns %>
3   </main>
```

It calls the internal render function with parameters for the view and module and displays the page as shown in Figure 10-3.

 **Phoenix generators**   Like other web frameworks, Phoenix provides several generators for creating models or HTML resources with controllers and views. It can also create models for JSON resources. All generators are mix tasks that start with `phoenix.gen` and information about them is displayed with `mix help` in a project with Phoenix as dependency.

It makes sense to study the generated code and also to try adding features without generators to understand the underlying architecture.

Users of other web framework will have had similar experiences with convention over configuration. The template engine used in Phoenix is EEx[18]. It is part of Elixir and provides a way to embed Elixir code in a string.

The controller for the API routes has more code; I only show the function index, in Example 10-63.

Example 10-63.

```
1   defmodule DarApi.ApiController do
2     use DarApi.Web, :controller
3
4     def index(conn, params) do
5       {:response, {:request, msg}} = DARRouter.process_message(DARRouter, {:get_as\
6       sets_all, params})
7       render conn, response: msg
8     end
9   end
```

Line 5 calls *DARRouter*, the one you added to the supervisor tree, to process the message. You know from the route definition that this function handles a request to get all assets. The parameter *param* may have more information like filters, filled with the query string key-value pairs.

DARRouter is a GenServer that creates internal messages for the workflow and sends the requests back to the API controller; see Example 10-64.

Example 10-64.

```
1   defmodule DARRouter do
2     use GenServer
3
```

---

[18]http://elixir-lang.org/docs/stable/eex/EEx.html

```
4    def start_link(name) do
5      GenServer.start_link(__MODULE__, :ok, name: name)
6    end
7
8    def process_message(server, msg) do
9      case msg do
10       {:get_assets_all,   params}   ->
11         GenServer.call(server, {:msg, msg})
12         _ -> {:failure, msg}
13     end
14
15   end
16
17   def init(:ok) do
18     {:ok,  ""}
19   end
20
21   def handle_call({:msg, msg}, _from, state) do
22     {action, params} = msg
23     case action do
24       :get_assets_all  ->
25         xmsg  =  %{
26           :name => "",
27           :actions   =>  [DARAction.retrievedoclist_all],
28           :actionfilter =>  params,
29           :comment => "",
30           :metaid => "",
31           :gfsid => ""
32         }
33         ret = DARWorkflow.process_message (DARModelInternalMessage.from_external\
34         _message  xmsg)
35         {:reply, {:response, {:request, ret}}, state}
36     end
37   end
38 end
```

I only show the code relevant to getting all assets. The exported function process_message, called by the controller, calls its callback *handle_call* where the actual work is done (line 21ff.). On line 33, the workflow is called and its response eventually sent back to the caller.

This example shows that it is easy to create, for example, a REST API with Phoenix. There may be lots of code involved from Phoenix's side, but a few lines of custom code can achieve the goals. Of course, a proper user interface and interaction with client frameworks has more work involved. You just scratched the surface.

CHAPTER 11

▓ ▓ ▓ ▓

Asset Processing

In the previous chapter, you created a server that allows the retrieval of binary data. Now you need to implement processing of this binary data. First of all, the data needs to be saved to data stores, in your case PostgreSQL and MongoDB. Then a simple workflow needs to be implemented to achieve transformations like watermarking images and creating PDF documents.

The choice of databases used in this chapter is based on experience with these data stores and specific project requirements. Erlang and Elixir and their libraries let you work with all major databases, relational or not. Also, I am not discussing technologies like ODBC, which is supported in Erlang[1].

Database Access

The project DAR uses two data stores to save its data. One, MongoDB GridFS, is a blob store used for storing images and PDF documents. The other is the metadata store and it uses PostgreSQL with a more relational data approach.

MongoDB GridFS

GridFS is one of MongoDB's least discussed features, but it may be its best feature. Many data stores have blob management, either NoSQL or relational databases, but GridFS is easy to use, chunked by default, and can be sharded.

Elixir does not have, at least according to my knowledge, a library that supports GridFS. The Erlang library Erlmongo[2] supports it, so we are using it.

Another, not fully satisfactory, option is to use the console application *mongofiles* directly, similar to what you will do with ImageMagick below.

The application for accessing documents in GridFS is written in Erlang; see Example 11-1.

---

[1]http://erlang.org/doc/man/odbc.html
[2]https://github.com/SergejJurecko/erlmongo

© Wolfgang Loder 2016

W. Loder, *Erlang and Elixir for Imperative Programmers*, DOI 10.1007/978-1-4842-2394-9_11

Example 11-1.

```
1    -module(dar_gfslib_process_files).
2
3    -ifdef(TEST).
4      -export([
5                  connect/0,
6                  read_binary/2,
7                  write_binary/3
8              ])
9    -endif.
10
11   -define (DARDB, "dar").
12   -export([
13                      read_from_gfs/2,
14                      save_to_gfs/3
15              ]).
16   -include_lib("erlmongo/src/erlmongo.hrl").
17
18   read_from_gfs(Name,DB)  ->
19         DB = ?DARDB,
20         {ok,B} = read_binary(Name,DB),
21         {ok,B,Name}.
22
23   save_to_gfs(Binary,Meta,DB) ->
24          DB = ?DARDB,
25          {ok, Name} = validate_meta(Meta),
26          {ok,N} = write_binary(Binary,   Name,DB),
27          {ok,N}.
28
29   validate_meta(M) ->
30         ok = dar_model:validate_meta(M),
31         #{name := Name} = M,
32         {ok,Name}.
33
34   write_binary(B,N,DB) ->
35         DB = ?DARDB,
36         true = connect(),
37         Mong = mongoapi:new(def,list_to_binary(DB)),
38         Mong:gfsIndexes(),
39         PID = Mong:gfsNew(N),
40         Mong:gfsWrite(PID,B),
41         Mong:gfsClose(PID),
42         {ok,N}.
43
44   read_binary(Name,DB) ->
45          DB = ?DARDB,
46          true = connect(),
47          Mong = mongoapi:new(def,list_to_binary(DB)),
48          Mong:gfsIndexes(),
49          PID = Mong:gfsOpen(#gfs_file{filename    =    Name}),
50          B = Mong:gfsRead(PID,5000000),
```

```
51              Mong:gfsClose(PID),
52              {ok,B}.
53
54
55   connect() ->
56              mongodb:singleServer(def),
57              mongodb:connect(def),
58              timer:sleep(200),
59              mongodb:is_connected(def).
```

The exported functions are on lines 18 to 27: read_from_gfs and save_to_gfs. They call private functions to read and write from GridFS. These private functions use Erlmongo to get the job done. The name of the MongoDB database is hard coded in a define (line 11) and functions check that no other database is used. See Example 11-2.

Example 11-2.

```
1    -define (DARDB, "dar").
2    % ...
3    DB = ?DARDB
```

The host is defined in a record def in Erlmongo and defaults to localhost when you try to connect to the data store. See Example 11-3.

Example 11-3.

```
1    connect() ->
2              mongodb:singleServer(def),
3              mongodb:connect(def),
4              timer:sleep(200),
5              mongodb:is_connected(def).
```

The private function connect connects to the server on localhost and checks if a connection can be established. The statement timer:sleep(200) is a workaround to let the library set the is_connected flag. Without sleeping, it would not be able to determine if a connection is available.

Testing private functions is always difficult and most of the time not necessary. In this case, you need to test the underlying private functions that do the actual work. It seems that these tests are testing only library calls into Erlmongo, but without tests the problem with checking for connections would not have been detected.

EUnit sets a constant named TEST when tests run, so you check this value and export the private functions during test runs; see Example 11-4.

Example 11-4.

```
1    -ifdef(TEST).
2      -export([
3                        connect/0,
4                        read_binary/2,
5                        write_binary/3
6                ]).
7    -define (FILETEST, "filetest").
8    -endif.
```

The test code looks like Example 11-5.

Example 11-5.

```
1    -module(dar_gfslib_process_files_tests).
2
3    -ifdef(TEST).
4    -include_lib("eunit/include/eunit.hrl").
5
6    -define (FILETEST, "Test.pdf").
7    -define (FILETESTWRITE, "Test.pdf").
8    -define (FILETESTCONTENT, <<"testbinary">>).
9    -define (DARDB, "dar").
10   -define (NOTDARDB, "notdar").
11
12   connect_to_server_test()  ->
13           R = dar_gfslib_process_files:connect(),
14           ?assertEqual(true, R).
15
16   read_binary_test() ->
17           R = dar_gfslib_process_files:read_binary(?FILETEST,?DARDB),
18           ?assertEqual({ok,?FILETESTCONTENT}, R).
19
20   write_binary_test() ->
21       R =   dar_gfslib_process_files:write_binary(?FILETESTCONTENT,?FILETESTWRITE,?D\
22       ARDB),
23               ?assertEqual({ok,?FILETESTWRITE}, R).
24
25   read_from_gfs_test() ->
26           R = dar_gfslib_process_files:read_from_gfs(?FILETEST,?DARDB).
27           ?assertEqual({ok,?FILETESTCONTENT,?FILETEST}, R).
28
29   save_to_gfs_test() ->
30           {ok, Bin} = file:read_file("/Users/Wolfgang/Projects/Mats.pdf"),
31           M = #{name => ?FILETESTWRITE,origin=>"test",timestamp=>100,  gfsid=>"66"},
32           R = dar_gfslib_process_files:save_to_gfs(Bin,M,?DARDB),
33           ?assertEqual({ok,?FILETESTWRITE}, R).
34
35   connect_to_server_noconnection_mocked_test() ->
36           meck:new(mongodb,[passthrough]),
37           meck:expect(mongodb, is_connected, fun(def) -> false end),
38           R  =  dar_gfslib_process_files:connect(),
39           ?assert(meck:validate(mongodb)),
40           ?assertEqual(false,  R),
41           ok = meck:unload(mongodb).
42
43   save_to_gfs_no_connection_mocked_test() ->
44           M = #{name => ?FILETESTWRITE,origin=>"test",timestamp=>100, gfsid=>"66"},
45           meck:new(mongodb,[passthrough]),
46           meck:expect(mongodb, is_connected, fun(def) -> false end),
47           ?assertError({badmatch,false}, dar_gfslib_process_files:save_to_gfs(?FILETES\
48           TCONTENT,M,?DARDB)),
49               ok = meck:unload(mongodb).
50
```

```
51   save_to_gfs_wrong_db_test() ->
52        M = #{name =>  ?FILETESTWRITE,origin=>"test",timestamp=>100, gfsid=>"66"},
53        ?assertError({badmatch,?DARDB}, dar_gfslib_process_files:save_to_gfs(?FILETE\
54        STCONTENT,M,?NOTDARDB)).
55
56   read_from_gfs_wrong_db_test() ->
57        ?assertError({badmatch,?DARDB}, dar_gfslib_process_files:read_from_gfs(?FILE\
58        TEST,?NOTDARDB)).
59
60   read_from_gfs_no_connection_mocked_test()  ->
61        meck:new(mongodb,[passthrough]),
62        meck:expect(mongodb, is_connected, fun(def) -> false end),
63        ?assertError({badmatch,false}, dar_gfslib_process_files:read_from_gfs(?FILET\
64        EST,?DARDB)),
65         ok = meck:unload(mongodb).
66
67   -endif.
```

The functions use defines for test constants and test all functions including connect. There are also mocked tests to see if the functions are behaving as expected when no connection can be established or other errors occur.

You call the Erlang library from Elixir via a RPC call. DARGfs is a GenServer and exposes function process_message, which is called from the workflow. Its purpose is to get a file from GridFS via the Erlang library; see Example 11-6.

Example 11-6.

```
1    defmodule DARGfs do
2        use GenServer
3
4        def process_message(node,module,function,params) do
5            case :rpc.call(
6                            node,
7                            module,
8                            function,
9                            params) do
10               {:ok, f, fname} -> f
11                _ -> "node down"
12           end
13       end
14
15       def start_link(name) do
16           GenServer.start_link(__MODULE__, :ok, name: name)
17        end
18
19       def init(:ok) do
20           {:ok,  ""}
21       end
22
23       def handle_call({:msg, msg}, _from, state) do
24       {:reply, "", state}
25       end
26   end
```

The call to process_message with parameters expanded looks like Example 11-7.

Example 11-7.

```
1   case :rpc.call(
2                  :"dargfslib@Wolfgangs-MacBook-Pro",
3                  :dar_gfslib_process_files,
4                  :read_from_gfs,
5                  ['filetestwrite','dar']) do
6       {:ok, f, fname} -> f
7       {:badrpc, reason} -> {:error, {:badrpc, reason}}
8       _ -> {:error, {:call, "Call failed"}
9   end
```

You use rpc.call, which is synchronous and uses a separate process. This allows the RPC server to handle more than one call. There are other functions for either blocking the RPC server (block_call) or using promises (async_call).

When a call is successful, the binary will be returned to the caller.

PostgreSQL

The access to the metadata database is done in the module *DarMetaData*. It uses Ecto for the low-level work and needs to define a schema for Ecto to know about the data. All parameters like table name, column names, and column types are deferred from one schema per model; see Example 11-8.

Example 11-8.

```
1   defmodule MetaData do
2       use Ecto.Schema
3
4       @primary_key {:id, :binary_id, autogenerate: true}
5
6       schema  "metadata" do
7           field :name,        :string
8           field :timestamp,   :integer
9           field :origin,      :string
10          field :haspdf,      :boolean
11          field :gfsid,       :string
12      end
13
14      def changeset(meta,params \\ :empty) do
15          meta
16      end
17  end
18
19  defmodule MetaDataImage do
20      use Ecto.Schema
21
22      @primary_key {:id, :binary_id, autogenerate: true}
23
```

```
24      schema "metadataimage" do
25          field :name,              :string
26          field :metaid,            :string
27          field :timestamp,         :integer
28          field :gfsid,             :string
29    end
30
31      def changeset(meta, params \\ :empty) do
32          meta
33      end
34  end
```

For Ecto to know which database type and which host to use, it needs to be configured in config.exs, as shown in Example 11-9.

Example 11-9.

```
1   config :dar_metadata, DARMetaData.Repo,
2       adapter: Ecto.Adapters.Postgres,
3       database: "dar",
4       hostname: "localhost"
5
6   config :dar_metadata, ecto_repos: [DARMetaData.Repo]
```

The configuration does not have *username* and *password* entries. They can either be hard coded in the configuration file or taken from an environment variable at runtime. As in other SQL databases, the command create user can be used in Postgres to set passwords for user accounts.

The implementation of the repository (defined on line 6 in the configuration) is simple; see Example 11-10.

Example 11-10.

```
1   defmodule DARMetaData.Repo do
2       use Ecto.Repo, otp_app: :dar_metadata
3   end
```

The statement use Ecto.Repo injects several functions that will be used to write or read data. When everything is in place and with Ecto.create the database initialized, you can create the actual access functions; see Example 11-11.

Example 11-11.

```
1    defmodule DarMetaData.DataAccess do
2        import Ecto.Query
3
4        def write_meta meta do
5            metax = %MetaData{
6                  name:  meta.name,
7                  origin: meta.origin,
8                  timestamp: meta.timestamp,
9                  gfsid: meta.gfsid,
10                 haspdf: meta.haspdf
11           }
```

```
12                cs = MetaData.changeset metax
13                case DARMetaData.Repo.insert!(cs) do
14                      meta  ->
15                              {:ok, meta}
16                end
17         end
18
19    def get_meta id do
20        query = from m in MetaData,
21                      where: m.id == ^id,
22                      select: m
23        DARMetaData.Repo.all(query)
24    end
25
26    def get_meta_all do
27        query = from m in MetaData,
28                      select: m
29        DARMetaData.Repo.all(query)
30    end
31
32    def get_imagemeta id do
33        query = from mi in MetaDataImage,
34                      where: mi.metaid == ^id,
35                      select: mi
36        DARMetaData.Repo.all(query)
37    end
38 end
```

Writing data is a matter of creating a changeset with the data values and calling the Repo function insert. The get functions create queries and call the function all. Queries are an interesting construct because they use certain Elixir DSL features to look like queries in SQL or for example Linq in .Net.

DarMetaData is a GenServer that starts the Repo and handles messages by forwarding them to the access module and sending the reply back to the caller; see Example 11-12.

Example 11-12.

```
1  defmodule DARMetaData do
2     use GenServer
3
4     def process_message(msg) do
5         GenServer.call(server, {:msg, msg})
6     end
7
8     def start_link(name) do
9       DARMetaData.Repo.start_link
10      GenServer.start_link(__MODULE__, :ok, name: name)
11     end
12
13     def init(:ok) do
14         {:ok,   ""}
15     end
16
```

```
17      def handle_call({:msg, msg}, _from, state) do
18          rep = DarMetaData.DataAccess.process_message(msg)
19          {:reply, rep, state}
20      end
21  end
```

Ecto has several features that make upgrades and downgrades possible, called migrations. You also can populate a database via a seeds script that is run from mix with the command mix run seeds.exs. See Example 11-13.

Example 11-13.

```
1   def seed_metadata do
2       t = Calendar.DateTime.now! ("Europe/Vienna")
3       meta  = %MetaData{
4           name:  "TestName2",
5           origin: "Seeds",
6           timestamp: t |> Calendar.DateTime.Format.js_ms,
7           gfsid: "",
8           haspdf: false
9       }
10      DARMetaData.Repo.insert!(meta)
11  end
12
13  def seed_metadataimage do
14      t = Calendar.DateTime.now! ("Europe/Vienna")
15      metaimage = %MetaDataImage{
16          metaid: "6a75e636-3e9d-41e7-9462-88980926a832",
17          name:  "TestName",
18          timestamp: t |> Calendar.DateTime.Format.js_ms,
19          gfsid: ""
20      }
21      DARMetaData.Repo.insert!(metaimage)
22  end
23
24  seed_metadata
25  seed_metadataimage
```

Workflow

The implementation of the workflow uses a state machine as the underlying architecture and gen_statem as an implementation concept.

ⓘ **Workflow vs. finite state machine**   Sometimes discussions come up about the differences of workflows and state machines. They are not the same, but some workflows can be expressed as state machines.

A workflow has states, but also needs orchestration. State machines normally react to external events, but it is also possible to switch the states internally during state handling. An orchestration actor or supervisor can then conduct the workflow.

The DAR workflow has several defined states, can be in any of the following states, and must be in one (Figure 11-1).

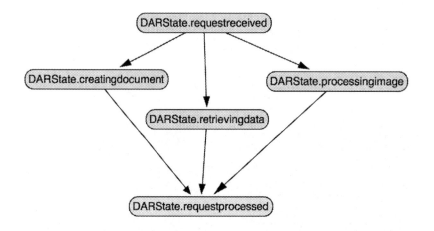

Figure 11-1. *Workflow states*

Figure 11-1 does not show error conditions for clarity. Any of the states with a green background can fail and the workflow would be in an error state. Let's assume that the messages passed around indicate errors.

When you switch to a view of the workflow orchestration, you get a different picture, as shown in Figure 11-2.

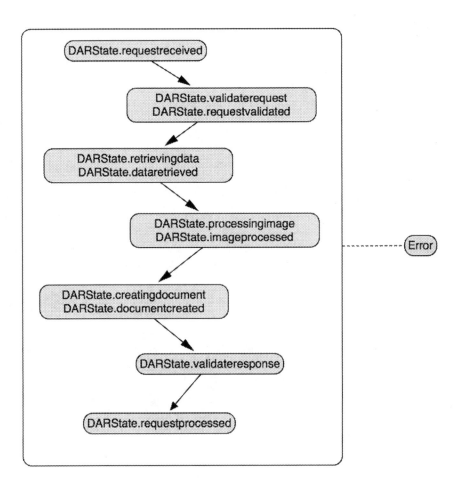

Figure 11-2. *Workflow orchestration*

The workflow is essentially sequential with possible error situations and optional skipping of steps. The implementation has three parts:

- Model definition
- State machine
- Orchestration

Model Definition

Models used in the workflow are partly used for communicating with internal modules in the workflow. Some will be used by the client and as JSON messages sent to the web server. These models are totally independent from the database models that are defined in Ecto.Schema format.

The state of the workflow is defined as module constants (actually macros) and functions that can be used to avoid typos. Unfortunately, these functions can't be used in all situations (for example, default values in functions), because the macro expansion does not work in those cases. See Example 11-14.

Example 11-14.

```
1   defmodule DARState do
2      @idle :idle
3      @requestreceived :requestreceived
4      @requestvalidated  :requestvalidated
5      @retrievingdata :retrievingdata
6      @dataretrieved :dataretrieved
7      @processingimage  :processingimage
8      @imageprocessed :imageprocessed
9      @creatingdocument  :creatingdocument
10     @documentcreated :documentcreated
11     @validateresponse :validateresponse
12     @requestprocessed:requestprocessed
13
14     def idle do
15       @idle
16     end
17
18     # truncated
19  end
```

The DARModelInternalMessage is for internal messages during the processing of the workflow; as in other models it is a *struct*. It holds information if, for example, a PDF of a requested document exists and also holds the id of a document in GridFS (gfsid). For simplicity, most ids are strings to avoid costly binary GUID transformations. See Example 11-15.

Example 11-15.

```
1   defmodule DARModelInternalMessage do
2      defstruct     gfsid:     "",
3                    name:      "",
4                    comment:   "",
5                    has_pdf:  false,
6                    state:     DARState.requestreceived,
7                    actions:   [DARState.retrievingdata],
8                    images:    %DARModelImageProcessing{}
9   end
```

Fields in lines 6 and 7 are initialized with the state functions discussed above. The field on line 8 refers to another model, shown in Example 11-16.

Example 11-16.

```
1   defmodule DARModelImageProcessing do
2      defstruct name:            "",
3               comment:         "",
4               imagelist:       [],
5               options:         []
6   end
```

This is a simple struct to hold information about images and image processing options. The struct DARModelExternalMessage in Example 11-17 is defined for communication with a client.

Example 11-17.

```
1    defmodule DARModelExternalMessage do
2      @derive [Poison.Encoder]
3      defstruct gfsid:          "",
4                name:           "",
5                comment:        "",
6                actions:        []
7                use ExConstructor
8
9      def from_json  m do
10       Poison.decode! m
11     end
12
13     def to_json m do
14       Poison.encode! m
15     end
16   end
```

It uses the library *Poison* to create internal messages from JSON and create JSON for the client from internal messages.

Orchestration

A workflow needs to be orchestrated to get from state to state or handle error conditions. You have a supervisor called *DARWorkflow* that processes messages coming from the client via the handler on the web server and DARRouter. See Example 11-18.

Example 11-18.

```
1    defmodule DARWorkflow do
2      use Supervisor
3
4      def process_message(m) do
5        case m.state do
6           :requestreceived  ->
7              DARWf.start_link m
8              DARWf.new_request
9
10          :requestvalidated ->
11             DARWf.retrieve_data
12
13          :dataretrieved  ->
14            if Enum.member?(m.actiongroups, DARActionGroup.images) do
15              DARWf.process_image
16            else
17              if Enum.member?(m.actiongroups, DARActionGroup.document) do
18                DARWf.create_document
```

```
19              else
20                DARWf.validate_response
21              end
22            end
23
24          :imageprocessed ->
25            if Enum.member?(m.actiongroups, DARActionGroup.document) do
26              DARWf.create_document
27            else
28              DARWf.validate_response
29            end
30
31          :documentcreated ->
32            DARWf.validate_response
33
34          :requestprocessed ->
35            DARWf.terminate
36            DARModelResponseMessage.get_json m
37
38          :errorstate  ->
39            DARWf.terminate
40            DARModelInternalMessage.get_json          m
41      end
42    end
43
44    def start_link do
45      Supervisor.start_link(__MODULE__, [], name: {:global,__MODULE__})
46    end
47
48    def init(_opts) do
49      children = [
50        worker(DARImageLib,[DARImageLib]),
51        worker(DARPdfLib,[DARPdfLib])
52      ]
53      supervise children, strategy: :one_for_one
54    end
55  end
```

The workflow supervisor keeps two workers for image processing and PDF creation in its tree. When a message arrives, the action that is taken in process_message depends on the state. Whatever happens as a next step is decided in this module, but the actual work is done in the state machine. In case of an error, the state machine will be terminated and an error message returned to the caller. When a new message arrives, a new state machine will be started and used in subsequent calls.

The workflow supervisor can be in a supervisor tree of the web server or preferably running on a different machine as named node.

State Machine

DARWf is implemented as GenStateMachine and is called from the workflow supervisor. Internally it uses GenStateMachine.call to invoke the callbacks of the state machine; see Example 11-19.

Example 11-19.

```
1   defmodule DARWf do
2     use GenStateMachine
3
4     # Client
5
6     def start_link(m) do
7       GenStateMachine.start_link(DARWf, {DARState.idle, m}, name: DARWf)
8     end
9
10    def terminate do
11      GenStateMachine.stop(DARWf, :normal)
12    end
13
14    def new_request do
15      r = GenStateMachine.call(DARWf, DARState.requestreceived)
16      DARWorkflow.process_message  r
17    end
18
19    def retrieve_data do
20      r = GenStateMachine.call(DARWf, DARState.retrievingdata)
21      DARWorkflow.process_message  r
22    end
23
24    def process_image do
25      r = GenStateMachine.call(DARWf, DARState.processingimage)
26      DARWorkflow.process_message  r
27    end
28
29    def create_document do
30      r = GenStateMachine.call(DARWf, DARState.creatingdocument)
31      DARWorkflow.process_message r
32    end
33
34    def validate_response do
35      r = GenStateMachine.call(DARWf, DARState.validateresponse)
36      DARWorkflow.process_message  r
37    end
38
39    # Server (callbacks)
40
41    def handle_event({:call, from}, :requestreceived, state, msg) do
42      case DARWorkflowOperations.validate_request msg do
43        {:ok, res} ->
44          {:next_state, DARState.requestvalidated,
45            %{msg | :state => DARState.requestvalidated, :actiongroups => res},
46            {:reply, from, %{msg | :state => DARState.requestvalidated, :actiong\
47             roups => res}}}
48        {_, err} ->
49          {:next_state, DARState.errorstate,
50            %{msg | :state => DARState.errorstate, :comment => err},
```

159

```
51              {:reply, from, %{msg | :state => DARState.errorstate, :comment => er\
52                r}}}
53         end
54    end
55
56    def handle_event({:call, from}, :retrievingdata, state, msg) do
57       case DARWorkflowOperations.retrieve_data msg do
58         {:ok, res} ->
59            {:next_state,DARState.dataretrieved,
60                %{msg | :state => DARState.dataretrieved, :metastruct => res},
61                {:reply, from, %{msg | :state => DARState.dataretrieved, :metastruct\
62                => res}}}
63         {_, err} ->
64            {:next_state, DARState.errorstate,
65                %{msg | :state => DARState.errorstate, :comment => err},
66                {:reply, from, %{msg | :state => DARState.errorstate, :comment => er\
67                r}}}
68         end
69    end
70
71    def handle_event({:call, from}, :processingimage, state, msg) do
72       case DARWorkflowOperations.process_image msg do
73         {:ok, res} ->
74            {:next_state, DARState.imageprocessed,
75                %{msg | :state => DARState.imageprocessed, :images => res},
76                {:reply, from, %{msg | :state => DARState.imageprocessed, :images =>\
77                res}}}
78         {_, err} ->
79            {:next_state, DARState.errorstate,
80                %{msg | :state => DARState.errorstate, :comment => err},
81                {:reply, from, %{msg | :state => DARState.errorstate, :comment => er\
82                r}}}
83         end
84    end
85
86    def handle_event({:call, from}, :creatingdocument, state, msg) do
87       case DARWorkflowOperations.create_document msg do
88         {:ok, res} ->
89            {:next_state, DARState.documentcreated,
90                %{msg | :state => DARState.documentcreated, :gfsid => res},
91                {:reply, from, %{msg | :state => DARState.documentcreated, :gfsid =>\
92                res}}}
93         {_, err} ->
94            {:next_state, DARState.errorstate,
95                %{msg | :state => DARState.errorstate, :comment => err},
96                {:reply, from, %{msg | :state => DARState.errorstate, :comment => er\
97                r}}}
98         end
99    end
100
```

```
101    def handle_event({:call, from}, :validateresponse, state, msg) do
102      case DARWorkflowOperations.validate_response msg do
103        {:ok, res} ->
104          {:next_state, DARState.requestprocessed,
105              %{msg | :state => DARState.requestprocessed},
106              {:reply, from, %{msg | :state => DARState.requestprocessed}}}
107            {_, err} ->
108          {:next_state, DARState.errorstate,
109              %{msg | :state => DARState.errorstate, :comment => err},
110              {:reply, from, %{msg | :state => DARState.errorstate, :comment => er\
111              r}}}
112      end
113    end
114
115    def handle_event(event_type, event_content, state, data) do
116      # Call the default implementation from GenStateMachine
117      super(event_type, event_content, state, data)
118    end
119  end
```

Each state has its own handle_event callback where another module is called to do the work and where error conditions are checked. The module called is *DARWorkflowOperations*; see Example 11-20.

Example 11-20.

```
1   defmodule DARWorkflowOperations do
2     def validate_request msg do
3       %{:name => pname} = msg
4       %{:metaid => pgmetaid} = msg
5       %{:actions => pactions} = msg
6       p = {pname,pgmetaid,pactions}
7       case p do
8         {_,_,pactions} when pactions == [] -> {:error, "Actions list empty"}
9         _ ->
10          ag = []
11          ag = if Enum.member?(msg.actions, DARAction.retrieveimage), do: List.\
12          insert_at(ag, 0, DARActionGroup.images), else: ag
13          ag = if Enum.member?(msg.actions, DARAction.retrievetext), do: List.i\
14          insert_at(ag, 0, DARActionGroup.document), else: ag
15          {:ok, ag}
16      end
17
18    end
19
20    def retrieve_data msg do
21      if Enum.member?(msg.actions, DARAction.retrievedoclist_all) do
22        metalist = DarMetaData.DataAccess.get_meta_all
23        {:ok, DARModelMetaData.from_schema_list(metalist)}
24      else
25        if Enum.member?(msg.actions, DARAction.retrievedoc) do
26          meta = DarMetaData.DataAccess.get_meta msg.metaid
```

```
27              case m = List.first(meta) do
28                nil ->
29                  {:error, "Retrieve Data error"}
30                _  ->
31                  {:ok, DARModelMetaData.from_schema(m)}
32              end
33            end
34          end
35        end
36
37        def process_image msg do
38          metaimage = DarMetaData.DataAccess.get_imagemeta msg.metaid
39          l = (for n <- metaimage, into:          [], do: n.id)
40          res = DARImageLib.Process.process_message l
41          {:ok, res}
42        end
43
44        def create_document msg do
45          pdfid = DARPdfLib.process_message msg
46          {:ok, pdfid}
47        end
48
49        def validate_response msg do
50          {:ok,  ""}
51        end
52      end
```

This module is the core of the workflow actions. It knows how to access the data stores and other workers. It also validates messages.

The workflow implementation has several modules to separate concerns and to make testing easier. Perhaps in the future a GenStage server implementation may have advantages compared to the state machine.

Image Processing

Image processing in DAR proves that it is not always necessary to have libraries available; you can also reuse existing console programs. ImageMagick[3] is an open source image processing program available on all major operating systems. It has more than enough features for most use cases.

This solution is not optimal, though. The application needs to be installed on a server or somewhere on the network that is accessible from the server the Elixir application runs on. It would not be advisable to have a similar solution from a web server.

You can use a library called *Mogrify* to call the console app; see Example 11-21.

---

[3]www.imagemagick.org

Example 11-21.

```
1   defmodule DARImageLib.Process do
2
3     @respath "~/Projects/creative-common-dar/Backend/dar/apps/dar_imagelib/test/re\
4     s/"
5
6     defmacro path_resource(file, path \\ @respath) do
7       Path.join(path,file)
8     end
9
10    # hard coded for testing
11    def resize do
12      Mogrify.open(path_resource("test.jpg"))
13          |> Mogrify.copy
14          |> Mogrify.resize("50x50")
15          |> Mogrify.save(path_resource("test_resize.jpg"))
16    end
17
18    def watermark(imageprocessingmodel) do
19      Mogrify.watermark(
20        getimagelist_as_string(imageprocessingmodel.imagelist),
21        getlist_as_string(imageprocessingmodel.options))
22
23    end
24
25    def getimagelist_as_string(imagelist) do
26      {_,s} = Enum.map_reduce(
27        (for n <- imagelist, do: n <> " "),
28        [],
29        fn(name,acc) -> {name,List.insert_at(acc,-1,add_path(name))} end)
30      List.to_string(s)
31    end
32
33    def getlist_as_string(list) do
34      for n <- list, into:      "", do: n <> " "
35    end
36
37    defp add_path(filename) do
38      Path.join(@respath,filename)
39    end
40  end
```

The code for calling for example the command line tool *composite* is shown in Example 11-22.

Example 11-22.

```
1   defp run_composite(inputfiles, optionlist) do
2     args = ~w(#{optionlist}  #{inputfiles})
3     System.cmd "composite", args, stderr_to_stdout: true
4   end
```

System.cmd allows you to call commands as if invoking them from the console.

ImageMagick is very powerful, but it is a bit difficult to compile all the different options. Also, the output is a file, and piping into a binary is possible, but depends on the operating system. Saving a temporary file for now is a first solution, although it won't scale in future.

PDF Creation

There are many options to create PDF documents on the fly, many of which are proprietary and commercial. Happily, in Erlang and Elixir, there are open source solutions: Erlguten[4] and Gutenex[5]. See Example 11-23.

Example 11-23.

```
1   {:ok,   pid} = Gutenex.start_link
2      |> Gutenex.set_page(1)
3      |> Gutenex.begin_text
4      |> Gutenex.set_font("Helvetica", 48)
5      |> Gutenex.text_position(40, 180)
6      |> Gutenex.text_render_mode(:fill)
7      |> Gutenex.write_text("ABC")
8      |> Gutenex.set_font("Courier", 32)
9      |> Gutenex.text_render_mode(:stroke)
10     |> Gutenex.write_text("xyz")
11     |> Gutenex.end_text
12     |> Gutenex.move_to(400, 20)
13   bin = Gutenex.export(pid)
14   Gutenex.stop
```

The library is very low level, as you can see. In the workflow, you have a GenServer DARPdfLib that processes the messages as the other workers do. The output is a binary that can then be cached in memory for delivery or optionally stored in GridFS.

---

[4]https://github.com/ztmr/erlguten
[5]https://github.com/SenecaSystems/gutenex

CHAPTER 12

▓ ▓ ▓ ▓

Deployment

So far you have an API and several components that help you implement and deliver the required features. This chapter explores the deployment of these components.

Security

The two previous chapters described the implementation of DAR and some of its features.

The Web API is a public service and, although the data this service provides in the open source version is publicly available, there are still aspects that need to be secured.

So what is meant by *security* in this context?

First, machines without a public face need to be secured with hardware access restrictions. Then authentication and authorization have to make sure that not everybody can access the non-public server and the database.

ⓘ **Authentication and Authorization**   Some developers are confused by the definitions of authentication and authorization. I always explain the terms this way:

Authentication tells if I am allowed to be somewhere.

Authorization tells what I am allowed to do once I am successfully authenticated.

Erlang or Elixir don't provide much help with this task. One measurement is the use of cookies, as you saw in the SayHello example. These cookies organize access to the node and are like a secret access code. This is not a problem for servers behind a firewall, but public-facing servers like web servers should not be secured by this method. In these cases, you either have to roll your own solution or rely on third-party solutions. You have to assume that servers are locked down by firewalls in the network.

If the focus is on authentication for the API server, you have to look at third-party libraries Guardian[1] and Openmaize[2] or a commercial service like Auth0[3].

---

[1]https://github.com/ueberauth/guardian
[2]https://github.com/elixircnx/openmaize
[3]https://auth0.com

© Wolfgang Loder 2016
W. Loder, *Erlang and Elixir for Imperative Programmers*, DOI 10.1007/978-1-4842-2394-9_12

Phoenix can integrate libraries like the ones mentioned above with the concept of plugging modules into the process pipeline. See Example 12-1.

Example 12-1.

```
1   pipeline :browser do
2       plug :accepts, ["html"]
3       plug :fetch_session
4       plug :fetch_flash
5       plug :protect_from_forgery
6       plug :put_secure_browser_headers
7       plug Openmaize.Authenticate
8   end
```

This is an excerpt from a Phoenix router integrating Openmaize. In a controller, more plugs have to be added, as shown in Example 12-2.

Example 12-2.

```
1    plug Openmaize.ConfirmEmail,
2       [db_module: Welcome.OpenmaizeEcto, key_expires_after: 30, 3 mail_function:
         &Mailer.receipt_confirm/1] when action in [:confirm]
4    plug Openmaize.ResetPassword,
5       [db_module: Welcome.OpenmaizeEcto, key_expires_after: 30, 6 mail_function:
         &Mailer.receipt_confirm/1] when action in [:reset_password]
7    plug Openmaize.Login,
8       [db_module: Welcome.OpenmaizeEcto, unique_id: &Name.email_username/1,
9       override_exp: 10_080] when action in [:login_user]
10   plug Openmaize.OnetimePass,
11      [db_module: Welcome.OpenmaizeEcto] when action in [:login_twofa]
12   plug Openmaize.Logout when action in [:logout]
```

Security is not only authentication and authorization but also, for public servers, cross-scripting issues, sniffing attacks, and similar. Phoenix is certainly taking care of these issues, but it is in the hands of the developers to make it work. Exposing databases and Erlang/Elixir nodes on the web server may bring more problems in the case of compromised servers than distributed architectures.

Distribution and Deployment

From the start of this book, I have emphasized Erlang's and Elixir's ability to distribute processes over several machines called nodes.

There is no difference if the application or applications run on one or one several machines, over a LAN, or over a WAN. Of course, in the latter case you must think about latency.

When Erlang was created, there existed clusters of multiple machines, but no multi-core machines, as we have now. Erlang/OTP implemented support for symmetric multiprocessing (SMP) in 2009. You can see if cores are supported on your machine by starting erl/werl and looking at the first line:

Erlang/OTP 17 [erts-6.3] [64-bit] [smp:8:8] [async-threads:10]

Smp[8:8] indicates that there are eight cores available and the Erlang VM can use all of them. Starting erl with –nosmp restricts the VM to one core.

You worked with nodes when you ran *SayHello*. You ran two nodes on a machine and since you gave them names they could communicate with each other. It does not matter which language implemented the node's code because they are all compiled to the binary language that the Erlang VM understands.

ℹ **Starting Phoenix applications with a name and cookie**   Phoenix applications can be started as a named node with a secret cookie to make it possible for nodes to communicate with each other if no cookie file is saved on the machines:

```
elixir –sname nodename –cookie secretcookie -S mix phoenix.server
```

Deployment can be done manually or per scripts, although it seems to me that the easier option is to use the manual approach.

When you have more than two nodes and the nodes communicate, then every node visited by another node will share its knowledge of nodes with the visitor. So if you have two disparate node sets and a node from one set is communicating with a node from the other set, then suddenly all the nodes from both sets know each other. This can lead to unexpected big node sets and may not be desirable.

All problems of networks are valid for distributed Erlang systems as well; for example, apart from security concerns discussed above, hardware failures, latency, or bandwidth problems can happen. Nodes communicate with each other per messages and a balance must be found between too small and too big messages. In DAR, we deal with images or PDF documents: should it be sent by messages from node to node or should it be retrieved from a cache node at the highest level in the hierarchy? The first one may impact bandwidth; the second solution may have latency problems.

One aspect of distribution can be to run the same application on a cluster of nodes to tackle issues when nodes fail or disappear. In this case, a system configuration file can hold the information for the failover cluster; see Example 12-3.

Example 12-3.

```
1   [{kernel,
2     [{distributed, [{myapp, 5000, [sayhello1@localhsot, {sayhello2@localhsot, sayh\
3   ello3@localhsot}]}]},
4       {sync_nodes_mandatory, [sayhello2@cave, sayhello2@cave]},
5       {sync_nodes_timeout, 5000}
6     ]
7   }
8   ].
```

All nodes need to have the configuration file, only differing in the list of the other nodes in the sync_nodes_mandatory key. This configuration ensures that all nodes are started together; if one node goes down, a distributed application controller process in the kernel will try to switch the application to another node if the restart of the application fails after the set timeout.

This method works in both Erlang and Elixir. In Elixir, you can start an application with the code in Example 12-4.

Example 12-4.

```
1   iex –sname sayhello1 -pa _build/dev/lib/sayhello/ebin/
2       –app sayhello –erl "-config config/sayhello1"
```

A Phoenix clustered application can be started with the code in Example 12-5.

Example 12-5.

```
1   elixir --name darapi@127.0.0.1 --erl "-config sys.config" -S mix phoenix.server
```

PART V

■ ■ ■

Patterns and Concepts

CHAPTER 13

Overview Patterns and Concepts

The following chapters discuss patterns and concepts that are important for programming with Erlang/OTP and Elixir.

In the object-oriented programming (OOP) world, patterns are widely used (and abused). The Gang of Four book[1] categorized many common design practices and had for a long time a monopoly on this subject. Other publications followed, but the search for patterns was mostly done by practitioners of OOP. The functional programming community was not so interested in them, similar to modeling, which is discussed in Appendix A. This said, there is a new initiative to collect Erlang patterns[2]. In fact, OTP is a collection of best practices and its implementation can be labeled as an implementation of patterns.

Most of the time, I personally avoid the word *pattern* because it is a loaded term. I prefer to talk of *concepts* in order to avoid lengthy discussions about whether a pattern is a pattern or not.

All of the chapters can be read on their own, although sometimes they build on each other in the order they are presented. Links between the concepts make it easier to jump to each section out of order.

A note that applies to all concepts discussed in this book: many definitions in computer science are not universally regarded as correct or valid and there are competing definitions. This is rather astonishing since most concepts are based on mathematical principles, but words are simply more open to interpretation and are less concise than symbols. So if you hear different definitions from what is discussed in this part of the book, remember to stay in the syntax of this book and the constraints or deficiencies of the author's knowledge and experience.

The discussed concepts are divided into three categories. These categories are more or less arbitrary and do not follow other categorizations. They just serve to divide the discussed concepts into logical sets.

Functional Concepts:

- Closures

- Continuation-Passing

- Higher Order Functions

- Immutability

- Lazy Evaluation

- Lists and Tuples

- Maps

- Pattern Matching

---

[1]http://en.wikipedia.org/wiki/Design_Patterns
[2]www.erlangpatterns.org

© Wolfgang Loder 2016
W. Loder, *Erlang and Elixir for Imperative Programmers*, DOI 10.1007/978-1-4842-2394-9_13

- Recursion
- Referential Transparency

Type Creation Concepts:

- Atoms
- Behaviors (*Behaviours*)
- DSL and Metaprogramming
- Dynamic Types
- Mixin
- Polymorphism

Code Structuring Concepts:

- Actor Model
- Concurrency
- Fault Tolerance
- Flow-based Programming
- Processes
- Separation of Concerns
- SOA
- Specific to Generic

CHAPTER 14

Functional Concepts

Pattern Matching

One of the most confusing concepts for an imperative programmer is *pattern matching*. The syntax looks like an assignment; the word *pattern* suggests something like RegEx.

Let's investigate **Erlang** first. Consider the expression shown in Example 14-1.

Example 14-1.

```
M = 2
```

Your imperative instincts will tell you that this is an initialization of the variable *M* with 2. This means that

```
M = 3
```

will simply assign *3* to the variable *M*.

In fact, typing this expression into the Erlang shell returns

```
exception error: no match of right hand side value 3
```

and the value of *M* is still *2*.

What is going on?

When you assign a value to a variable, the state of this variable changes from *unbound* to *bound*, as shown in Figure 14-1.

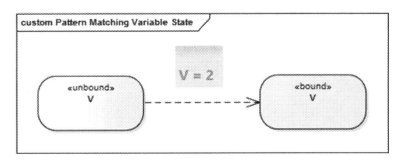

Figure 14-1. *Unbound to bound*

© Wolfgang Loder 2016
W. Loder, *Erlang and Elixir for Imperative Programmers*, DOI 10.1007/978-1-4842-2394-9_14

Any further assignment will try to match the right-hand side with the assigned value. The right-hand side can be any valid expression or function call. Consider the function in Example 14-2.

Example 14-2.

```
1    always_return_42()  ->
2            42.
```

Statements

```
1   L42 = 42.
2   L42 = patternmatching:always_return_42().
```

will return *42* to indicate a successful pattern match.

Pattern matching is a very powerful concept and can replace imperative language constructs like *if* and *while* including their variations.

Let's look at this function with an if-statement in Erlang; see Example 14-3.

Example 14-3.

```
1    return_42_if_when_true(Flag)  ->
2      if
3        Flag =:= true ->
4           42;
5        true ->
6           0
7      end.
```

If you set the flag to true, it will return 42. The `if` statement compares the argument with Boolean true and false and returns 42 or 0 accordingly. Example 14-4 will succeed.

Example 14-4.

```
L42 = patternmatching:return_42_if_when_true(true).
```

The `if` statement is not very intuitive. Erlang does not have an else branch, so an arbitrary *true* statement is used. The `if` expression looks for a true branch; if there is none, it comes back with an exception (*no true branch found when evaluating an if expression*).

The best is to forget that `if` exists in Erlang, because there are better alternatives. One alternative is `case`. It is the next step up from the imperative construct `if`. See Example 14-5.

Example 14-5.

```
1    return_42_case_when_true(Flag) ->
2      case Flag of
3        true -> 42;
4        _ -> 0
5      end.
```

This code does the same thing the `if` statement did. It is similar to switch/case statements in languages like C#, Java etc. The differences are that all case statements are in one block separated by semicolons and the placeholder _, which acts as an indicator for the default-branch. So Example 14-6 will succeed as before.

Example 14-6.

```
L42 = patternmatching:return_42_case_when_true(true).
```

The examples so far are trivial. Erlang is in the tradition of Lisp dialects that are famous (or infamous) for their list treatment. You will examine lists later. Let's look now at two valid pattern matching examples in Example 14-7.

Example 14-7.

```
{L42,3} = {patternmatching:return_42_case_when_true(true),3}.
```

Here you compare a tuple with a variable and a number with a tuple that has a function call and a number. Now see Example 14-8.

Example 14-8.

```
{L42,_} = {patternmatching:return_42_case_when_true(true),3}.
```

This example is similar to the one above; it only uses the placeholder _ on the left side. This means *I compare the right side that has a tuple with two members, but I am not interested in the second one.*

The return value for both statements is {42,3}.

A special case is the left side having one or more unbound variables. If the number of members in the tuple on the left and right side are the same, then the unbound values will be initiated and bound. Example 14-9 will bind the unbound variable *X* to *42* as before. Example 14-10 will fail because the number of the members does not match.

Example 14-9.

```
{X,_} = {patternmatching:return_42_case_when_true(true),3}.
```

Example 14-10.

```
{X,Y,_} = {patternmatching:return_42_case_when_true(true),3}.
```

This type of pattern matching with lists or tuples is used extensively in functions both with function arguments and return values. See Example 14-11.

Example 14-11.

```
1   incorrect_case(a,b) ->
2     case a == b of
3       true -> -1;
4       false -> 0
5     end;
6   incorrect_case(a,Y) ->
7     case Y > 0 of
8       true -> 42;
9       false -> 0
10    end;
11  incorrect_case(_,Y) ->
12    case Y > 0  of
13      true -> 43;
```

```
14      false -> 0
15    end.
16
```

For imperative programmers, it looks fine, but in Erlang you will get one of the following:

- A call *incorrect_case(a,b)* will always return *0*.

- A call *incorrect_case(42,1)* will return an exception (*no function clause matching*).

The compiler will actually display a warning when the above code is compiled (*the guard for this clause evaluates to 'false'*) but it is easy to miss it if there are more warnings.

The cause of these exceptions lies in the difference between atoms and variables, which can only be distinguished by their case. Elixir makes this easier by prefixing atoms with a colon. Having a function signature like *incorrect_case(:a,:b)* makes the error more obvious.

If you call the Erlang function like this, you will get another exception: *no function clause matching*. This means there was no matching function signature, because *42* is not an atom. Something like incorrect_case(X,Y) as signature with X and Y meaning numbers would be fine in a language with polymorphism. Erlang has a similar approach, but it's implemented differently with pattern matching; see Example 14-12.

Example 14-12.

```
incorrect_case(42,3).
```

Erlang is dynamically typed and you can express polymorphic parameter types with *guards*, as shown in Example 14-13.

Example 14-13.

```
1   guard_function(Flag) when Flag == true -> 42;
2   guard_function(Flag) when Flag == false -> 0.
```

This code implements the if function with guards. Viewing the code, it is clear what is meant, once you get over the syntax with the semicolon and the dot. This code is an example of an ad hoc polymorphism.

Which of the described concepts to use is partly an individual decision. I prefer guards where possible because they are concise, easy to understand, and leave completely out the if statement. The *case...of* construct is useful in simple functions and apparently the resulting byte code is very similar without an advantage towards any implementation.

How can you implement the Erlang examples in Elixir? They have a slightly different syntax, but are otherwise functional equivalent, as you can see in Example 14-14.

Example 14-14.

```
1   def always_return_42 do
2       42
3   end
```

The function is defined in a def block, which indicates a public or exported function. Private functions can be defined in a defp block.

This trivial function can also be defined in a different syntax on one line, as shown in Example 14-15.

Example 14-15.

```
1   def always_return_42_short, do: 42
```

The do: keyword is necessary to tell the compiler that a function definition is on the same line. Pattern matching in Elixir works as in Erlang. One difference is the assignment of variables; see Example 14-16.

Example 14-16.

```
1   v1 = 2 # -> 2
2   v1 = 3 # -> 3
3   ^v1 = 4 # -> (MatchError) no match of right hand side value: 4
```

In the Erlang world, line 2 should throw an exception, because v1 is immutable once assigned a value on line 1. In Elixir, a reassignment creates a new immutable variable in the background, but keeps the name. If you use the caret (^, called a *pin operator*) as in line 3, you are back to the original Erlang behavior and an exception will be returned if you try to assign a value to ^v1.

The introduction of this reassignment shortcut can lead to problems in certain situations, so the Elixir compiler will print out warnings when a reassignment can have adverse effects (see the discussion of immutability in the next section).

Immutability

Immutability is part of the "gold standard" of functional programming. According to many functional developers, immutability separates the good programming languages from the bad.

So what is it? Let's assume you are writing assembler code and you have a *variable* in a memory location that is used as an argument in a *method*. Assembler code does not define constructs like variable or method. On the other hand, this is the purest example to discuss immutability; see Figure 14-2.

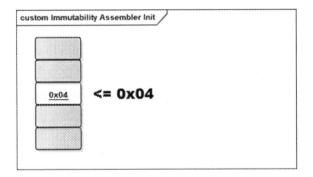

Figure 14-2. *Memory location*

Your variable is just a memory location, and any code in the same program can change the value in that location. In fact, the same is true for many programming languages, even if they are not so bare-bones as Assembler. The C family of programming languages especially had and has problems with mutable variables, although on different danger levels. It is very easy to overwrite arrays beyond their limits (assuming you have 8-bit memory and big endian format). See Figure 14-3.

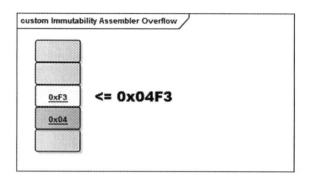

Figure 14-3. *More memory location*

The 16-bit data overrides the memory location with the red background, most probably unintended by the programmer.

Object-oriented languages are not immune to immutability problems. A class with public properties, fields, or whatever they are called in the language, can't protect those values to be overwritten by a consumer of the class or a derived class.

Most developers are aware of this and are careful to protect the values either by definition or by convention. The former may be baked into the language, such as a protected, private, or sealed keyword; the latter depends on the development team to focus on the effects of their code. It is obvious that the approach by convention is error prone and not really feasible. Protection in the language only goes so far and also needs the developers to anticipate future uses of the class, method, or property.

The critical problems of mutable memory locations are side effects and difficult-to-analyze defects at runtime. Objects or classes in OOP bind state and behavior, where state can be public or private. Figure 14-4 shows bad programming, but this can be seen in many programs. The function Peel() just updates the property Peeled and returns void.

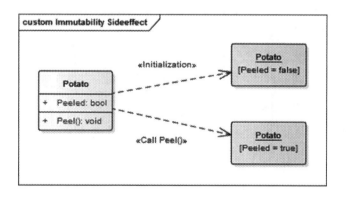

Figure 14-4. *Bad programming*

The next call to Peel() would not do anything or, worse, would throw an exception "Already peeled". The programmer has to check Peeled first, before calling the method. The state of the object instance Potato is changed, and if you share this instance between different consumers, the code accessing the object needs to be implemented in a defensive way to cater for possible side effects.

This is a trivial example and it can't be fixed with immutable memory locations. It is an inherent flow of OOP. A library function could be written with an object instance of Potato as argument, as in Example 14-17.

Example 14-17.

```
1   Potato Peel(Potato p) {
2     Potato _p = p.clone();
3     _p.Peel();
4     return _p;
5   }
```

This function returns a new Potato instance, but the property can still be changed at a later time. Only by using a language that supports immutability will the side effect problem be fixed. Of course, programming discipline can prevent side effects as well, but it should not be the programmer's responsibility to do this, and it is too error prone as well.

What happens if you have concurrent access to a memory location? You have to start using locks and other workarounds to prevent side effects, but this introduces a bunch of new problems, especially deadlocks. If you have had to use concurrency in your applications, you can certainly remember a time when the machine was frozen and needed to be restarted. After the machine was running again, you stood in front of it with the task of debugging the program. Writing logs to a file and restarting the machine again and again was and often still is the "solution," if the management did not get you one of the expensive external debuggers.

Pure functional concepts consider writing data to disks or printing as side effects. Also, assignments are seen as side effects, but a more pragmatic approach will allow the assignment of local variables in functions and disallow global variables and their modification.

What are the advantages of immutable values ("variables")?

Code Quality and Debugging

Having data immutable takes away many pitfalls. Especially compared to OOP, with immutability you simply know when data is pushed into a function as argument that this data can't be changed by the caller or by the function. If, and this is in fact a second advantage, you debug a program, you don't have a situation when data is suddenly changed and you don't have any idea when this happened and where in the code this happened. Code maybe easier to read as well.

Data Consistency and State

Data consistency and state are in fact a paradigm change. OOP is about the state. Objects have an internal-only state or state exposed to the outside of an object. In the functional paradigm, you are managing data. You are passing immutable data around, such as messages. The messages can contain the data model values and I could argue that the data is the state. In some way, a program has a state at any given time. In the concept of *event sourcing*, the events are the immutable data, and invoking events means creating or recreating the state of the program.

Cache and Sharing

Since data is immutable, you can easily cache it without fear that you change the state when you read the data back. You can be sure that the value of the data is what it is intended to be. Nobody could have changed it in the meantime. The same applies to sharing. Going back to the example of sending messages between processes, you can send messages from a supervisor to a number of processes. The messages won't change; they will be the same if sent to one or ten processes.

Hash Keys

Immutable data is perfect for keys. In maps in Erlang, any valid term can be used as key, which is only possible because of the immutable nature of data.

Functional Correctness

Immutable data helps to ensure functional correctness of a function.

Not everything is either true or false, or black or white. Many imperative languages are in fact hybrid languages, such as Java, Scala, C#, F#, and Python. They integrate the object-oriented paradigm with the functional paradigm and know closures or lambda expressions, functions as parameters, and may have immutable data structures like strings.

Having described the advantages, a pure functional approach with all data immutable has disadvantages as well.

Bi-Directional Data Structures

Not everything can be easily expressed with immutable data, for example bi-directional structures. It is easy to implement a structure like trees or directed graphs, but bi-directional is more of a challenge. Add a node to such a structure and you will have to update the (by definition) immutable parent node of the newly created child node.

Workarounds

If immutability should be used with OOP languages, you have to code workarounds. The C# example above clones the in-parameter in order not to change it. In fact, it creates a new object in a different memory location and manipulates that object. The return value is then the new object and the old one is unchanged.

This is not real immutability, of course; it is just a tweak to let the original object appear immutable. The caller can still change the return value or copy the values into the original object.

In a previous project, I had to invent an "immutable" list to prevent other developers from overriding the values. Essentially this means creating new lists and copying the values from the old to the new list. The copying can affect performance and in any case it is an overhead. Functional languages have to *copy* as well, but it is baked into the language and can do reference tricks to not copy values.

Resistance

Resistance is a problem that is not a real disadvantage of the concept, but since switching to the concept of immutability is a change in hard-wired programming behaviors, many developers reject the concept.

"I have always done it like that. I won't change." How often have we heard this and probably said it ourselves?

Immutable data needs a different thinking and a different software design. Without a language that supports immutability, it needs additional code that needs to be tested and can potentially introduce new defects. The resistance is real and needs to be overcome with training or use of libraries to help with the task.

The discussion in the last paragraphs only touches some parts of immutability. The biggest advantage hasn't been mentioned yet.

Concurrency

Erlang also means working with concurrent processes, and to make sure not to run into data inconsistencies, you need to have immutable data. It can still happen as a side effect of I/O. If a database or a mutable queue implementation is used, than the immutable data in the language won't help. It is the programmer's responsibility to avoid this trap. Discipline is required to avoid the pitfalls of mutability.

Elixir has, as you saw in Chapter tk, changed the syntax of assignment, although not the meaning. Even if a variable is reassigned with a different value, the compiler will still create a different variable in a different memory location.

Consider Example 14-18.

Example 14-18.

```
1    def assignment_warning(flag, v1) do
2      ret = if (flag) do
3               v1 = v1 + 21
4                :processed
5             else
6                :notprocessed
7             end
8      {ret, v1}
9    end
```

This is imperative code written in Elixir. The crucial lines are 3 and 8. In line 3, the argument *v1* is reassigned the value plus 21. In line 8, *v1* is returned to the caller. What value should v1 have? The imperative programmer would expect the value from line 3; the functional programmer would expect the argument's value.

The Elixir compiler will throw a warning shown in Example 14-19.

Example 14-19.

```
warning: the variable "v1" is unsafe as it has been set inside
a case/cond/receive/if/&&/||.
Please explicitly return the variable value instead.
```

The example has shortened the output; there is more text to explain what the warning means. When you run the function, the result is shown in Example 14-20.

Example 14-20.

```
1    iex(1)> Assignment.assignment_warning true,21
2    {:processed,  42}
3    iex(2)> Assignment.assignment_warning false,21
4    {:notprocessed,  21}
```

The problem here stems from the possibility of reassigning variables, which encourages imperative style programming. The more idiomatic way to implement this function is shown in Figure 14-21.

Example 14-21.

```
1  def noassignment_nowarning(flag, v1) do
2    case flag do
3      true -> {:processed, v1+21}
4      _    -> {:notprocessed,  v1}
5    end
6  end
```

According to a short e-mail exchange I had with Joe Armstrong, the difference between Erlang and Elixir is that Erlang checks the referenced value, and if the values don't match, an error will be raised. In Elixir, the name of a variable is a reference to a value as well, but the reference is changed so a reassignment can be made as in imperative languages, although with restrictions like context.

Maps

Maps are a new type in Erlang since version 17 and were enhanced for large maps in version 18. Other programming languages call them hashes or dictionaries. Basically, maps are collections of key-value pairs. In earlier versions of Erlang, *records* were the preferred way to express a data structure similar to a database record. With maps, it is now possible to express, for example, a JSON string as key-value pairs in a map that can then be pattern matched.

The creation of a map is a little verbose, but intuitive. Say you want to bake a pizza with different toppings; see Example 14-22.

Example 14-22.

```
1   pizza_toppings_map() ->
2       #{{tomatosauce,spoon} => 3,
3         {mozzarella,slices} => 8,
4         {ham,slices} => 6,
5         {mushroom,spoon} => 2,
6         {spinach,spoon} => 2,
7         {onion,spoon} => 2,
8         {onionring,spoon} => 2,
9         {sausage,piece} => 1
10       }.
```

The operator $\Rightarrow$ sets the value of an element and associates the key with the value. Once the map is defined, you can use it to match it to a pattern, update values, or run built-in functions from the standard library.

Pattern matching is achieved with the operator := as you can see in Example 14-23.

Example 14-23.

```
1   pizza_topping_match_valid() ->
2       M = pizza_toppings_map(),
3       #{ {mozzarella,slices} := I} = M,
4       I.
5   % mapsexample:pizza_topping_match_valid(). -> 8
```

If the pattern does not exist, the runtime will throw an exception as it does in other pattern matching cases. See Example 14-24.

Example 14-24.

```
1   pizza_topping_match_invalid()  ->
2       M = pizza_toppings_map(),
3       #{ {butter,teaspoons} := I} = M,
4       I.
5   % mapsexample:pizza_topping_match_invalid().
6   % -> exception error: no match of right hand side value #{{ham,slices} =>     6,
7   % {mozzarella,slices}  =>    8,
8   % {mushroom,spoon} => 2,
9   % {onion,spoon}  =>    2,
10  % {onionring,spoon}  =>    2,
11  % {sausage,piece}  =>    1,
12  % {spinach,spoon}  =>    2,
13  % {tomatosauce,spoon}       =>      3}
```

If you try to use the ⇒ operator for pattern matching, an *illegal pattern* compile error will occur.

Both operators can be used for updating values, but they behave slightly different; see this blog post from Joe Armstrong: http://joearms.github.io/2014/02/01/big-changes-to-erlang.html. Updating, of course, is creating a new list; the original list is immutable. The := keeps the keys in one memory place, shared by multiple instances of the same map type, and only associates values to them for the new map. See Example 14-25.

Example 14-25.

```
1   pizza_topping_update_v1() ->
2       M = pizza_toppings_map(),
3       M1 = M#{{mozzarella,slices} := 5},
4       M1.
5   % -> #{{ham,slices} => 6,
6   %    {mozzarella,slices} => 5, % changed from 8 to 5
7   %    {mushroom,spoon} => 2,
8   %    {onion,spoon} => 2,
9   %    {onionring,spoon} => 2,
10  %    {sausage,piece} => 1,
11  %    {spinach,spoon} => 2,
12  %    {tomatosauce,spoon} => 3}
13
14  pizza_topping_update_v2() ->
15      M = pizza_toppings_map(),
16      M1 = M#{{mozzarella,slices} => 6},
17      M1.
18  % -> #{{ham,slices} => 6,
19  %    {mozzarella,slices} => 6, % changed from 8 to 6
20  %    {mushroom,spoon} => 2,
21  %    {onion,spoon} => 2,
22  %    {onionring,spoon} => 2,
23  %    {sausage,piece} => 1,
24  %    {spinach,spoon} => 2,
25  %    {tomatosauce,spoon} => 3}
```

You create a new map with the same keys, but with new values. Alternatively, you can add new keys while updating; see Example 14-26.

Example 14-26.

```
1   pizza_topping_add()  ->
2       M = pizza_toppings_map(),
3       M1 = M#{{mozzarella,slices} := 5, {pepperoni,piece} => 3},
4       M1.
```

In this case, you use both operators: := for updating and keeping the key in one memory place and ⇒ for adding a new key-value-pair. It is possible to use only := but then the keys will be stored redundantly.

The main advantage for the := operator is to avoid adding keys by accident. The compiler checks if a key is in the map and stops compilation with an error if it is not.

Creating and pattern matching maps are only basic tasks. The standard library[1] provides many useful functions that work on maps.

Elixir has to two data structures to express key-value pair collections. The first one is a *map* as in Erlang. The creation of your examples in Elixir is syntactically similar to Erlang, as you can see in Example 14-27.

Example 14-27.

```
1    def pizza_toppings_map() do
2        %{{:tomatosauce,:spoon} => 3,
3          {:mozzarella,:slices} => 8,
4          {:ham,:slices} => 6,
5          {:mushroom,:spoon} => 2,
6          {:spinach,:spoon} => 2,
7          {:onion,:spoon} => 2,
8          {:onionring,:spoon} => 2,
9          {:sausage,:piece} => 1
10        }
11   end
```

The biggest difference to Erlang is that there is a mixture of library calls and map syntax to implement the same functionality and a difference of output depending on the key type, if atom or not.

Consider Example 14-28.

Example 14-28.

```
1    m1 = %{1 => "m1"}
2    m2 = %{:a1 => "m2"}
3    m1[1]              # -> "m1"
4    m1[2]              # -> nil
5    m2.a1              # -> "m2"
6    m2.b               # -> ** (KeyError) key :b not found in: %{a1: "m2"}
7    m2[:a1]            # -> "m2"
8    m2[:b]             # -> nil
```

---

[1]http://erlang.org/doc/man/maps.html

The comments on each line display the output in a shell. The *dot* syntax, also called the *strict* syntax, is only valid with atoms and returns an exception if the key does not exist (lines 5 and 6). With the dynamic syntax, the output is the same and non-existing keys will cause *nil* to be returned.

The functions to handle maps as in your Erlang examples look like Example 14-29.

Example 14-29.

```
1   def pizza_topping_match_invalid() do
2       m = pizza_toppings_map()
3       Map.get m,{:butter,:teaspoons}
4   end
5
6   def pizza_topping_match_valid() do
7       m = pizza_toppings_map()
8       Map.get m,{:mozzarella,:slices}
9   end
10
11  def pizza_topping_update() do
12      m = pizza_toppings_map()
13      %{m | {:mozzarella,:slices} => 5}
14  end
15
16  def pizza_topping_add() do
17      m = pizza_toppings_map()
18      Map.put(m, {:pepperoni,:piece}, 3)
19  end
20
21  def pizza_topping_get_value() do
22      m = pizza_toppings_map()
23      %{{:mozzarella,:slices} => value} = m
24      value
25  end
```

There are different results depending on the method used to retrieve a value.

Line 23 shows a pattern matching access; the value in value will be what the key's value is. This is only valid if the key exists; otherwise an exception will be raised. In lines 3 and 8, you use the *Map* library to get the value of a key. If the key does not exist, *nil* will be returned.

Adding a key-value pair to a map is achieved with Map.put. The update syntax on line 13 returns an error if the key does not exist. In Erlang, you can update and add in one statement. Elixir's update syntax with | reminds us of the list processing with header and tail.

Elixir has a special data structure for ordered lists with atoms as keys where the same key can be in the list multiple times. They are called keyword lists and you can see them in Example 14-30.

Example 14-30.

```
1   def create_pizza_order() do
2     [{:margerita, 1},{:calzone, 2}]
3   end
4
5   def add_to_order() do
6     kwl = create_pizza_order
7     kwl ++ [roma: 1]
```

```
 8    end
 9
10    def jump_the_queue() do
11      kwl = create_pizza_order
12      [roma: 1] ++ kwl
13    end
14
15    def add_the_same() do
16      kwl = create_pizza_order
17      kwl ++ [margerita: 2]
18    end
```

The create function on line 2 shows that keyword lists are actually lists with tuples as elements. All list operations can be used on keyword lists as well. For example, lines 7, 12, and 17 show the concatenation operator. Keyword lists have a special library module *Keyword* similar to maps and lists.

This specialized data structure is used for options passing in Elixir functions. Together with optional parentheses and a keyword list as a last parameter, it can be used to create DSLs.

Lists and Tuples

Lists and tuples are similar data types; the main difference is that the number of elements is fixed in tuples and not fixed in lists. A different syntax is used to indicate this.

Example 14-31 shows it in Erlang.

Example 14-31.

```
1   % tuple
2   {mozzarella,slices, 5, fun(a,b) -> {a,b} end }.
3
4   % list
5   [mozzarella,slices, 5, fun(a,b) -> {a,b} end].
```

Example 14-32 shows it in Elixir.

Example 14-32.

```
1   # tuple
2   {:mozzarella,:slices, 5, fn(a,b) -> {a,b} end}
3
4   # list
5   [:mozzarella,:slices, 5, fn(a,b) -> {a,b} end]
```

Both lists and tuples can hold any value type, as shown in the examples above, mixing atoms, numbers, and functions.

Internally lists are represented as linked lists of elements and tuples are held in memory in order of the element definitions. Therefore, getting elements by index in a tuple is fast; other list-related operations like additions or updates are slow. Since you can have the same value types in lists and tuples, the use of either depends on the desired operations.

In many examples in this book you have tuples as return values of function calls. They can transport additional information, for example in case of an error. In fact, it is astonishing that in imperative languages we did not do the same for a long time. Which older Windows developer does not remember the sequence shown in Example 14-33 of statements in C/C++[2]?

Example 14-33.

```
1    #include <windows.h>
2    #include <strsafe.h>
3
4    void ErrorExit(LPTSTR lpszFunction)
5    {
6        LPVOID lpMsgBuf;
7        LPVOID  lpDisplayBuf;
8        DWORD   dw = GetLastError();
9        FormatMessage(
10           FORMAT_MESSAGE_ALLOCATE_BUFFER |
11           FORMAT_MESSAGE_FROM_SYSTEM |
12           FORMAT_MESSAGE_IGNORE_INSERTS,
13           NULL,
14           dw,
15           MAKELANGID(LANG_NEUTRAL, SUBLANG_DEFAULT),
16           (LPTSTR) &lpMsgBuf,
17           0, NULL );
18       lpDisplayBuf = (LPVOID)LocalAlloc(LMEM_ZEROINIT,
19           (lstrlen((LPCTSTR)lpMsgBuf) + lstrlen((LPCTSTR)lpszFunction) + 40)
20                           * sizeof(TCHAR));
21       StringCchPrintf((LPTSTR)lpDisplayBuf,
22           LocalSize(lpDisplayBuf) / sizeof(TCHAR),
23           TEXT("%s failed with error %d: %s"),
24           lpszFunction, dw, lpMsgBuf);
25       MessageBox(NULL, (LPCTSTR)lpDisplayBuf, TEXT("Error"), MB_OK);
26       LocalFree(lpMsgBuf);
27       LocalFree(lpDisplayBuf);
28       ExitProcess(dw);
29   }
30
31   void main()
32   {
33       if(!GetProcessId(NULL))
34           ErrorExit(TEXT("GetProcessId"));
35   }
```

In Erlang or Elixir, you simply return the code shown in Examples 14-34 and 14-35.

Example 14-34.

```
1    {error,<<"description">>}.
```

---

[2]https://msdn.microsoft.com/en-us/library/windows/desktop/ms680582(v=vs.85).aspx

Example 14-35.

```
1   {:error,"description"}
```

Especially in functional languages we find lists implemented as singly linked lists, whereas OO languages implement lists as arrays similar to tuples described above. Linked lists can easily be used in recursive functions and with immutable data. The disadvantages are that in singly linked lists there is no easy and performant way to update or delete the element before a given element. This is why we see many list algorithms in Erlang and Elixir with *head* and *tail* operations. Concatenation of lists means to link the new list to the existing list as a tail; see Example 14-36.

Example 14-36.

```
1   append([H|T], Tail) ->
2       [H|append(T, Tail)];
3   append([], Tail) ->
4       Tail.
```

This code takes two lists and arguments, and splits the head from the tail recursively until the head is empty and the tail is the list with *list two* appended to *list one*. See Example 14-37.

Example 14-37.

```
1   1> listsexample:append([1,2,3],[4,5]).
2   [1,2,3,4,5]
```

The same example in Elixir is shown in Example 14-38.

Example 14-38.

```
1   def append([h|t], tail) do
2       [h|append(t, tail)]
3   end
4   def append([], tail) do
5       tail
6   end
```

Of course you don't need to do this manually all the time and can use an operator, as in Example 14-39.

Example 14-39.

```
1   1> [1,2,3] ++ [4,5].
2   [1,2,3,4,5]
```

The recursive head-tail functionality will be useful in Chapter 14. In the introduction of this book, you saw an example similar to Example 14-40.

Example 14-40.

```
1   [I*10 || I <- lists:seq(1,10), I rem 2 == 0].
```

This is called *list comprehension* and is related to the *map* part in *map and reduce* algorithms. The statement means

- Generate a list with the number from 1 to 10.

- Filter this list by computing modolo 2 for each list element and taking all values that can be divided by 2.

- Output a new list with the filtered elements multiplied by 10 A list comprehension takes a generator

```
I <- lists:seq(1,10)
```

and a filter

```
I rem 2 == 0
```

The same list comprehension expressed in Elixir is shown in Figure 14-41.

Example 14-41.

```
1   def comprehension_ex1() do
2     mod2? = fn(i) -> rem(i, 2) == 0 end
3     for i <- 1.10, mod2?.(i), do: i*10
4   end
```

You define an anonymous function for convenience and use it in the list comprehension as the filter function.

Elixir also knows the :into option to have the output converted to a different data structure, so you can write an example to concatenate strings, as in Example 14-42.

Example 14-42.

```
1   def comprehension_ex2(list) do
2     for n <- list, into:  "", do: n <> " "
3   end
```

The function takes a list of string elements and returns a string of all concatenated list elements. The into option can't cast into arbitrary types, but it is useful for string or map transformations.

One important operation on lists is the reduction. For example, you want to sum up all arithmetic values in a list, as shown in Example 14-43.

Example 14-43.

```
1   def reduce(list) do
2     sum = fn(x, y) -> x + y end
3     list |> Enum.reduce(0, sum)
4   end
```

The reduce function of the module *Enum* takes a list, an accumulator, and a function.

ⓘ Pipe Operator, |> This operator takes the output of the left side (in the example, the *list*) and passes it as the first argument of the right side function.

Some library functions handling lists, maps, or tuples have the order of arguments changed in Elixir compared to Erlang. This is not only normalizing the arguments order, but is also necessary for the pipe operator to work. The first argument is always the object that needs to be processed, and all other arguments follow.

A statement like

ListExample.reduce [2,5,3.14]

will return the value *10.14*, the sum of all numbers in the list.

The *Enum* module in Elixir has a map_reduce function. Example 14-44 is from the project's *dar_imagelib* module, written in Elixir.

Example 14-44.

```
1   def getimagelist_as_string(imagelist) do
2     {_,s} = Enum.map_reduce(
3       (for n <- imagelist, do: n <> " "),
4       [],
5       fn(name,acc) -> {name,List.insert_at(acc,-1,add_path(name))} end)
6     List.to_string(s)
7   end
8
9   defp add_path(filename) do
10    Path.join(DarImagelib.Mixfile.getconstant(:respath),filename)
11  end
```

The example takes a list of image names, computes a URI by adding the name to a constant path, and returns each URI with a space at the end.

Line 2 is the relevant statement. The Enum.map_reduce function takes a list, actually anything that implements the protocol Enumerable, and also an accumulator with a function that does the actual work.

The accumulator is necessary to keep the result between the recursive enumeration steps, because the list you are processing is immutable. The reduce function takes the processed list argument and the accumulator as arguments and returns a tuple with the element and the updated accumulator. In the example, the new element is not just appended, but inserted in the right position (*-1*) to keep the original order of the image list.

Example 14-45 shows how a call of this function looks.

Example 14-45.

```
1   iex(1)> getimagelist_as_string(["image1","image2"])
2   "/path/to/res/image1 /path/to/res/image2 "
```

There are many other operations on lists in both Erlang and Elixir libraries defined. They are described in the Erlang[3] and Elixir[4] manuals.

Recursion

It is little bit misleading to call *recursion* a functional concept. In fact, it is a concept that is used in all programming languages. What is different in languages like Erlang and Elixir is that *tail calls* to the same function are not growing the call stack and can be used for iterations.

What is a tail call? Example 14-46 shows a normal non-recursive tail call in C/C++:

Example 14-46.

```
1   int tailCall(int data) {
2        f1(data);
3        return f2(data);
4   }
```

Here, f2 is the last ("tail") call. Example 14-47 shows a recursive version.

Example 14-47.

```
1   int recursiveTailCall(int data) {
2        f1(data);
3        return   recursiveTailCall(data);
4   }
```

Our experience will tell us that `recursiveTailCall` will crash, because it runs indefinitely until the stack allocation is full and the runtime environment will crash. Of course, this example is deliberately wrong to show the problem. Having an infinite recursion has to be considered a bug.

Programming in, for example, C and C++ had and still has the danger of running into exactly this stack problem, not only with recursive calls. The solution was and still is either to let the compiler insert stack check code, which sometimes significantly affects performance and does not fix the problem, or avoid recursion at all.

In Erlang (and Elixir), every tail call will be optimized, which is called *tail call optimization*. This means that the stack frame will be eliminated. It also means that you can create infinite loops, as shown in Example 14-48.

Example 14-48.

```
1   tailrecursiveloop(N) ->
2        io:format("~w~n", [N]),
3        tailrecursiveloop(N+2).
4
5   nontailrecursiveloop(N)  ->
6        io:format("~w~n", [N]),
7        2 * nontailrecursiveloop(N).
```

---

³http://erlang.org/doc/man/lists.html
⁴http://elixir-lang.org/docs/stable/elixir/Enum.html#content

Only `tailrecursiveloop` will hold the memory consumption of the Erlang VM stable; the `nontailrecursiveloop` function will grow memory steadily and eventually crash, because the recursive call is in an expression and can't be optimized. Run the example from the Rebar3 shell and then monitor the memory of the beam process on your machine.

As mentioned, recursion with tail optimization is a good tool for loops and is used widely in libraries for manipulating data structures like lists or trees.

Example 14-49 doubles all list element values with a recursive function.

Example 14-49.

```
1   doublebody([H|T]) -> [2*H | doublebody(T)];
2   doublebody([]) -> [].
```

If the list argument is empty, the returned list will be an empty list as well. In any other case, the statement in line 1 will process recursively the list until the tail portion *T* is empty. The output of the function called like

recursionexample:`doublebody([1,2,3]).`

will be

`[2,4,6]`

This is an example of a *body recursive* function. In the past, such functions were slower than tail recursive functions, but the Erlang/OTP guide states that this is not the case anymore (see Myth: Tail-Recursive Functions are Much Faster Than Recursive Functions[5]).

You can write the function example in a tail recursive way, as shown in Figure 14-50.

Example 14-50.

```
1   doubletailreversed(L) -> doubletailreversed(L, []).
2
3   doubletailreversed([],Acc) -> Acc;
4   doubletailreversed([H|T],Acc) -> doubletailreversed(T,[2*H|Acc]).
```

The function gets a list as argument and calls a private function with an accumulator as second argument. In this case, the accumulator is an empty list, but it could be a number for other cases.

Why use an accumulator? This is a concept to construct tail recursions. The accumulator will be filled with the result after each successful recursive call. Another element in the concept is that there must be an end condition to stop the recursion. In the case of lists, this is an empty list.

In the example, line 1 calls the private function in lines 3 and 4. The argument for the private function is the original list argument and an empty list as accumulator. Line 3 checks if the list to process is empty and returns the accumulator. If you pass an empty list to the exported function, you will also get an empty list *[]* returned. Line 4 uses the head (the first element) of the list and the tail (the rest of the elements) to pass in a recursive call with the tail as argument, which could be empty, and updates the accumulator with the doubled value of the head element. In your case, the *update* of the accumulator means that you add the result as head to the accumulator list. Attaching a list element to the beginning of the list is more performant than appending (see Lists and Tuples).

---

[5]`http://erlang.org/doc/efficiency_guide/myths.html`

The call
recursionexample:doubletailreversed([1,2,3]).
will result in

[6,4,2}

Is this the result you want? The handling of the lists resulted in a reversed order. Fixing this is easy; see Example 14-51.

Example 14-51.

```
1   doubletail(L) -> doubletail(L,  []).
2
3   doubletail([],Acc) -> lists:reverse(Acc);
4   doubletail([H|T],Acc) -> doubletail(T,[2*H|Acc]).
```

The only change, apart from the function name, is in line 3. You call list:reverse on the accumulator to correct the order.
The call

recursionexample:doubletail[1,2,3]).

will now result in

[2,4,6}

as expected.
Interesting is the implementation of lists:reverse in Erlang; see Example 14-52.

Example 14-52.

```
1   reverse([]  =  L)  ->
2       L;
3   reverse([_]  =  L)  ->
4       L;
5   reverse([A,  B])  ->
6       [B,  A];
7   reverse([A, B | L]) ->
8       lists:reverse(L, [B, A]).
```

The function lists:reverse(list) (arity 1) for non-trivial lists will call function lists:reverse with arity 2. The reverse algorithm is actually implemented as built-in function (BIF) to take advantage of C, because reverse is very often used as tail call in recursive functions. The call lists:reverse on line 8 calls the BIF. Also, if you look at the implementation of Elixir's enumerable protocol, you see that it is calling the same BIF; see Example 14-53.

Example 14-53.

```
1   # enumerable  protocol
2   def reverse(enumerable) when is_list(enumerable) do
3   :lists.reverse(enumerable)
4   end
```

Elixir has the same approach for creating recursive functions. Assume you have a map with a value that has nested lists and maps, as in Example 14-54.

Example 14-54.

```
1   defmodule NestedMaps do
2
3     def nested_map() do
4       %{"configs" =>
5         [
6           [%{"kind" => "compute#accessConfig",
7             "name" => "External  NAT",
8             "natIP" => ["146.148.0.0","127.0.0.1"],
9             "type" => "ONE_TO_ONE_NAT"}
10          ],
11          [{:otherconfig,"Router"}]
12        ]
13      }
14    end
15
16    def get_nested_list(nm) do
17      %{"configs" => nestedmaplist} = nm
18      nestedmaplist
19    end
20
21    def get_nested_map_from_list(nm, nestedlevel) when nestedlevel < 1 do
22      nm
23    end
24
25    def get_nested_map_from_list(nm, nestedlevel) do
26      l = List.first(nm)
27      get_nested_map_from_list(l,nestedlevel-1)
28    end
29
30    def get_nested_map_value(nm, val) do
31      Map.get  nm,val
32      end
33  end
```

The function get_nested_map_from_list gets a nestedlevel number to indicate how many lists you have nested. Once the number goes to 0, then the guard nestedlevel < 1 kicks in and the nested map or list is returned. With that you can then retrieve the value you need (in this example, from the first list only) but the example can be changed to either set the list index to retrieve or send a function parameter that will be applied to the list.

Lines

```
1   NestedMaps.nested_map
2     |> NestedMaps.get_nested_map
3     |> NestedMaps.get_nested_map_from_list(2)
4     |> NestedMaps.get_nested_map_value("natIP")
```

return the value ["146.148.23.208","127.0.0.1"].

If a recursive function calls another recursive function, then the function is called *trampolined*. This concept is used in Lisp implementations, but it can also be used to implement tail call recursion in stack-based languages. In this case, an outer function calls an inner function, but this inner function returns the address of another function that is then called by the outer function. When returning the stack of the first inner function is cleared. The downside is that arguments need to be passed as global variables and the performance is worse than direct calls. This is related to continuation passing style programming.

Higher Order Functions

A *higher order function* is a function that takes other functions as argument or returns a function, also at the same time. The concept derives from the *lambda calculus* in mathematics, but it can be used without understanding the underlying theory.

Historically, higher order functions are not only a domain of functional languages; see Example 14-55.

Example 14-55.

```
1   #include <stdio.h>
2   #include "printlib.h"
3
4   int int_print_func(int x)
5   {
6           printf( "%d\n", x );
7   }
8
9   int main()
10  {
11          // declared in printlib.h as: void print_func(void*(*func)(int));
12          print_func(int_print_func(42));
13
14          return 0;
15  }
```

This short C++ program defines a function int_print_func that obeys the declaration void*(*func) (int). This declaration is a *function pointer* declaration and int_print_func implements it. The _print_ func takes the address of the implemented function ("pointer") as an argument; it says, *just give me a function that takes an argument of type int and returns anything*. This is a simple example in C++ from the past; nowadays we would use lambda functions, which have a more insane syntax. Printing out "Hello world" in the console would be auto func = [] () { cout << "Hello world"; }; func(); if this code was included in a normal main() function.

Erlang and Elixir allow functions as argument with a simple syntax, either as anonymous function or via a variable. See Example 14-56.

Example 14-56.

```
1   call_function(F, A) -> F(A).
2
3   call_with_fun() ->
4       call_function(fun(N) -> N*N end, 5).
5
6   call_with_variable() ->
7       Sqfunc = fun(N) -> N*N   end,
```

```
 8        call_function(Sqfunc,4).
 9
10    direct_call() ->
11        fun(N) -> N*N end(3).
```

You define a function named `call_function` with two arguments: one function F and one argument for the function F. The body then calls F with A.

The function `call_with_fun` uses `call_function` with an anonymous function and the argument 5, so the result is 25. The function `call_with_variable` defines the function variable Sqfunc first and then calls `call_function` with Sqfunc as the first argument and 4 as the second, so the result is 16. The function `direct_call` just invokes the anonymous function with arguments and returns 9.

The Elixir implementation is equivalent to Erlang's implementation with a few syntax differences; see Example 14-57.

Example 14-57.

```
 1    def call_function(function,a) do
 2        function.(a)
 3    end
 4
 5    def call_with_fn() do
 6        call_function(fn n -> n*n end,5)
 7    end
 8
 9    def call_with_variable() do
10        sqfunc = fn n -> n*n  end
11        call_function(sqfunc,4)
12    end
13
14    def direct_call() do
15        fn n -> n*n end.(3)
16    end
17
18    def call_with_variable_shorthand() do
19        sqfunc = &(&1*&1)
20        call_function(sqfunc,4)
21    end
22
23    def direct_call_shorthand() do
24        (&(&1*&1)).(3)
25    end
```

Note the syntax on line 2. The dot is required to invoke the function; otherwise the compiler is complaining that `function/1` is undefined. The dot also makes sense looking at the function `direct_call`, where the anonymous function is defined and the dot tells the compiler that it will be invoked (line 15).

Elixir has a shorthand syntax for anonymous functions, which is shown in lines 19 and 24. The ampersand and the parentheses tell the compiler that an anonymous function is defined and the &1 means the first argument passed into this anonymous function.

You can find usage of function arguments in the standard library where predicate functions are used for iterators, filters, and reduce implementations. This is also valid for OOP languages like C#.

A chapter about high order functions would not be complete without mentioning *currying*. This is a technique that was made popular by the mathematician Haskell Curry[6] in the 1960s. The essence is to create functions with arity 1, which means one argument, from functions with arity greater than 1, which means multiple arguments.

The language Haskell not surprisingly supports currying automatically, so all functions have only one argument. A statement in Haskell like

```
take 2 [1, 3, 5, 7, 9]
```

will apply 2 to *take* and returns a function that takes a list as argument and returns the first 2 elements of this list. You could do this yourself, again in Haskell:

```
take2 = take  2
take2 [1, 3, 5, 7, 9]
```

In Erlang (Example 14-58) and Elixir (Example 14-59) you can achieve currying by writing additional functions to create partial evaluation.

Example 14-58.

```
1    multiply(X, Y) -> X*Y.
2    doubler() -> fun(X) -> multiply(2, X) end.
3
4    curry() ->
5        C = doubler(),
6        C(21).
```

Example 14-59.

```
1    def multiply(x,y) do
2        x*y
3    end
4
5    def doubler() do
6        fn x -> multiply(2,x) end
7    end
8
9    def curry() do
10       c = doubler()
11       c.(21)
12   end
```

The function doubler returns a function that calls multiply with 2 as the first argument. Calls to the returned function will subsequently call multiply with the first argument fixed to 2 and double the second argument. The result of both examples is 42. You have *curried* a function with arity 2 (multiply) to a function with arity 1 (doubler).

---

[6]https://en.wikipedia.org/wiki/Haskell_Curry

Continuation-Passing

Continuation-passing is one of the concepts that are used without knowing it. For example, C# has the keywords async and await (which soon may make an appearance in ECMAScript 7 as well); see Example 14-60.

Example 14-60.

```
1   async Task<int> GetData() {
2          return await LengthyOperation();
3          // declared as async Task<int> LengthyOperation()
4   }
```

The execution will be suspended on line 2 and other operations will continue. When the return value is received, GetData() will return to the calling function, which is also async. In other terms, we can say that on line 2 a *continuation* is saved, which is the execution state at the time of the call to LenghtyOperation.

If you think now of a *monad*, you are right (see Continuation Monad[7] in Haskell). You are also right when you think of a *goto*. Jumping in the code dependent on asynchronous events makes it very difficult to debug or understanding the control flow of a program.

Writing in continuation-passing style (CPS) means that you can pass continuations as functions explicitly to other functions. These continuation functions will "tell it what to do next." By calling the continuation function, the calling function indicates that it is ready to continue.

CPS can be used for interface programming or for computations that take a long or unknown time. Interesting examples are lazy sequences, for example streams. The language *Clojure* has it implemented in a way[8] that a function similar to an iterator object in other languages returns both a value and a continuation function. This helps to iterate through potentially infinite sequences.

Erlang and Elixir don't support continuations in the language, but with anonymous functions and tail-recursion, the continuation-passing style can be achieved.

The following code shows generic continuation-passing style examples. The function *initiate* calls the next function and so on until you send a *stop* message to terminate the process.

For Erlang, see Example 14-61.

Example 14-61.

```
1    continue(A,F) ->
2        F(A).
3
4    initiate(A) ->
5        case A of
6            {ok,1} -> continue({ok,2},fun continueB/1);
7            _ -> error
8        end.
9
10   continueB(A) ->
11       case A of
12           {ok,2} -> continue({stop},fun continueC/1);
13           _ -> error
14       end.
15
16   continueC(A) ->
```

---

[7]http://hackage.haskell.org/package/mtl-2.0.1.0/docs/Control-Monad-Cont.html
[8]http://clojure.org/reference/lazy

```
17       case A of
18           {stop} -> {stopped}
19       end.
```

For Elixir, see Example 14-62.

Example 14-62.

```
1    def initiate(a) do
2        case a do
3            {:ok,1} -> continue({:ok,2},&continueB/1)
4            _  ->  :error
5        end
6    end
7
8    defp continue(a,f) do
9        f.(a)
10   end
11
12   defp continueB(a) do
13     case a do
14       {:ok,2} -> continue({:stop},&continueC/1)
15       _ -> :error
16     end
17   end
18
19   defp continueC(a) do
20     case a do
21       {:stop} -> {:stopped}
22       _ -> :error
23     end
24   end
```

The generic example is very simple; a more advanced code can be found in this stackexchange answer[9] by Elixir's creator Jose Valim. Hint: the ampersand in the Elixir example denotes the definition of an anonymous function (see the *Higher Order Functions* section).

Notes:

- Continuation passing without tail-recursion optimization will eventually grow the stack and cause runtime problems.

- Using continuation functions means that a potentially concurrent process will be broken down into lambda expressions that are computed one after another, probably on a single thread.

Closures

The concept of closures is part of many programming languages, functional or imperative. The names vary from *lambda* (Java) to *delegate (C#) to _block* (Objective C).

---

[9]http://codereview.stackexchange.com/a/51548

Closures keep immutable state in context by binding the value to the environment. Values are defined outside of a function during the creation of this function and do not change until invocation of the function. A closure is an instance of a function; an anonymous function is the literal of a function type, similar to *class* and *object instance*.

The examples map a list of atoms (initiate_closure) to anonymous functions and print it to the console in print_closure. See Example 14-63.

Example 14-63.

```
1    initiate_closure() ->
2        [tomato,onion,cheese].
3
4    print_closure() ->
5        L = initiate_closure(),
6        lists:map(fun(A)-> io:format("~p~n", [A]) end, L).
```

The Elixir implementation is more obvious and easier to read thanks to the pipe operator |>, although the anonymous & operator makes it more abstruse; see Example 14-64.

Example 14-64.

```
1    def initiate_closure do
2        [:tomato,:onion,:cheese]
3            |> Enum.map &(fn () -> &1 end)
4    end
5
6    def print_closure do
7        initiate_closure
8            |> Enum.each &(IO.puts(&1.()))
9    end
```

In initiate_closure you map the atoms to functions, and the return value is a list of functions. This list is then used to print the atom strings out.

Lazy Evaluation

When code in any programming language comes across an expression, it needs to decide, if it is able to decide, if the expression is evaluated immediately or at a later point in time when the value of the expression is needed.

ⓘ Lazy evaluation vs. short-circuit evaluation   Assume you have a statement like

if (1 == 2 && 1 = 1) {do_something();}

There is no way that the function do_something() will ever be called. You are interested if the second expression (1 = 1) will ever be evaluated. If not, you are talking about short circuit evaluation.

As often in our industry, there are discussions if this is lazy evaluation. Since the second expression in this example is never evaluated, it is certainly not in a strict sense.

Deferred evaluation is needed when it would be too time- or memory-intensive to get the result at once. Examples are data streams or lists, especially when they are retrieved from data stores.

In functional languages, you can force lazy evaluation by wrapping an expression in an anonymous function, as in Example 14-65.

Example 14-65.

```
next(N) -> [N|fun() -> next(N+1) end].
```

The expression is only evaluated when the function wrapping is called. In fact, this is an example of continuation passing. When you call next the first time, it is not clear to the caller what will be returned. The anonymous function in the example just gives the next number, but it could be more complex and, for example, retrieve the next value from a stream.

Anonymous and recursive functions are language features that may be used when implementing lazy evaluation.

Related to lazy evaluation implementation is memorization, which is an optimization technique to reduce computational complexity of a program. The complexity is often expressed in the big O- notation, as $O(n)$ or $O(n \log n)$ and similar. The essence of the technique is to cache results of a computation so it does not need to be computed more than once if an expression has to be evaluated more than once as well. I am not aware of a programming language that has automatic memoization. If you want to use it, you have to implement it ourselves. As mentioned before, the sole reason for the use of memoization is performance.

The library functions in the module *Stream* in Elixir use lazy evaluation, while the functions in the module *Enum* are eager, which means they evaluate immediately.

Referential Transparency

Functional programming concepts in this chapter are often based on mathematical principles. When we apply a function in mathematics we can replace the function with the value of the function without changing the overall result. In programming, we can't always be sure of this; for example, consider errors or exceptions.

Referential transparency in programming means that it does not matter if I *reference* an expression or the result of this expression. It should be *transparent* to the rest of the program and should not change the outcome of the program at all.

ℹ **Referential transparency and determinism and idempotence** A deterministic program or function will always return the same result for a given input. According to this definition, all deterministic expressions are also referentially transparent.

The opposite is not true: a non-deterministic function may be one that returns a random number or encrypts based on random input like time. This function will still be referentially transparent, although this is disputed.

Idempotence is similar to both determinism and referential transparency: run a function with the same input several times and it will always return the same results *after the first run*. Inserts into a data store should not change the data if applied a second time. A (surprising) example is a C include file: if it prevents another include after the first time with the help of #ifdef/#define then it would be considered idempotent.

Let's reexamine the functions discussed with currying. See Example 14-66.

Example 14-66.

```
1   def multiply(x,y) when is_number(x) and is_number(y) do
2       x*y
3   end
4
5   def doubler() do
6       fn x when is_number(x) -> multiply(2,x)    end
7   end
```

The function multiply multiplies two numbers and the function double returns a function with one argument to *multiply* fixed to 2, so a given number will be multiplied by 2.

You can call the function doubler with numbers and will always get the same result. If you call with a string as argument, you get an error; therefore the function is not deterministic for all inputs. See Example 14-67.

Example 14-67.

```
1   iex(1)> c = Currying.doubler
2   #Function<0.125872190/1 in Currying.doubler/0>
3   iex(2)> c.(1)
4   2
5   iex(3)> c.("a")
6   ** (FunctionClauseError) no function clause matching in anonymous fn/1 in Curryi\
7   ng.doubler/0
8       currying.ex:18: anonymous fn("a") in Currying.doubler/0
```

Well, is it now referentially transparent or not? Some will say yes, some will say no. It is certainly not *pure*, but this is a totally different discussion I won't get into. It seems clear that we can't simply replace the function call with the result; the result can be either a number or an exception. On the other hand, we could have guards on the functions to indicate that we only want to deal with number type arguments. If we would use a statically typed language, the call would never compile. So it depends on the context if the above functions are referentially transparent or not.

In Erlang and Elixir, we can achieve referential transparency, but the languages are not helping us much. We as developers have to ensure that we overcome the problems of dynamic types.

An interesting idea is to merge designing unit tests with the concept of referential transparency. If all *units* tested are referentially transparent, then the quality of all tests will presumably be higher. Otherwise, we have to fear that one side effect or input variant was not tested at all and may emerge as error at runtime.

Referential transparency was certainly introduced by functional programming, but there is no constraint in OOP languages not to introduce the same idea in OOP as well.

## CHAPTER 15

Type Creation Concepts

DSL and Metaprogramming

Domain-specific languages (DSL) have their origin in declarative programming. The idea is to go up the logical domain chain until we have very high level functions, thus hiding some of the complexity of the implementation and invocation of functions.

A good example is SQL. Just write *CREATE TABLE*, provide a name and optionally a database name, and the system will create a database table with default settings. The user does not need to know how this is implemented and a non-developer can work with this declarative style.

Other examples in the developer world are HTML and CSS. DSLs outside of software development are text-based adventure or role-playing games. Commands like *turn*, *attack*, and *view* are shortcuts to more or less complex functions in the code of the game. Mouse clicks on a pixel area of the screen to *attack* or *defend* could be defined as a visual DSL.

ℹ Metaprogramming *Meta* has Greek roots with a simple meaning of *after* or *beyond*. Philosophers theorize about metaphysics, the abstract world beyond the physical world. During reception into other languages the meaning changed slightly and it was used as *about*. Douglas Hofstadter (Goedel, Escher, Bach, 1979) made the term "meta" popular. In software development, we often speak of metadata and mean *data about data*. Metaprogramming is programming on a higher abstract level, taking a program or programming language as the data. The developer can manipulate the code, write code at runtime, or analyze it.

In programming, a DSL is used for metaprogramming. You will look into macros first and then explore other more sophisticated ways.

Since the early programming languages we've had macros. MASM is the *Macro Assembler*. C was famous (or infamous, depending on your love of C) for macros like that in Example 15-1.

Example 15-1.

```
#define multiply( x1, x2 ) ( x1 * x2 )
```

The preprocessor expands the macro into the source code when it is used, so it is a way to define a DSL restricted by constraints of macro definitions.

Erlang has macros as well. The syntax is a bit odd, but it works. There are predefined macros like *?MODULE* or *?FILE,* which are used regularly in source code files.

Example 15-2 defines some macros in lines 1 to 3 and uses them in the function read_- binary_test.

Example 15-2.

```
1    -define (FILETESTCONTENT, <<"test_from_gfslib">>).
2    -define (FILETEST, "filetest").
3    -define (DARDB, "dar").
4
5    read_binary_test() ->
6        R = dar_gfslib_process_files:read_binary(?FILETEST,?DARDB),
7        ?assertEqual({ok,?FILETESTCONTENT},    R).
8
9    % expanded to:
10   read_binary_test() ->
11       R = dar_gfslib_process_files:read_binary("filetest","dar"),
12       ?assertEqual({ok,<<"test_from_gfslib">>}, R).
```

Erlang macros work like C macros and in fact replace strings in the code before the actual compilation of the code into bytes. In Example 15-3, the macro simply injects string constants, but the macro body can be a little bit more complex than just a string constant.

Example 15-3.

```
1    -define(IF(A,T,F),
2       begin
3         (case (A) of true->(T); false->(F) end)
4       end).
5
6    is_true(A) ->
7      ?IF(A,{ok,A},{error,A}).
8
9    % expanded to
10   is_true(A) ->
11     case (A) of true->{ok,A}; false->{error,A} end.
```

Here you define an *IF* macro to test if a Boolean expression is true or false. The function is_true uses this macro to just return *ok* or *error*.

When you call the function, you get the expected result; see Example 15-4.

Example 15-4.

```
1    1> macrosexample:is_true(1<2).
2    {ok,true}
3    2> macrosexample:is_true(1>2).
4    {error,false}
```

Of course, a macro could define other statements like calling a function; see Example 15-5.

Example 15-5.

```
1    -define(IF2(B,T,F),
2       begin
3         (case (B) of true-> (T()); false->(F()) end)
4       end).
```

```
 5
 6    send_message_to_next_actor(B) ->
 7      ValidOrder = {pizza,margherita},
 8      T = fun() -> self() ! {order, {pizza,margherita}, takeaway} end,
 9      F = fun() -> self() ! {noorder, B} end,
10      ?IF2(B == ValidOrder,T, F).
```

This example defines the macro *IF2* that expects functions as arguments T and F and calls them according to the Boolean expression B. Your functions send a message to the module itself to be able to test, but it could be another module or registered node.

As mentioned, macros are only one way to achieve metaprogramming in software development. Another way is to directly manipulate the AST (abstract syntax tree[1]).

You can manipulate the AST in Erlang as well, but Elixir brings metaprogramming to a new dimension. Part of the language is built on top of macros which are, in a difference to Erlang, not just extenders, but manipulate the AST. The macros run at compile time and produce byte code.

ℹ Homoiconic languages   The term *homoiconic language* means that the internal representation of a program written in this language can be expressed by the syntax of the language. This also means that code can be manipulated as data. One example for such a language is Lisp[2]. Elixir is considered to be a homoiconic language as well.

A simple example to define a macro in Elixir is to check if a number is even or not; see Example 15-6.

Example 15-6.

```
1    defmodule Macros do
2      defmacrop even?(n) do
3        quote do rem(unquote(n),2) == 0 end
4      end
5
6      def is_even?(n) do
7        even?(n)
8      end
9    end
```

The macro in the example is private (*defmacrop*) to the module and is used in the function is_even?.

The magic is done in *quote* and *unquote* which are themselves macros. *quote* provides the internal representation of the expressions; see Example 15-7.

Example 15-7.

```
1    iex(1)> num = 3
2    3
3    iex(2)> quote do rem(unquote(num),2) == 0 end
```

---

[1]https://en.wikipedia.org/wiki/Abstract_syntax_tree
[2]www.mprove.de/diplom/gui/kay69.html

```
4    {:==, [context: Elixir, import: Kernel],
5     [{:rem, [context: Elixir, import: Kernel], [3, 2]}, 0]}
```

The representation is a tuple with nested lists and tuples.

- The first element in the example is the atom :== which is the name of the function.

- The second element is metadata, in your case the module the function is imported from.

- The third element is a list of arguments, in your case two arguments: the first one is a tuple for the function rem (the left side of ==) and the second argument is 0 (the right side of ==).

- The rem function (atom :rem) has the same metadata as == and a list of two arguments as well. The second one is 2, which is a constant in the macro.

- The first argument of the rem function is num, the macro's argument. *unquote* gets the value from the variable defined in line 1 and injects it into the representation.

This tuple is in fact the abstracted syntax tree expressed in Elixir and this is the reason why Elixir falls into the category of a homoiconic language.

You can also get the textual representation of the macro; see Example 15-8.

Example 15-8.

```
1    iex(1)> num = 3
2    3
3    iex(2)> Macro.to_string(quote do rem(unquote(num),2) == 0 end)
4    "rem(3, 2) == 0"
```

The function to_string from the module *Macro* takes the AST and returns a string with the macro text as it will be injected into code.

ⓘ Internal and external DSL   The macros in Elixir can be used to create an *internal* DSL, which is a domain-specific language that uses language constructs to appear to be a different language or, as in Elixir's case, to extend the language. For example, *defmodule* is a macro, although it appears to be a language keyword.

External DSLs need to be parsed to be transformed into another language. For example, LESS is a DSL for defining web page styles that are then translated into CSS.

What can you do with all this knowledge?

Example 15-9 is a statement you can write with Ecto[3], a DSL to interact with databases.

Example 15-9.

```
1    query = from w in Weather,
2             where: w.prcp > 0 or is_nil(w.prcp),
3             select: w
```

---

[3]https://github.com/elixir-ecto/ecto

Some readers will be reminded of C#, which has a DSL for *Linq* expressions in the .Net framework. In C#, anonymous functions are used to achieve this DSL. Elixir uses macros; for example, *from* is the macro shown in Example 15-10.

Example 15-10.

```
1   # from https://github.com/elixir-lang/ecto/blob/master/lib/ecto/query.ex
2   defmacro from(expr, kw \\ []) do
3       unless Keyword.keyword?(kw) do
4         raise ArgumentError, "second argument to `from` must be a keyword list"
5       end
6
7       {quoted, binds, count_bind} = From.build(expr,__CALLER__)
8       from(kw,__CALLER__, count_bind, quoted, binds)
9   end
```

The macro takes an expression (in your case, *w in Weather*) and a keyword list as arguments. Example 15-9 shows the keyword list on lines 2 and 3. The syntax of keyword lists allows the square brackets to indicate the list to be optional if the keyword list is the last argument in the function. All arguments are then used to build an expression for a function call to a function *from*; see line 8 in Example 15-10. Similar macros can be found in the web framework *Phoenix*, for example to define routes.

Macros in Elixir are powerful because they can run code at compile time and so can be used to raise exceptions or log messages at compile time. They can also be used to define mixins.

Mixin

The concept of mixins means to *inject* code without changing the recipient, which can be a class in OO languages, an object in languages like JavaScript, or a module as in Ruby.

The reason for mixins is to reuse code for general functionality without having to rely on inheritance implementations in OO languages. Interfaces and similar are no real substitute because they just define the behavior and have to be implemented individually for each case.

Erlang does not have a mechanism for mixins. Elixir makes use of its macro features to provide a way to define a mixin.

When you *include* a module, you can do it in different ways. Using *use* you tell the compiler to run a special macro in the module you want to include; see Example 15-11.

Example 15-11.

```
1   defmodule RecipeMixins do
2     defmacro __using__(_opts) do
3       quote location: :keep do
4         def print(l) do
5           IO.puts(inspect l)
6         end
7         defoverridable [print: 1]
8       end
9     end
10  end
11
12    defmodule VegetableStew do
13      use RecipeMixins
```

```
14      def cook() do
15        l = %{{:carot,:piece} => 3,
16             {:onion,:piece} => 2,
17             {:tomato,:piece} => 2
18            }
19          # do something
20            print(l)
21        end
22      end
23
24      defmodule BeefStew do
25        use RecipeMixins
26        def cook() do
27          l = %{{:carot,:piece} => 3,
28               {:onion,:piece} => 2,
29               {:tomato,:piece} => 2,
30               {:beef,:grams} => 250
31              }
32            # do something
33            %{{:beef,:grams} => g} = l
34            print(g)
35        end
36
37        def print(g) do
38        IO.puts(("How much beef? " <> inspect g) <> " grams")
39        end
40      end
```

The macro *using* starting on line 2 simply defines a function that takes a variable as argument and sends its value to the console.

The two other modules do not define a print function, but after the line

```
use RecipeMixins
```

the modules can use the print function that is defined in the *using* macro in the module *RecipeMixins*. Line 7 in the example defines the function print with arity 1 overridable:

```
defoverridable [print: 1]
```

The module *BeefStew* does this and overrides the function. When you run the print version of both modules you get a different output; see Example 15-12.

Example 15-12.

```
1   iex(1)> VegetableStew.cook
2   %{{:carot, :piece} => 3, {:onion, :piece} => 2, {:tomato, :piece} => 2}
3   iex(2)> BeefStew.cook
4   How much beef? 250 grams
```

In OO languages, the pattern *decorator* can be used to inject behavior even at runtime. This works by defining an interface and implementing it in the types that should use that behavior. A similar approach can be taken in Elixir by defining a *protocol* and implementing it for certain types (see Chapter tk).

Another OO pattern similar to mixins is the *visitor* pattern that is implemented with abstract classes (C++, C#) or interfaces (Java).

Polymorphism

Polymorphism is a set of different concepts, and many of the definitions overlap. What they have in common is that a type can change appearance without changing the original functionality.

In the object-oriented world, polymorphism mostly means subtypes (*inclusion polymorphism*) and templates or generics (*constrained parametric polymorphism*). Then there is the term *ad hoc polymorphism*. This can refer to operator overloading and function overloading; it's sometimes also called virtual functions.

All these types can be seen in Java, C++, and C#. With these mechanisms OO developers build hierarchies of types that share behavior or functionality.

In dynamically typed languages, we speak of unconstrained parametric polymorphism, also called *duck typing*, if no type information is available.

Erlang can express polymorphism, but it is different from OO languages. Let's first look at Example 15-13 of type-based (sort of) polymorphism.

Example 15-13.

```
1   cookstew_typebased({S,I}) when {S,I} == {vegetable,I} ->
2     io:fwrite("It is a vegetable stew~n");
3   cookstew_typebased({S,I}) when {S,I} == {beef,I} ->
4     io:fwrite("It is a beef stew~n");
5   cookstew_typebased(_) ->
6     io:fwrite("Unknown stew~n").
```

The function cookstew_typebased behaves differently depending on the argument. To call it, use the code in Example 15-14.

Example 15-14.

```
polymorphism:cookstew_typebased({beef,[]}).
```

Or you can call it as shown in Example 15-15.

Example 15-15.

```
polymorphism:cookstew_typebased({beef,{ingredients,[]}}).
```

It will return "It is a beef stew".

This example does not seem very elegant and in fact it is not considered to be good Erlang code. Let's refactor the function to use pattern matching; see Example 15-16.

Example 15-16.

```
1   cookstew_patternmatching({vegetable,_I}) ->
2     io:fwrite("It is a vegetable stew~n");
3   cookstew_patternmatching({beef,_I}) ->
4     io:fwrite("It is a beef stew~n");
5   cookstew_patternmatching(_) ->
6     io:fwrite("Unknown stew~n").
```

This looks more like the Erlang we are expecting, although the limits lie in the first element of the tuple, which must be one of the positive pattern atoms. Also, the argument always needs to be a tuple and there need to be exactly one argument. This construct (as with the one with the guards above) looks more like a virtual function of OOP languages without the option to be overwritten.

If the argument passed is a record or a map, then it will be possible to change the record and still match positively, because the additional fields will be ignored; see Example 15-17.

Example 15-17.

```
1   beef_map() ->
2                     #{ stewtype => beef,
3             {beef,grams} => 200
4             }.
5
6   beef_map_extended() ->
7                      #{ stewtype => beef,
8             {beef,grams} => 200,
9             ingredients => []
10            }.
11
12  cookstew_map(#{stewtype := vegetable}) ->
13    io:fwrite("It is a vegetable stew~n");
14  cookstew_map(#{stewtype := beef}) ->
15    io:fwrite("It is a beef stew~n");
16  cookstew_map(_) ->
17    io:fwrite("Unknown stew~n").
```

You can use the map in beef_map or beef_map_extended and they will both match in the function cookstew_map. The pattern match is only interested that a key stewtype is in the map and that its value is beef.

Elixir can do what I have described for Erlang, but also adds *protocols*. They are inspired by *Clojure* and are a mechanism to define functions or modules with dynamic polymorphism.

According to Jose Valim[4],

"Elixir protocols are not interfaces. Behaviors would be the closest thing to interfaces. However, typed contracts are not exclusive to OO languages. Protocols build on top of behaviors to add data-type polymorphism (a form of ad hoc polymorphism). Polymorphism is not a concept exclusive to OO as well. Protocols in Elixir provide the same kind of polymorphism as Haskell type classes."

Protocols certainly look like *interfaces* in OO languages where they define the *behavior* of a type or class. Once the interface is implemented in the class, consumers of this class can rely on the fact that they can call the methods defined in the interface.

C# knows extension methods, which are somewhere in the middle between an interface and a mixin. They are bound to the type, but as static methods they are defined and implemented outside of the class they affect. The implementation of an extension method is part of the class, though, and the code is injected into its own implementation.

In Elixir, it is not the type that implements the protocol, but the protocol itself needs to be implemented for different types; see Example 15-18.

---

[4]https://elixirforum.com/t/why-avoid-mocks/1396/9

Example 15-18.

```
1   defmodule Stewtype do
2     defstruct stewtype: :veg, ingredients: []
3   end
4
5   defmodule Protocols do
6     defprotocol Stew do
7       def print(data)
8   end
9
10    defimpl Stew, for: Stewtype do
11      def print(s) do
12        case s.stewtype do
13          :veg ->
14            "It's a vegetable stew"
15          :beef ->
16            "It's a beef stew"
17          _ ->
18            "Unknown stew"
19        end
20      end
21    end
22  end
23
24    defmodule StewProtocol do
25      def what_is_it?(stew) do
26        Protocols.Stew.print(stew)
27      end
28  end
```

This example contains three modules in one file for easier compilation. The module from line 5 defines first the protocol *Stew* and then implements it on lines 10-22 for the type Stewtype. This type is defined in the module *Stewtype* and it is a struct.

The implementation of the protocol in the example is just to print out a string. The interesting part is that this implementation checks the conditions (in your case, which data comes in the struct) and processes the data accordingly.

The module *StewProtocol* is a simple usage of the implementation. The function what_is_it? uses the protocol implementation to print out a string depending on the data. If you call this function, you get the output shown in Example 15-19.

Example 15-19.

```
1   iex(1)> s = %Stewtype{}
2   %Stewtype{ingredients: [], stewtype: :veg}
3   iex(2)> Stew.print(s)
4   "It's a vegetable stew"
5   iex(3)> sb = %{s|stewtype: :beef}
6   %Stewtype{ingredients: [], stewtype: :beef}
7   iex(4)> StewProtocol.what_is_it?(sb)
8   "It's a beef stew"
9   iex(5)> su = %{s|stewtype: :chicken}
```

```
10    %Stewtype{ingredients: [], stewtype: :chicken}
11    iex(6)> StewProtocol.what_is_it?(su)
12    "Unknown stew"
```

Line 1 defines the struct you use. It contains default values :veg for the stewtype key and an empty list for the ingredients key. Lines 5 and 9 create new structs from the first one and just change *stewtype* to another atom. When you call your protocol implementation, you get the correct output.

The Elixir standard library has defined a few protocols like *Enumerable* that are used heavily. An interesting protocol, which you have encountered in the examples, is the *inspect* protocol, shown in Example 15-20.

Example 15-20.

```
1    # https://github.com/elixir-lang/elixir/blob/master/lib/elixir/lib/inspect.ex
2    defprotocol Inspect do
3      @fallback_to_any true
4      def inspect(term, opts)
5    end
```

The protocol defines the function inspect that takes an Elixir term and options. In tests, you have written lines like

```
Enum.each context, &IO.puts(inspect &1)
```

This line prints out all the key-value pairs in the context of the test. Since the types can't always be expressed as strings, they need to be transformed first. This is what *inject* does.

Line 3 in Example 15-20 defines that the protocol should fall back to the implementation for the type *Any* if no implementation for a certain type is found.

If you call Example 15-20 like Example 15-21, you will get an error.

Example 15-21.

```
1    iex(1)> StewProtocol.what_is_it?(2)
2    ** (Protocol.UndefinedError) protocol Stew not implemented for 2
3        protocols.ex:5: Stew.impl_for!/1
4        protocols.ex:6: Stew.print/1
```

You must change the protocol implementation so you catch any type that is not implemented; see Example 15-22.

Example 15-22.

```
1    defmodule Protocols do
2      defprotocol Stew do
3        @fallback_to_any true
4        def print(data)
5      end
6
7      defimpl Stew, for: Stewtype do
8        def print(s) do
9          case s.stewtype do
10            :veg ->
```

```
11              "It's a vegetable stew"
12              :beef ->
13              "It's a beef stew"
14          _   ->
15              "Unknown stew"
16
17        end
18      end
19    end
20
21    defimpl Stew, for: Any do
22      def print(_) do
23          "This is not stew data!"
24      end
25    end
26  end
```

The implementation for type *Any* together with @fallback_to_any set to true on line 3 returns the string in Example 15-23, as expected.

Example 15-23.

```
1  iex(1)> StewProtocol.what_is_it?(2)
2  "This is not stew data!"
```

Protocols are implemented in a way that OO developers will find the wrong way around. In OO, a class knows everything about the type, including all behavior. Protocols separate this into a different module, away from the type. It also means that the logic of how to handle a behavior request, say a function, is defined and implemented outside of a type. This is a good example of the functional paradigm where the functions handle data, not the data type handling functions.

Behaviors (*Behaviours*)

So far you have seen two ways to affect the original implementation (or the behavior) of a module or type: mixins and polymorphism via pattern matching and protocols.

Erlang and Elixir know a construct called *behaviour* which is confusingly named like the description we use in OOP for an interface. In addition, the Erlang *behaviour* is slightly different than an Elixir *behaviour*.

The idea of the Erlang behaviour goes back to the concept of generic and specific. The *behaviour* module is the generic part and another module (the specific one) implements the callbacks. It is closely related to OTP, for example to define a gen_server; see Example 15-24.

Example 15-24.

```
1  -module(darapi).
2  -behaviour(gen_server).
```

The behaviour keyword indicates that there may be callbacks defined in the generic module that need to be implemented in the consuming module.

This sounds familiar, and in fact we could say that a *behaviour* is an *interface*. Callbacks are called when certain events occur, for example when messages arrive. We could also say the behaviour defines a contract between the generic module and its implementer.

Elixir behaviours work as explained above, also with a slightly different syntax; see Example 15-25.

Example 15-25.

```
1  defmodule Stewtype do
2    defstruct stewtype: :veg, ingredients: []
3  end
4
5  defmodule Printer do
6    @type stew :: Stewtype.t
7    @callback print(stew) :: {:ok, term} | {:error, term}
8  end
```

The definition of the callbacks is a specification declaration as it is used to document code, for example to give type hints to Dialyzer. The @type declaration defines the type for use in the callback declaration. The callback declares a function called print that takes the specified type stew on line 6 as an argument. The right side after the double colon (::) indicates the return value. In this case, we say that one of two tuples may be returned, with the first element a well-specified atom and the second a *term* which, in Erlang- and Elixir-speak, means any valid expression. We call the example behaviour *Printer*.

A consumer of this behaviour has to implement the callback; otherwise a compiler error will be thrown. See Example 15-26.

Example 15-26.

```
1   defmodule VegStew do
2     @behaviour Printer
3     def print(s) do
4       case s.stewtype do
5         :veg ->
6           {:ok, "It's a vegetable stew"}
7         _ ->
8           {:error, "Unknown  stew"}
9
10      end
11    end
12  end
13
14  defmodule BeefStew do
15    @behaviour Printer
16    def print(s) do
17      case s.stewtype do
18        :beef ->
19          {:ok, "It's a beef stew"}
20        _ ->
21          {:error, "Unknown stew"}
22      end
23    end
24  end
```

The @behaviour directive says that the modules *VegStew* and *BeefStew* implement the behaviour *Printer*, so they are both implementing the print function.

Calling the print functions in the modules returns the expected outputs as you have seen in previous examples; this time it's a tuple of an :ok or :error atom with a string. See Example 15-27.

Example 15-27.

```
1   iex(1)> s = %Stewtype{}
2   %Stewtype{ingredients: [], stewtype: :veg}
3   iex(2)> sb = %{s|stewtype: :beef}
4   %Stewtype{ingredients: [], stewtype: :beef}
5   iex(3)> su = %{s|stewtype: :chicken}
6   %Stewtype{ingredients: [], stewtype: :chicken}
7   iex(4)> VegStew.print(s)
8   {:ok, "It's a vegetable stew"}
9   iex(5)> sb = %{s|stewtype: :beef}
10  %Stewtype{ingredients: [], stewtype: :beef}
11  iex(6)> su = %{s|stewtype: :chicken}
12  %Stewtype{ingredients: [], stewtype: :chicken}
13  iex(7)> VegStew.print(sb)
14  {:error, "Unknown stew"}
15  iex(8)> BeefStew.print(sb)
16  {:ok, "It's a beef stew"}
17  iex(9)> BeefStew.print(s)
18  {:error, "Unknown stew"}
19  iex(10)> BeefStew.print(su)
20  {:error, "Unknown stew"}
21  iex(11)> VegStew.print(su)
22  {:error, "Unknown stew"}
23  iex(12)> VegStew.print(s)
24  {:ok, "It's a vegetable stew"}
```

The relationship between protocols and behaviours in Elixir is that the former dispatches based on data, the latter dispatches based on functions.

Dynamic Types

There exists a very old discussion between proponents of different programming languages and the style of typing. For example, Haskell, Java, and C# are statically typed, and Ruby and JavaScript are dynamically typed. If a developer can indicate that a variable, return argument etc. has a certain type and I want to use it, even complex types, the compiler can tell me any error and won't compile the executable or can give me a warning.

Dynamic types mean that the type is not set, for example in Ruby and JavaScript. This can mean more freedom in writing code with no constraints, but there are also problems with it. With dynamic types, the developer has to rely on tools that check types in the compiled executable. These tools can do this with static analysis. Or a developer has to check at runtime the type of variables to rule out exceptions. Languages with dynamic types need many tests and it is not uncommon to have the same lines of code for tests than for the actual feature code.

Static type languages in OO languages are not free from problems either. Due to the constraints of types, changes in complex types may require runtime versioning code to be able to process several generations of that complex type. Many developers use a hash or a dictionary to circumvent this problem.

Erlang and Elixir are dynamically typed, and a tool named *Dialyzer* can be used to find not only type errors, but also other problems. To give the tool a hint which type was meant to be implemented with special attributes or directives, see Example 15-28.

Example 15-28.

```
1    -module (specifications).
2    -compile(export_all).
3
4    -type returnvalue() :: {ok} | {error}.
5    -export_type([returnvalue/0]).
6
7    -spec numberfunction(number()) -> returnvalue().
8    numberfunction(T) ->
9      case T of
10       42 -> {ok};
11       _ -> {error}
12    end.
```

You define a type on line 4. It is called `returnvalue` and is a tuple with two possible values, `{ok}` and `{error}`. Exporting this type (line 5) makes this type available in other modules.

On line 7, you define a specification for a function called `numberfunction` which takes a number as an argument and returns your newly defined custom type, `returnvalue`. The last lines of the example show the implementation. The module compiles fine and you can call it as shown in Example 15-29.

Example 15-29.

```
1    1> specifications:numberfunction({1}).
2    {error}
```

Your call does not pass a number as defined in the specification; at least the return value is `{error}` to indicate something is wrong. You have defined a contract, but at runtime this contract is not checked. There are other ways to catch the error, for example with guards, but you don't want to have too much defensive code.

In Elixir we can implement the same example as shown in Example 15-30.

Example 15-30.

```
1    defmodule Specifications do
2      @type returnvalue :: {:ok} | {:error}
3      @spec numberfunction(number) :: returnvalue
4
5      def numberfunction(t) do
6        case t do
7          42 -> {:ok}
8          _ -> {:error}
9        end
10     end
11   end
```

Whatever you throw at `numberfunction`, it will always return `{:error}` if the argument is not *42*. Chapter tk explains how to use specifications to detect type errors in Erlang and Elixir.

Atoms

Atoms are a confusing concept for many people, although they are implemented in OO programming languages with different syntax and names. The overall term for atoms is *symbols*.

Sometimes atoms are thought of as a special form of constants. In Erlang and Elixir, we can define constants with macros, but in difference to atoms they are processed at compile time and have a value besides their name that is expanded into the code.

For an Erlang example, see Example 15-31.

Example 15-31.

```
1  -define(LIMIT, 10000).
2  -define(FONT, "Courier")
```

For Elixir, see Example 15-32.

Example 15-32.

```
1  defmacro limit do
2    10000
3  end
4
5  defmacro font do
6   "Courier"
7  end
```

Atoms are similar to enumerable in other languages; for example in C++, it looks like Example 15-33.

Example 15-33.

```
1  enum AfricanAnimal
2  {
3      Lion = -3,
4      Hyena, // assigned -2
5      Giraffe, // assigned -1
6      Hippo = 5,
7      Buffalo = 5, // shares same value as Hippo
8      Antilope // assigned 6
9  };
```

The implementation of atoms in the Erlang VM is geared towards fast access with a lookup table in memory and the value as number, but it is not possible to get the value, which is only used internally.

In Erlang, every "variable" with a lowercase first character is an atom, but it is also possible to define atoms with any characters as long as they are enclosed in single or double quotes; see Example 15-34.

Example 15-34.

```
1  dog.
2  2dogs.
3  dog_with_collar.
4  "DOG".
5  theDog.
```

```
6    '453627'.
7    "&*$%".
```

Elixir defines atoms with colon as prefix and can have lowercase and uppercase characters and certain special characters (_,!,@). Other combinations need to be enclosed in quotes. See Example 15-35.

Example 15-35.

```
1    :dog
2    :"2dogs"
3    :dog_with_collar
4    :DOG
5    :theDog
6    :'453627' # => "453627"
7    :"&*$%"
```

The atom lookup table is implemented in C[5] and can hold up to 1GB of atoms, with one atom having a maximum of 255 characters. Running the function memory() in an Erlang shell reveals, among other information, the space atoms use. See Example 15-36.

Example 15-36.

```
1    1> memory().
2    [{total,16300408},
3     {processes,4234480},
4     {processes_used,4233360},
5     {system,12065928},
6     {atom,194289},
7     {atom_used,172278},
8     {binary,124384},
9     {code,4173842},
10    {ets,284464}]
```

Even a shell without any application running uses a few MB for atoms the system defines. Examples are *false, true,* and others like the atoms in the tuples the *memory* function prints out.

It is possible to create atoms dynamically at runtime with the Erlang function list_to_atom or with the Elixir function String.to_atom. This is not encouraged because the atom table is limited and atoms are not garbage collected, so memory leaks could be the result.

---

[5]https://github.com/erlang/otp/blob/e1489c448b7486cdcfec6a89fea238d88e6ce2f3/erts/emulator/beam/atom.c

CHAPTER 16

■ ■ ■

Code Structuring Concepts

Separation of Concerns

A *separation of concerns* is an old concept, probably coined by E. W. Dijkstra[1] in 1974. It means, in general interpretation, that one computational unit should be concerned with only one functionality.

In the past (and I hope not to see it again), we have seen *spaghetti code* in Assembler or Basic where everything was in one file, so runtime it jumped around from one line to another far away in the source code. The debugging and maintenance cost of such programs is high; sometimes it was cheaper to rebuild the program in a different language.

To counter this problem, we have separation of concerns in different ways:

- The simplest form is a function. It separates one computation from another in theory, but it can easily be abused by putting everything that needs to be computed into one function and branch with *if/else* statements.

- In C and later C++, we have file-based imports with includes of header files, compiling corresponding C/C++ files and linking them all together. These files may have the implementation for only one concern, but it can be a mix of more concerns.

- The next step is to create modules and wrap functions in them. Files in C do this, but lack the namespace to avoid name conflicts.

- OO defines types as classes to wrap state and behavior. Classes in Java or C# have and are namespaces because functions outside of classes are not allowed. This goes so far as to create classes for general functionality. I am sure many of the readers have seen these types named *General* or *Constants*.

- Recently, we have seen the extension of separation of concern to services. While 15 years ago we had services with huge functionality and lots of overhead with calling protocols like SOAP, the trend nowadays goes to small services with clearly defined functionality, called *microservices*.

Erlang and Elixir provide a modular approach with *modules* (implementation) and *processes* (runtime).

In Erlang, the compilation is dependent on the file name and each module lives in its own file. If you run the code in Example 16-1 in a shell, you need to have a file named sayhello.erl in the current directory the shell runs in, but also the module name (with -module) defined as sayhello.

---

[1] www.cs.utexas.edu/users/EWD/transcriptions/EWD04xx/EWD447.html

© Wolfgang Loder 2016

W. Loder, *Erlang and Elixir for Imperative Programmers*, DOI 10.1007/978-1-4842-2394-9_16

Example 16-1.

```
1   Erlang/OTP 18 [erts-7.1] [source] [64-bit] [smp:8:8] [async-threads:10] [hipe] [\
2   kernel-poll:false] [dtrace]
3
4   Eshell V7.1 (abort with ^G)
5   1> c(sayhello).
6   {ok,sayhello}
```

If you change the module name (but not the file name) to sayhello2, you get the error shown in
Example 16-2. You can find the full code of sayhello.erl in Chapter 9.

Example 16-2.

```
1   Erlang/OTP 18 [erts-7.1] [source] [64-bit] [smp:8:8] [async-threads:10] [hipe] [\
2   kernel-poll:false] [dtrace]
3
4   Eshell V7.1 (abort with ^G)
5   1> c(sayhello).
6   sayhello.beam: Module name 'sayhello2' does not match file name 'sayhello'
7   error
```

Elixir relaxes the naming rules and the module name can be different from the file name.

Separation of concerns is only one side of the coin. Having many small computational units makes it
necessary to have a means of composing these units. Examples are UNIX tools piping or *fluent interfaces* that
take one type of data, process it, and return the processed data.

The Erlang VM is built on the premise of running modules in processes that are not OS processes. With
OTP, these processes can then be composed into bigger units like applications. Again, modules in Erlang
and Elixir can be abused by packing too much functionality into one module.

Up to now I have not defined what a *concern* actually is. As with many definitions in software
development, the answer is a little bit fuzzy and depends on the scope. For many, *functionality* is the main
separator, for example data store access or business logic.

Despite the differences in definitions, the advantages seem to be clear cut. Smaller and functionally
restricted units, whether modules or functions or anything else, reduce coupling between parts of the code
and make it easier to test, debug, understand, and maintain code.

SOA

The term *service-oriented architecture* (SOA) got a bad name a decade and more ago. SOA at that time
was bound to SOAP and at the end everything got out of hand. It became a service protocol that could do
everything, but then other services like discovery services or the infamous ESB (enterprise service bus) were
needed. The big companies could sell training and consultation in addition to complicated systems. In the
end, this concept failed.

For me, SOA is not this Big Bang approach. It was always a service that is doing exactly one thing. In
the spirit of *separation of concerns*, we don't want one service for everything. For example, we implement
a communication service, and I am guilty of doing this, that does e-mail, SMS, and has other features,
and then somebody wants to integrate other social media. Eventually the code needs to be changed
to accommodate everything and it is likely that we will introduce new bugs, not to mention internal
dependencies that are difficult to test.

Nowadays there is a new buzzword: *microservices*. Is it clear what a microservice is? I don't think so. We have some microservice architectures with thousands of services and others with a handful. I am not sure if the management of thousands of services is easier than the big services from the past (and the present, in many cases). Often, the microservice architecture is used to solve a people-and-management problem. Each microservice is run by one team; they code, deploy, and maintain the service. The concept is not fully worked out yet, and I stick to the definition of SOA as an architecture of small services that work together to solve a problem. Architecture and design questions decide the granularity of the processes.

Microservice implementations need loose coupling of services, scalability of individual services, and distribution over machines. Erlang with OTP supports this concept of scaleable services communicating with messages. It also defines its own protocol to pass data between its nodes and processes, so there is no need to use more verbose protocols like JSON.

This said, the introduction of microservices may not always be the best way, because it can also introduce coordination costs. Sometimes libraries are the better approach for small projects that don't need to scale in the foreseeable future. Also, front-end code won't have access to the internal protocol, so there will be an additional layer to translate that into something the front-end code can understand, most likely JSON.

Actor Model

The Actor Model is an important pattern in Erlang/OTP and Elixir where actors are implemented as lightweight and operating system-independent *processes*.

Before we go into details, let's look at the original definition of the Actor Model by Carl Hewitt[2]. There are three axioms in this model and a valid implementation of the Actor Model must satisfy the following axioms:

I. An actor can create more actors.

II. An actor can send messages to known actors, including itself.

III. An actor can make local decisions and can select how to handle the next message.

A generic model looks like Figure 16-1.

---

[2]https://arxiv.org/pdf/1008.1459.pdf

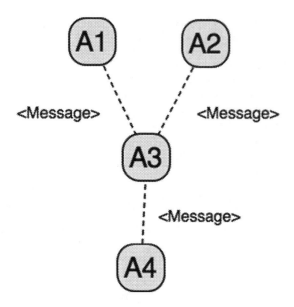

Figure 16-1. *Actor Model, generic*

This diagram is simple, because the Actor Model is simple in its raw form. Please note the following:

- The model does not specify where an actor gets the knowledge about other actors from.

- Actors send messages to each other directly. If there was a channel facilitating communication between actors, it would be an actor.

- Messages are received in any order and there is no guarantee in the model that messages sent will arrive at the receiving actor. The message will be sent once and the time until arrival is not determined.

- Actors have addresses. Conceptually an address is a capability of an actor to send messages only.

- If an actor sends a message to itself, it can do so using *futures* or *promises* to avoid deadlocks. A simple definition of a *future* is that it is a wrapper around a computation result that will or will not be valid in future time. If you think now of a *Monad*, you are not far off, but I won't go into details in this book.

- The *address-to-actor* relationship is in relational terms a *m-n* relationship. One actor can have many addresses and one address can point to many actors. The consequence is that it is not possible to determine the number of actors in a system at any given time by counting addresses.

- Following from the last note, an address is not an identity of an actor.

Sometimes the Actor Model is described as being *non-deterministic*, but according to Hewitt[3] this is not correct. Non-determinism means that there are two rules that refer to the same input and imply two different outputs. In pseudocode,

---

[3]https://channel9.msdn.com/Shows/Going+Deep/Hewitt-Meijer-and-Szyperski-The-Actor-Model-everything-you-wanted-to-know-but-were-afraid-to-ask

if x then do a

if x then do b

The system can only decide by guessing, flipping a coin, or similar methods. This is not happening in the Actor Model, which is *indeterministic*. An actor can decide with deterministic rules, but the arrival time and order of messages can't be determined. For example, an actor can send a stop message to itself, but there is no way to say when it will arrive, and another message could be processed before the stop message.

More rules:

- The Actor Model does not say anything about the state of the system.

- The Actor Model does not say anything about side effects.

- The Actor Model is designed to decentralize computation.

- The Actor Model is based on the physical world and not on Algebra.

- The Actor Model does not specify how or if messages are stored in an actor.

- A requirement for the Actor Model to work is that latency is very small in order to minimize time between sending and receiving messages.

So far, this is the description of the conceptual Actor Model.

There were many efforts to implement the model in a language or library, including Java and C#. If you search for Actor Model on the Internet you will find many discussions about pure and impure implementations, right and wrong, programming paradigm ideology, and so on. This is why I will not comment if Erlang is actually implementing the Actor Model or if that implementation is correct. Common opinion is that Erlang/OTP has an implementation of the Actor Model with processes as actors. A process can be anything from a full blown web server to a small computational unit that provides, for example, a random number. There are also *nodes* in OTP, which are distributed processes and are controlled by a supervisor. See Figure 16-2.

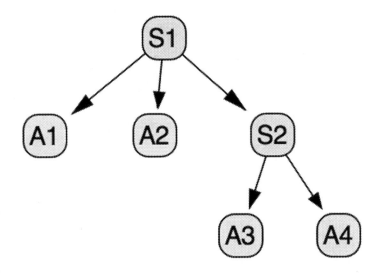

Figure 16-2. Erlang/OTP, supervisor

An example is the Digital Asset Repository that is discussed in this book. It has a number of client-facing nodes that process and maintain web sockets/TCP connections and distribute worker nodes. See Figure 16-3.

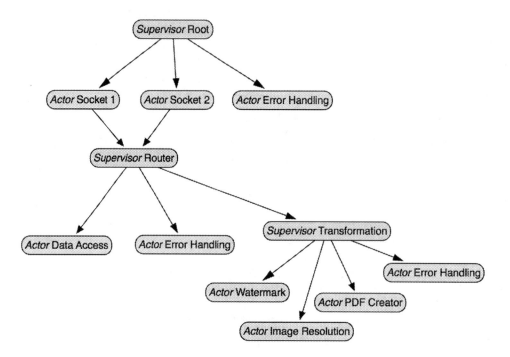

Figure 16-3. *Actor Model, example*

Processes do not share state in memory, but they change state and pass it around in messages or persist it for general access. This implies that state needs to be identifiable. For example, having a socket open with a client creates a state that identifies this client connection in a unique way within the system.

If the system is designed properly, then no deadlock or other concurrency problems are possible. A proper architecture design and implementation is also necessary to achieve maximum concurrency performance.

Erlang's, and Elixir's, implementation of the Actor Model is based on the premises of having a fault tolerant and reliable system that performs at its optimum in distributed systems with lightweight processes as actors and message pass between them without sharing any data beyond the message contents.

Specific to Generic

The concept of *specific to generic* is heavily used in OTP and comes from an experience many developers had and have. During our programming lives we come into situations when we implement some function or class and then later realize that we need this code elsewhere. Of course, we don't want to copy, so we refactor it into a more generic class, function, module, library, or other construct.

The reason is to be able to reuse code. The downside is that the more generic code has to cover different uses cases, and we may end up with more code and configuration work than expected. In fact, this book uses this concept by presenting specific implementations in Part 4 and then tries to extract and describe generic concepts in Part 5.

In OOP, we may implement a factory pattern and push specialized code into a class to retrieve polymorphic types. We can also use interfaces to define a generic behavior that needs to be implemented by the consumer in a specific way. Erlang/Elixir/OTP does the latter with generic servers and defining *behaviors*. Example 16-3 defines a gen_server in Erlang.

Example 16-3.

```
1    -module(genservertemplate).
2
3    -behaviour(gen_server).
4
5    -export([start_link/0]).
6    -export([init/1,  handle_call/3,  handle_cast/2,  handle_info/2]).
7    -export([code_change/3]).
8    -export([stop/0, terminate/2]).
```

The implementation needs to implement and export all callbacks defined by the behavior; see Example 16-4.

Example 16-4.

```
1    terminate(normal, _State) ->
2      ok;
3    terminate(shutdown, _State) ->
4      ok;
5    terminate({shutdown, _Reason}, _State) ->
6      ok;
7    terminate(_Reason, _State) ->
8      ok.
```

This example only shows the implementation of different function signatures of the callback `terminate`. The code does not need to think about how the server is actually stopped; it is just concerned with cleaning up specific processes that have been used. In this example, it just returns *ok*.

The two parts, definition and implementation, can reside in different modules and separate specific from generic for easier maintenance. The gen_ templates in OTP are the result of the refactoring by many people over a long time and are best practices that have been successfully used. Further, it is possible to define custom behaviors and create other generic templates for server or other needs.

OTP helps to implement complicated designs. One disadvantage with using templates certainly is that developers may not understand the underlying concepts and implementations. On the other side, there are built-in functionalities in the generic templates like logging or statistics that come for free and don't need to be implemented for every project.

Fault Tolerance

Erlang propagates the *let it crash* approach, which does not sound very fault tolerant. In fact, it seems to be the opposite. What does fault tolerance mean regarding data and processes?

- The user does not care if data is lost, so nothing needs to be done from the user's point of view.

- The user has no chance of knowing if data is lost.

- Data can easily be recreated.

- Processes are isolated from each other with their own state and can be restarted without downtime.

There are certainly other scenarios regarding hardware or network failures, but in general it comes down to data consistency and computing processes availability. In OOP, we program defensively to check various failure situations in code at runtime. Not doing this reduces code, but also increases the chance of crashes or expensive exceptions.

Erlang and Elixir are based on sending messages between processes, which is intrinsically error-prone in distributed and concurrent systems. Without further measurements, failures would not be found. OTP provides the concept of supervising nodes and restart failing nodes or node trees. Messages are kept in queues on each process, so a restarting process will also delete its queue contents and with them all pending messages.

Every project has to define its own fault tolerance. Let's examine a few scenarios and possible solutions in Erlang and Elixir.

Message services like *Twitter* and *WhatsApp* are eventually consistent systems by default. The sender of a message does not know if and when the message arrives. Of course, these services do not want to be seen as losing messages, so they need to have software or hardware solutions to avoid this.

In Erlang/OTP, we can augment the default mechanisms with additional queues or message locking in redundant data stores. We can have a supervisor that sends all messages to another supervisor that runs processes for these tasks; see Figure 16-4.

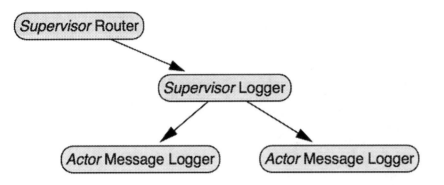

Figure 16-4. *Logger*

Timeouts on the client side and acknowledgement messages from the first process in the back-end system give the user at least some security if a message had arrived. Other messages to the client can notify if an intended recipient has received a direct message. For example, e-mail systems have done this on demand.

In cases of failures, it may be possible to retrieve the not-processed messages from the backup queue and process them if no timeout was hit. When a message is processed, it may be necessary to avoid duplicate processing, so the system has to handle this.

Transactional systems like banking applications can't afford to lose requests. In this scenario, all the mechanisms of the last scenario are valid, but in addition three may be the logging of events, called *event sourcing*. Event data is stored and can be used to play back events if the system crashes. Erlang/OTP processes can use the replicated data store Mnesia[4] , which is part of OTP, to implement this.

As in other scenarios, it is a good design to have small supervised services that do only one thing and can be easily scaled. When they fail, they are replaced by a new instance without side effects.

Processes

Processes in the Erlang VM do not mean operating system processes or threads; rather they sit on top of them.

In an Erlang shell, we can see all processes of a VM and info about them; see Example 16-5.

---

[4]http://erlang.org/doc/man/mnesia.html

Example 16-5.

```
1> rp(registered())
[user,inets_sup,user_drv,erlangexamples_server,
 erlangexamples_sup,code_server,application_controller,
 standard_error,sasl_sup,erl_prim_loader,httpd_sup,
 rebar_agent,kernel_safe_sup,erts_code_purger,inet_db,
 release_handler,tls_connection_sup,ssl_sup,alarm_handler,
 rex,standard_error_sup,global_group,tftp_sup,kernel_sup,
 sasl_safe_sup,global_name_server,httpc_rebar,file_server_2,
 ssl_manager,error_logger,httpc_sup,init,disk_log_sup,
 httpc_profile_sup,disk_log_server,httpc_manager,
 httpc_handler_sup,ssl_listen_tracker_sup,ftp_sup]
ok
2> erlang:process_info(whereis(erlangexamples_server), memory).
{memory,2848}
3> erlang:process_info(whereis(erlangexamples_sup),    memory).
{memory,2888}
4> erlang:process_info(whereis(sasl_sup),    memory).
{memory,7080}
```

The function `registered()` lists all functions in the VM. Then you ask for the memory footprint of some processes. The output is in bytes and you can see that the notion of lightweight processes in Erlang is valid. *SASL* is the support libraries app with support for error handling and it is a bit bigger. All the values include stack and heap.

Erlang's efficiency guide[5] speaks of 338 words of memory footprint for a process, including 233 words heap. A *word* is 8 bytes on 64-bit systems.

It is easy to create and terminate a process at runtime. You did this in your introductory example, shown in Example 16-6, called SayHello.

Example 16-6.

```
spawn(sayhello, say_hello, ["Hello", 2, InitNode]).
```

When a process does not have code to execute anymore, it will terminate itself. When a process terminates, it gives a reason; without error this will be the atom *normal*. You can initiate termination in code by calling `exit` or `erlang:error`. In supervised OTP applications, processes may also get exit messages with a reason different from *normal* and then it either handles this situation itself or terminates itself. This way an error bubbles up to the highest supervisor in the supervisor tree, which can then decide what to do based on the configured supervisor strategy.

SayHello also shows the registration of processes; see Example 16-7.

Example 16-7.

```
register(precipient, spawn(sayhello, recipient, [])).
```

A name, in this case `precipient`, is associated with the process and saved in a network global data store. The function `whereis` returns the process id (PID); see Example 16-8.

---

[5]http://erlang.org/doc/efficiency_guide/advanced.html#id68294

Example 16-8.

```
1> whereis(precipient).
<0.115.0>
```

In Chapter 8, you looked at monitoring processes.

Concurrency

Concurrent systems are sometimes confused with parallel systems. When you prepare your breakfast, you may put cereal in a bowl, set up milk on the stove to heat it up, and put water into the kettle to boil it for tea. All this is done seemingly at the same time, but in fact you do it time slices; you do it concurrently. The kettle and the milk heating on the stove are done at the same time, in parallel.

The first graphical user interfaces, running on one CPU with one core, tried to trick us into thinking that they worked parallel, but in fact the time slice was so short that we did not realize it was concurrent.

A more computer scientific definition of concurrency is that it is concerned with a *nondeterministic composition* of programs. We may have a number of processes or threads working together on one problem, but their behavior is not deterministic. From outside we can't say at any given time when one process is working, finished, or starting. For example, an actor in an Actor Model system can change behavior according to incoming messages. In a banking application, one actor may be responsible for payouts. We may have one actor for each customer that approves paying out money and there may come a message that the customer is overdrawn. Next time the actor's behavior will be that no money will be paid out to the customer. We can't say, apart from studying log files later, which state the actor is in.

Parallelism, on the other hand, is concerned with *asymptotic efficiency* of programs with *deterministic* behavior. We know that deterministic, asymptotic efficiency means that a system tends towards efficiency, for example a computer system with given internal memory and CPU. Parallel execution of programs will try to make the best use of the machine, since it knows that all the programs are deterministic and they don't change input and output. The *manager* of this system can try to make this execution parallel and as efficient as possible.

The Erlang VM uses concurrency with actors, called processes, which pass messages to other actors and share no data and also no code. This concept is not unique to Erlang, though. Many architectures of systems implemented in any language try to decouple processes or threads with message systems by using queues or, less efficient, data stores to invoke indirectly pieces of code. In addition, Erlang's and OTP's architecture is meant to be asynchronous; "meant to be" because it is possible to implement a completely synchronous and blocking solution, for example, with RPC calls.

Interesting side note: Joe Armstrong mixes *concurrent* and *parallel* in his discussion about red and green callbacks[6], so the distinction may just be academic.

Flow-Based Programming

Flow-based programming (FBP) was invented by J. Paul Morrison[7] who was working as an engineer at IBM. I mention this concept here because it is related to functional programming, the Actor Model, and Erlang's processes, but it is also related to hardware design with electronic components. I recommend looking into the free-to-read first edition of the book[8] *Flow-Based Programming*, written in the 90s with ideas going back to the 70s.

---

[6]http://joearms.github.io/2013/04/02/Red-and-Green-Callbacks.html
[7]www.jpaulmorrison.com/fbp/
[8]www.jpaulmorrison.com/fbp/book.pdf

The basic concept is simple; see Figure 16-5.

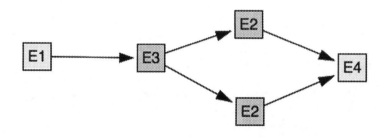

Figure 16-5. *FBP*

Data flows from *E1* to *E4* passing through *E3* and, in our example, two *E2* that are running concurrently. The ideas of the concept are

- The design is data-based and describes the *flow* of the data from one *entity* to another *entity*.

- The *entities* are black boxes and can be processes, functions, or similar.

- Every *entity* has a number of *in-ports* and *out-ports*.

- *Entities* can be accessed concurrently and have no side effects.

- The connections between *entities* are well defined.

FBP is a concept and there are several implementations, some programmed by Morrison himself. In fact, he still develops FBP for several programming languages and publishes the implementations on GitHub[9].

As mentioned, the *entities* are self-contained processes as we know it, for example from Erlang, and the connection can be a message. The process needs to be able to interpret the message and work on the data. When a FBP system is designed, it creates a network (in fact, a graph) of connected *black boxes*. This approach goes so far that the black-box processes are delivered in compiled form in some implementations to ensure that they cannot be changed. The only interface is the ports in and out; not necessarily only one of each, but as many as needed for different use cases.

It is interesting that the creation of this concept is rooted in the critique of the von Neumann system. Even 40 years ago, the problems with that architecture were obvious, first in the mainframe world and then later in the PC world. The problems have to do with the paradigm of running synchronously through instructions to manipulate memory locations. A component-based approach like FBP creates many independent von Neumann-machines and assembles them into a system where those components can run independently from each other in a concurrent architecture built on several CPUs or CPU cores.

The concept has more features than listed in these few paragraphs; you can read about them in the mentioned book. There are current implementations available, for example in JavaScript[10], and it will be interesting if an Erlang/Elixir implementation of this concept surfaces in the future.

---

[9]https://github.com/jpaulm/csharpfbp
[10]http://noflojs.org/

Where To Go From Here?

Elixir is built on top of Erlang's syntax and claims to make it better and easier to use the Erlang/OTP system. This is more or less an individual decision and most probably also driven by the language someone learned first. My personal opinion is that the syntax is not a big divider; there are strange constructs in each language. As somebody who used C/C++ professionally for more than 10 years in the 80s and 90s, I can't be "scared" by syntax anymore.

The Elixir community has absorbed some of the *Ruby* and *Ruby on Rails* community and it shows in the efforts to bring many of Rails goodies to Elixir's libraries. This is not necessarily a bad thing, but focuses heavily on web projects.

The current development world has a heterogeneous approach, and monolithic frameworks seem to be pushed to the background. Have a look at Figure 16-6.

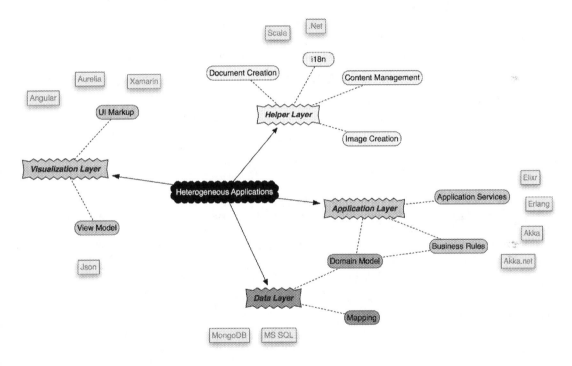

Figure 16-6. *Heterogeneous system*

My own work has included all of these technologies over the last years and architectures like SOA (or in its "modern" form, microservices) support this heterogeneous approach. An API does not care if it is accessed by a phone, a desktop, a gaming console, or anything else as long as the supported protocols are obeyed. The Erlang VM world with Elixir, Erlang, and other[11] languages[12] that sit on top of the VM support the idea of being language agnostic, similar to the JavaScript world where several languages like TypeScript, ClosureScript, or Elm are transpiling to vanilla JavaScript.

---

[11]http://lfe.io
[12]http://efene.org

Elixir and Erlang provide the technology suited for back-end processes, being excellent for dealing with concurrency and fault tolerance and fitting into this heterogenous world. The web framework *Phoenix* makes web application development in many aspects easy and makes use of all the Elixir features available.

There are differences between Erlang and Elixir:

- Erlang was not built to handle strings, so Elixir's string library is a nice wrapper around this.

- Elixir's protocols are a nod towards *interfaces* in imperative languages. They are not the same, but bring polymorphism to the language.

- *Mix* provides a modern project management tool. The Erlang community has responded with Rebar3, which has improvements compared to the older versions. Hopefully the tools will converge eventually and in future it won't make a difference if the source of a package is Elixir or Erlang.

Elixir also goes beyond the Erlang/OTP base:

- GenStage is a new generic server that does not have a counterpart in Erlang/OTP.

- Generic servers have default implementations of callbacks without the need to implement all of them.

- Assigned variables appear mutable by allowing reassignments with the same name.

- Many helper functions for enumerable are provided.

- Macros are an integral part of the language (and sometimes they are used to implement language constructs).

It seems that Elixir is progressing on a way to reduce the 1:1 relation to Erlang, hopefully without making it impossible to mix Erlang and Elixir modules. Of course, Erlang itself is not standing still, although on a much slower pace than Elixir.

This accelerated pace of Elixir also made it difficult to keep up with and adjust the contents of the book. During the last months the tendency in my own implementation was to move more to Elixir. This is also reflected in the code that accompanies this book. A year ago, more Erlang libraries were part of the solution; now it's down to one.

When I started the book I hoped to discuss more tools and features. Unfortunately they did not make it into this book, for example:

- Containers

- Releases

- Continuous integration and delivery (scripts, third-party services)

- Distributed deployments with cloud services

- Streaming

- Security

We will see what the coming months and years bring for the Erlang/Elixir/OTP ecosystem. There are many developers in the community now, and many more will join in future. The development of Elixir is open, so it lies with every developer who uses the language to determine where it will go.

APPENDIX A

■ ■ ■

Modeling

Modeling and designing: developers love it or hate it. Many fall into the latter category.

However, if a few developers are sitting together and are discussing a software problem, most probably one will get up to draw on a whiteboard. It may not be pure UML, but it will be some "dialect" everyone in the room agrees on.

A study about UML use[1] concludes that a big percentage of the developers that were interviewed in the study do not use UML at all, although they consider alternatives. The group interviewed is too small to draw broader conclusions, but it correlates with my own experience. Most projects I have worked on did not use any modeling, apart from informal diagrams drawn on a whiteboard. Sometimes fellow developers almost aggressively argued against the use of any modeling.

For me, modeling is a way to sort my thoughts before starting development, but also to formalize requirements, design, deployment, and similar. I use modeling *before* writing code. Once the circle of writing tests, coding, and refactoring starts, keeping lower-level designs up-to-date is very cumbersome. There may be updated versions of diagrams before major deployment to go hand in hand with documentation, but this is rather the exception than the norm.

Modeling and UML or similar are very much rooted in the object-oriented programming world. Not many of us used real concurrent programming, not to speak of modeling such systems. UML and derivates can handle many different paradigms if not applied rigorously and with the goal in mind to show designs in a clear and understandable way.

Erlang/OTP is all about processes, which are essentially implementations of actors in the sense of the Actor Model. Processes are only one layer; the implementation of the actors themselves is done in a functional way. OOP with sending messages between objects is modeled top-down; functional composition is modeled bottom-up.

In any case, development starts with requirements, which can be easily expressed in UML. The example is taken from this book, based on this sentence in the prose requirements:

During the retrieval of images, a transformation provides smaller, low resolution images, and the full resolution image is only accessed on demand.

Let's first examine the OO model.

You need a *transform component* that simply takes an instance of an image object, processes it, and outputs another instance of an image object. See Figure A-1.

---

[1]http://oro.open.ac.uk/35805/8/UML%20in%20practice%208.pdf

© Wolfgang Loder 2016

W. Loder, *Erlang and Elixir for Imperative Programmers*, DOI 10.1007/978-1-4842-2394-9

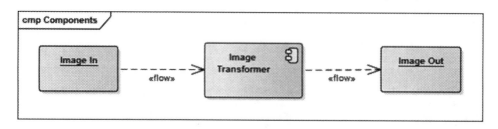

Figure A-1. *Transform component*

The model for the transformer is shown in Figure A-2.

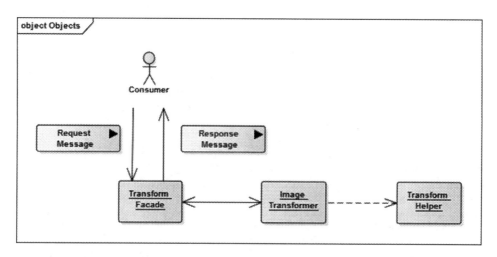

Figure A-2. *Transform objects*

The component receives a request message, processes it, and then sends back a response message. This model shows a `facade` and a `helper` class supporting the actual `transformer`. The implementation could be different without affecting the consumer of this component, which only knows the messages as the interface to the component.

In OO, there will be a class diagram with properties and methods and interaction diagrams to show how these classes work together.

How can you translate this into Erlang/OTP/Elixir? You don't!

Instead, let's look for the functions you need to implement this feature. See Figure A-3.

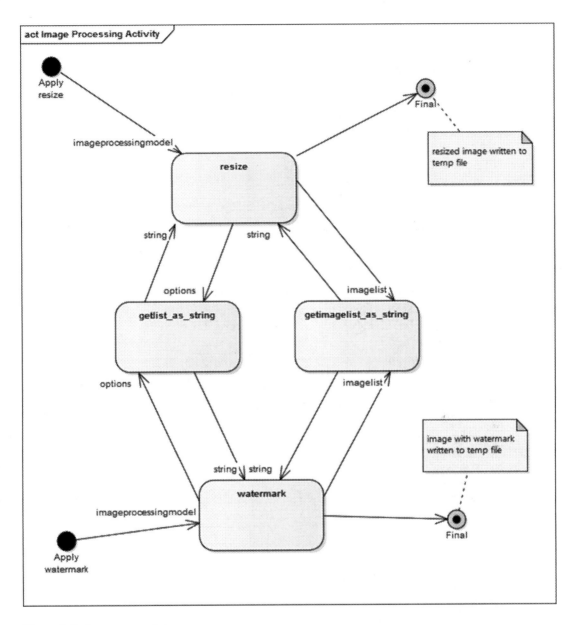

Figure A-3. *Image processing*

This diagram assumes that an external program is used that writes processed images to temporary files, for example *ImageMagick*. You use an activity diagram where functions are shown as activities and control flows indicate input and output parameters. The two main functions, resize and watermark, have two helpers (getlist_as_string and getimagelist_as_string) to provide the parameters in a form the external program understands. Both helper functions return a string as input for the external program and have themselves as input internal models, *option* and *imagelist*. An example of an option string would be *"30% -gravity south"* and an example of an imageless string would be *"image.png logo.jpg image_watermark.jpg"*.

The functions process a type `imageprocessingmodel`, as shown in Figure A-4.

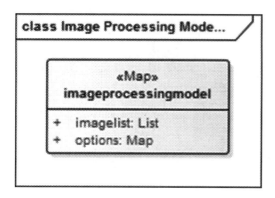

Figure A-4. *Image processing model type*

This is a simple class diagram and it displays the elements as attributes. The stereotype `<<Map>>` gives you the hint that you may implement this model as a type `map`.

The last step is to define the higher level processes (or actors) that are implementing the image processing functions; see Figure A-5.

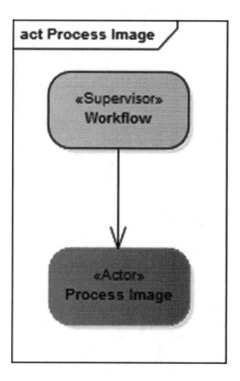

Figure A-5. *Workflow actors*

This just says that there is a workflow process that supervises (among others) the worker/actor *Process Image*. Figure A-6 shows more details.

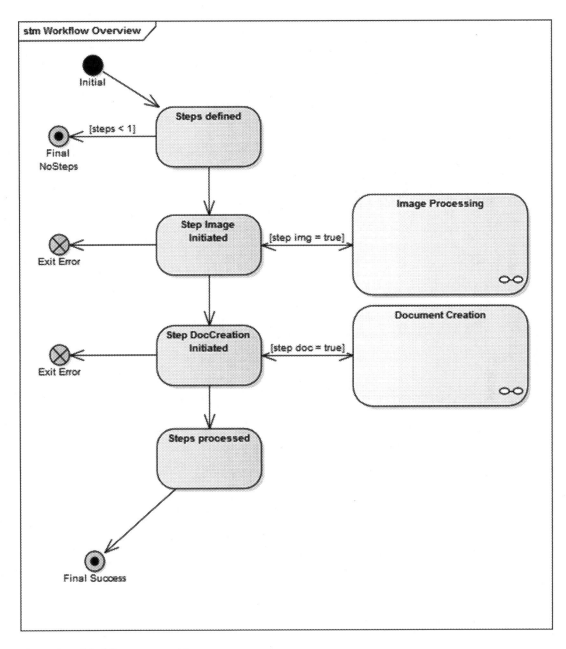

Figure A-6. *Workflow state machine*

You see that the workflow is a state machine and calls into another state machine called *Image Processing*, as shown in Figure A-7.

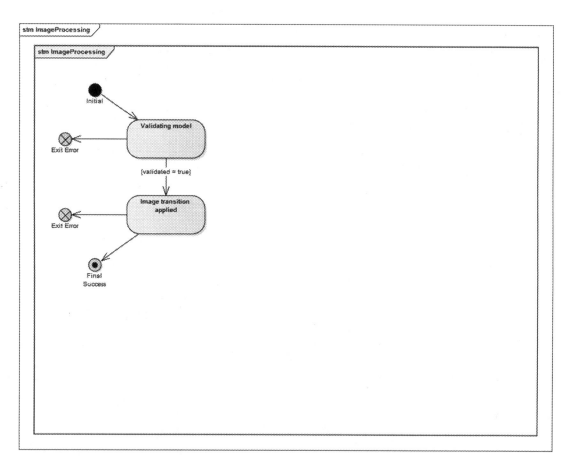

Figure A-7. *Image Processing State Machine*

This state machine is implemented with the functions in the above diagram, *Image Processing*. You are not detailing if an OTP concept is used or not. As said at the top of this appendix, I use modeling to make the initial design in an easy way. Going deeper is most of the time not necessary because code is documenting the implementation (and, sometimes, documentation in source code files explains further details).

In other parts of the book, I use diagrams to show requirements and I also use use-case diagrams. These together with the diagrams discussed here make it possible to describe a system that uses Erlang and Elixir.

Resources

Erlang: www.erlang.org
Elixir: http://elixir-lang.org
List on GitHub: Awesome Elixir: https://github.com/h4cc/awesome-elixir
List on GitHub: Awesome Erlang: https://github.com/drobakowski/awesome-erlang
Erldocs (searchable Erlang documentation): http://erldocs.com
Erlang Central: http://erlangcentral.org
Erlang Solutions, Downloads: www.erlang-solutions.com/resources/download.html
Libraries.io Elixir: https://libraries.io/languages/Elixir

Books

Armstrong, Joe. *Programming Erlang*, 2nd Edition. Pragmatic Programmers, 2013.
Ballou, Kenny. *Learning Elixir*. Packt Publishing, 2016.
Eisenberg, J. David. *Études for Erlang*. O'Reilly Media, 2013.
Eisenberg, J. David. *Études for Elixir*. O'Reilly Media, 2014.
Jurić, Saša. *Elixir in Action*. Manning Publications, 2015.
McCord, Chris. *Metaprogramming Elixir*. Pragmatic Programmers, 2015.
Pereira, Paulo A. *Elixir Cookbook*. Packt Publishing, 2015.
Thomas, Dave. *Programming Elixir 1.2*. Pragmatic Programmers, 2016.
Vinoski, Steve and Francesco Cesarini. *Designing for Scalability with Erlang/OTP*. O'Reilly Media, 2016.

Articles and Papers

Armstrong, Joe. "A History of Erlang." 2007, http://dl.acm.org/citation.cfm?id=1238850&dl=ACM&coll=D
L&CFID=495241682&CFTOKEN=12700222

Online Learning

Learn You Some Erlang: http://learnyousomeerlang.com
Elixir School: https://elixirschool.com

© Wolfgang Loder 2016   239
W. Loder, *Erlang and Elixir for Imperative Programmers*, DOI 10.1007/978-1-4842-2394-9

Blogs

Plataformatec Elixir: `http://blog.plataformatec.com.br/tag/elixi/`
The Erlangelist: `www.theerlangelist.com`
Joe Armstrong: `http://joearms.github.io`
Robert Virding: `http://rvirding.blogspot.com`
Erlang Solutions: `www.erlang-solutions.com/blog.html`

Fora

Elixir Forum: `https://elixirforum.com`
Reddit Erlang: `www.reddit.com/r/erlang/`
Reddit Elixir: `www.reddit.com/r/elixir/`
Slack Erlang: `http://erlanger.slack.com`
Slack Elixir: `http://elixir-lang.slack.com`

■ ■ ■

Features/Framework/Concepts Matrix

This diagram shows all features, concepts, and patterns used and described in this book. Dotted lines indicate a relationship within a group, directed lines with arrows indicate usage.

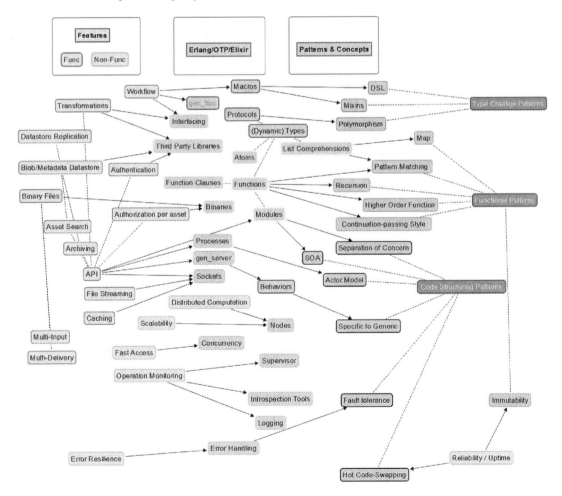

Figure C-1. *Feature/Framework/Concepts Matrix*

© Wolfgang Loder 2016
W. Loder, *Erlang and Elixir for Imperative Programmers*, DOI 10.1007/978-1-4842-2394-9

On the left are both functional and non-functional service-features as partly described in **Part 2**. These features use Erlang/OTP/Elixir language constructs for the implementation, which can be seen in the middle of the diagram. The right side shows more generic concepts and patterns and how they are grouped in the chapters of **Part 5**.

■ ■ ■

Quick Guide to Erlang and Elixir

The following code examples show the different syntax of Erlang and Elixir. For more information, Appendix B lists some resources to learn the languages.

Code Comments

Erlang - Comments

```
% Oneline comment or inline comment
%% This should be used to comment functions.
%%% This should be used to comment modules.

% There is no multiline comment construct in Erlang.
```

Elixir - Comments

```
# Oneline comment or inline comment

# Documentation has its own syntax different from comments.

# There is no multiline comment construct in Elixir.
```

Variables

Erlang - Variable

```
% All variable names must start with an uppercase letter.
VarString = "hello world".
```

Elixir - Variable

```
varstring = "hello world"
```

© Wolfgang Loder 2016

W. Loder, *Erlang and Elixir for Imperative Programmers*, DOI 10.1007/978-1-4842-2394-9

Atoms

Erlang - Atom

```
% Atoms start with lowercase characters unless in quotes.
v.
'atom with space'.
is_atom('atom with space'). % -> true
is_atom(false). % -> true
```

Elixir - Atom

```
:v
:"atom with space"
is_atom(:"atom with space") # -> true
is_atom(false) # -> true
```

Data Types

Erlang - String

```
S1 = "hello world".
S2 = [104,101,108,108,111,32,119,111,114,108,100]. % list of integers
S3 = [$h,$e,$l,$l,$o,$ ,$w,$o,$r,$l,$d]. % ASCII values of character
S4 = <<"hello world">>. % one byte per character
```

Elixir - String

```
s1 = "hello world"
s2 = [104,101,108,108,111,32,119,111,114,108,100] # list of integers
s3 = [?h,?e,?l,?l,?o,?\s,?w,?o,?r,?l,?d] # ASCII values of character
s4 = <<"hello world">> # one byte per character
```

Erlang - String Operations

```
S = "hello world".
string:len(S). % -> 11
string:equal(S,"hello"). % -> false
string:concat("hello", " world"). % -> "hello world"
string:tokens(S,[$ ]). % -> ["hello","world"]
string:to_upper(S). % -> "HELLO WORLD"
```

Elixir - String Operations

```
s = "hello world"
String.length(s) # -> 11
String.equivalent?(s,"hello") # -> false
"hello" <> " world" # -> "hello world"
String.split(s) # -> ["hello","world"]
String.upcase(s) # -> "HELLO WORLD"
```

Erlang - Number

```
V1 = 1.0.
V2 = 3.
N1=16#FF. % -> 255; base 16
V1 + V2. % -> 4.0
```

Elixir - Number

```
v1 = 1.0
v2 = 3
n1 = 0xFF # -> 255; base 16
v1 + v2 # -> 4.0
```

Erlang - Binary

```
% Bin is a list of three integers encoded with 8, 8, and 3 bits.
Bin = <<16:8, 1:8, 1:3>>. % -> <<16,1,1:3>>
% BinList is a list of three integers encoded with 8 bits.
BinList = <<16:8,2,1>>. % -> <<16,2,1>>
binary_to_list(BinList). % -> [16,2,1]
```

Elixir - Binary

```
# b1 is a list of three integers encoded with 8, 8, and 3 bits.
b1 = <<16::size(8), 1::size(8), 1::size(3)>> # -> <<16,1,1:3>>
# binlist is a list of three integers encoded with 8 bits.
binlist = <<16::size(8),2,1>> # -> <<16,2,1>>
to_char_list(binlist) # -> [16,2,1]
```

Operators

Erlang - Operators`

```
V1 = 1.0.
V2 = 3.
V3 = 2.
L1 = [1].
L2 = [2,3].
L3 = [2].

V1 == V2. % -> false
V1 + V2. % -> 4.0
V2 rem V3. % -> 1

L1 ++ L2. % -> [1,2,3]
L2 -- L3. % -> [3]
```

Elixir - Operators

```
v1 = 1.0
v2 = 3
v3 = 2
l1 = [1]
l2 = [2,3]
l3 = [2]

v1 == v2 # -> false
v1 + v2 # -> 4.0
rem v2,v3 # -> 1

l1 ++ l2 # -> [1,2,3]
l2 -- l3 # -> [3]
```

Conditionals

Erlang - Conditionals

```
Flag = false.


case Flag of
  true -> 42;
  _ -> 0
end.


if
  Flag =:= true ->
    42;
  true ->
    0
end.
```

Elixir - Conditionals

```
flag = false

case flag do
  true -> 42
  _ -> 0
end

if flag == true do
    42
else
    0
end
```

Pattern Matching

Erlang - Pattern Matching

```
P = {ok,{note,""}}.
{ok,_} = P. % -> {ok,{note,[]}}
{Ret,_} = P. % -> {ok,{note,[]}}
Ret. % -> ok
[] = P. % -> exception error: no match of right hand side value {ok,{note,[]}}
```

Elixir - Pattern Matching

```
p = {:ok,{:note,""}}
{:ok,_} = p # -> {:ok, {:note, ""}}
{ret,_} = p # ->{:ok, {:note, ""}}
ret # -> :ok
[] = p # -> (MatchError) no match of right hand side value: {:ok, {:note, ""}}
```

Guards

Erlang - Guards

```
% Guards in if and case see in section "Conditional"

return_boolean(N) when N =:= 42 -> true;
return_boolean(N) -> false.

FunReturnBoolean =
  fun
    (N) when N =:= 42 -> true;
    (N) -> false
  end.
```

Elixir - Guards

```
# Guards in if and case see in section "Conditional"


def return_boolean(n) when n == 42 do
  true
end
def return_boolean(_n) do
  false
end

def fun_return_boolean() do
  fn n when n == 42 -> true
    n -> false
  end
end
```

Functions

Erlang - Functions

```
F = fun(X,Y) -> X+Y end.
F(1,2). % -> 3
```

Elixir - Functions

```
f = fn(x,y) -> x+y end
f.(1,2) # -> 3
```

Data: Lists, Records, Maps, and Structs

Erlang - Lists

```
L = [1,2,3].
hd(L). % -> 1
tl(L). % -> [2,3]
length(L). % -> 3
T = {hd(L),tl(L),"hello world"}. % -> {1,[2,3],"hello world"}
tuple_size(T). % -> 3
element(2,T). % -> [2,3]
setelement(2,T,[0]). % -> {1,[0],"hello world"}
T. % T unchanged -> {1,[2,3],"hello world"}
```

Elixir - Lists

```
l = [1,2,3]
hd(l) # -> 1
tl(l) # -> [2,3]
length(l) # -> 3
t = {hd(l),tl(l),"hello world"} # -> {1, [2, 3], "hello world"}
tuple_size(t) # -> 3
elem(t,1) # -> [2,3]
put_elem(t,1,[0]) # -> {1, [0], "hello world"}
t # t unchanged -> {1, [2, 3], "hello world"}
```

Erlang - Records

```
-record(documentrecord, {docid, name}).

R = #documentrecord{docid=123, name="name"}.
  % -> #documentrecord{docid = 123,name = "name"}

R#documentrecord.name. % -> "name"

F = fun(#documentrecord{docid=DocId} = D) ->
            D#documentrecord{docid=DocId+1} end.
F(R). % -> #documentrecord{docid = 124,name = "name"}
R. % R is not changed -> #documentrecord{docid = 123,name = "name"}
```

Elixir - Records

```
require Record
Record.defrecord :documentrecord, docid: 0, name: ""
@type documentrecord::record(:documentrecord, docid: integer, name: String.t)

r = documentrecord(docid: 123,name: "name")
    # -> {:documentrecord, 123, "name"}

documentrecord(r,:name) # -> "name"

f = fn (d) ->
 documentrecord(docid: documentrecord(d,:docid)+1,name: documentrecord(d,:name))
end
f.(r) # -> {:documentrecord, 124, "name"}
r # r is not changed -> {:documentrecord, 123, "name"}
```

Erlang - Maps

```
M = #{{tomatosauce,spoon} => 3,
      {mozzarella,slices} => 8,
      {ham,slices} => 6
     }.

#{{ham,slices} := I} = M % get value
  % -> #{{ham,slices} => 6,{mozzarella,slices} => 8,{tomatosauce,spoon} => 3}
I. % -> 6

M#{{mozzarella,slices} => 6}. % update
  % -> #{{ham,slices} => 6,{mozzarella,slices} => 6,{tomatosauce,spoon} => 3}

M#{{mozzarella,slices} := 5, {pepperoni,piece} => 3}. % update and add
  % ->  #{{ham,slices} => 6,
  %      {mozzarella,slices} => 5,
  %      {pepperoni,piece} => 3,
  %      {tomatosauce,spoon} => 3}
```

Elixir - Maps

```
m = %{{:tomatosauce,:spoon} => 3,
      {:mozzarella,:slices} => 8,
      {:ham,:slices} => 6
     }

Map.get m,{:ham,:slices} # get value -> 6

%{m | {:mozzarella,:slices} => 6} # update
  # -> %{{:ham, :slices} => 6, {:mozzarella, :slices} => 6,
  #      {:tomatosauce, :spoon} => 3}

Map.put(m, {:pepperoni,:piece}, 3) # add
```

```
# -> %{{:ham, :slices} => 6,
#       {:mozzarella, :slices} => 8,
#       {:pepperoni, :piece} => 3,
#       {:tomatosauce, :spoon} => 3}
```

Elixir - Structs

```
defmodule Documentrecord do
  defstruct docid: 0, name: ""
end

%Documentrecord{} # -> %Documentrecord{docid: 0, name: ""}

d = %Documentrecord{docid: 123, name: "name"}
  # -> %Documentrecord{docid: 123, name: "name"}
d.docid # -> 123

%{d | name: "Joe"} # updating
  # -> %Documentrecord{docid: 123, name: "Joe"}
d # d is unchanged -> %Documentrecord{docid: 123, name: "name"}

is_map(d) # -> true (structs are maps with fixed set of fields)
```

Pipeline

Elixir - Pipeline

```
"hello world" |> String.upcase |> String.split # -> ["HELLO", "WORLD"]
```

Erlang Shell

- `erl` -Start shell
- `c(Module).` -Compile module
- `b().` -Show all variables
- `f().` -Remove all variable bindings
- `i().` -List processes
- `memory().` -Print memory information
- `q().` -Quit shell
- `regs().` -List registered processes
- `rr(Module).` -Load record definitions from module
- `pwd().` -Return current working directory
- `cd(Dir).` -Change working directory

Elixir Shell

- `iex` -Start shell
- `c` "`filename.ex`" -Compile file
- `i var` -Print type information for var
- `v n` -Print session history for step n
- `pwd` -Return current working directory {pagebreak}

Index

Get the eBook for only $4.99!

Why limit yourself?

Now you can take the weightless companion with you wherever you go and access your content on your PC, phone, tablet, or reader.

Since you've purchased this print book, we are happy to offer you the eBook for just $4.99.

Convenient and fully searchable, the PDF version enables you to easily find and copy code—or perform examples by quickly toggling between instructions and applications.

To learn more, go to http://www.apress.com/us/shop/companion or contact support@apress.com.

Printed in the United States
By Bookmasters